too Precious to Die

My Daughter's Journey to Heaven

Precious in the sight of the Lord
is the death of His saints.
Psalm 116:15

Trudy Colflesh

Bridal Cry

Too Precious To Die
Original Copyright © 1984 by Bridge Publishing, Inc.
Revised Edition Copyright © 2013 by Trudy Colflesh
All rights reserved

Printed in the United States of America
ISBN 978-0-9848599-9-3

BridalCry Publishing
Colorado Springs, CO

Cover design by Nathan D. Fisher www.nathanfisher.com

To buy additional copies go to:
Amazon.com or
Search: Trudy Colflesh Books on Amazon
www.encouraginghope.com/books

Contents

Dedication

This book is dedicated to our
Heavenly Father
who gave us the story to write
and to our daughter Karen
who bravely lived it out in faith and trust

Acknowledgments

It is with much love I extend grateful acknowledgment to the following:

Eternal gratitude to the Women of the Aglow Fellowship of Southern Florida who were sisters of strength and encouragement throughout our ordeal; and to the greater Body of Christ, the supernatural community of Spirit-filled believers of our city who came together in one accord in the battle for Karen's life; for rallying around us in love and faithful, continuous, support; for their ministry in the gifts of the Spirit, spiritual warfare, prayer power, and expectant faith and hope. Special thanks to Nancy Hedlund for preparing Karen for heaven through telling the prophetic story of the "City of His Brilliance".

Dr. Sergio DeLamerens and the staff at Variety Children's Hospital for their expert medical skill combined with friendship and care.

Emilie Gewecke, Sussex Aglow president and the Sussex, New Jersey chapter of Women's Aglow Fellowship for the "typing parties," Eileen Schott for continual encouragement, Gail Bjork for fine editing, Peggy Kibler for careful proofreading, and Kathy Albert for quality typing; all expressed with great love and many prayers.

Most especially to my husband George for his love and patience, support and backing; to my sons Christopher and Michael for their interest and encouragement; my mother Gertrude Patterson for her love and strength.

Eternal gratitude and praise to my wonderful Savior and Lord, Jesus Christ, my Rock and Strength throughout my writing; and to the precious Holy Spirit who enabled me to remember and express everything I wrote.

Preface

1984

I have experienced both joy and pain in putting this book together. It has been a joy to share the mighty works of God in our lives as He reveled himself throughout Karen's illness. It has, however, also brought me pain to relive many of the events described in this book.

But through the elation and the anguish I have known God's peace and healing. It is my prayer that through our daughter Karen's story you will experience a special blessing in exactly the way the Lord chooses.

This book explains how God led our family to deal with Karen's illness. When this trial came into our lives, my husband and I were not "super-Christians" that made it possible for us to endure where others could not. The events you are about to read describe ordinary people – but people who serve a very extraordinary God.

We would not expect God to lead those involved in similar circumstances in exactly the same way He led us. We do know, however, that God is intimately involved in the lives of His people and will direct and guide whomever seeks Him according to the perfect plan He has for them.

We found that God has supplied *all* our needs in Christ Jesus – our faith, trust and hope; the fruits and gifts of the Spirit; our physical, emotional and financial needs – all came from our source in Him. As we leaned on and expected from God, He abundantly supplied. Everything He called us to do, He enabled us to do!

As you read of our wonderful Lord, know that we bow in reverence before Him, offering Him all the praise, for He alone is worthy and it is His glory we desire you to see and to experience.

Love in Jesus,
Trudy Colflesh

High Crest Lake
West Milford, New Jersey

Addendum

2013

It has been almost 30 years since I first wrote the above Preface. Our lives have gone on, our two sons have graduated from college and both married. Michael worked in the field of insurance before his (we are praying, temporary) disability because of a stroke.

Christopher entered the field of medicine and is now an electro physiologist (heart doctor). He and his wife have given us three beautiful granddaughters and a fine handsome grandson.

After traveling across the country sharing the story you are about to read, I realized I loved ministering to people and identifying with them in their pain. I was able to show them a road of hope, even as the Lord had brought us into healing from the deep grief of our daughter's death.

God had put the desire for a new career into my heart. Up until then, I was a career Mom and volunteer. When our youngest son left for college, I enrolled in our local university and studied to become a counselor.

I graduated with a Master's Degree from Montclair State University in 1990.

I have loved ministering to broken and wounded individuals as a Christian Professional Counselor for over 20 years now. I know first hand how suffering tenderizes us, and how God can heal.

My husband and I have now moved from New Jersey to Colorado Springs, Colorado where we are "semi-retired." Since our four grandchildren (as well as their parents) live in Colorado Springs, it wasn't difficult to decide where to relocate.

I still enjoy counseling clients on a scaled down basis and continue to see God's hand of healing on broken hearts.

I sense Karen's "Way to go, Mommy " approval, and know she had a big part in preparing me for counseling others. Sometimes I feel we're a team. She remains very dear to my heart. As you read her story, I think you will find her very dear to yours as well.

Even though I wrote Karen's story in 1978, the year of her death, it remains relevant for today. The reality of God's partnering with His people in the midst of our suffering remains an abiding truth.

I pray the Lord will minister to your heart and bring you healing and hope in whatever situation you are in as you read *Too Precious To Die*.

To Jesus Christ be all the glory.

Trudy Colflesh,
Colorado Springs,
Colorado

Prologue

"Childhood Leukemia" was the feature article in the morning paper. Myrna's coffee lay untouched as her mind absorbed the moving stories of afflicted children and their families. A concern for all who must walk through the shadow of this tragic disease gradually engulfed her until it assumed the full weight of a physical burden.

Placing her hands on the newsprint spread on the table before her in the early June sunlight, Myrna's spirit yielded to the prayer that had begun to move within her.

The weeping and travail that followed seemed to carry her to the heart of God himself, overwhelming her with the depth of His love and compassion for His creation. Little did our dear friend realize that the Holy Spirit had called her to a deep intercession at the very moment Karen and I so desperately needed it . . . .

1
Shelter in the Storm

"What could possibly be wrong with her?" The question raced through my mind as I forced myself to concentrate on driving. Karen lay on the front seat beside me, listless, crying softly.

I glanced at my six-year-old daughter. The sun's rays illuminated her nutmeg-colored hair, reflecting reddish highlights on the brown. Pain showed in her big, brown eyes as they met mine. "When will we get to the doctor's, Mommy?" she pleaded.

"It won't be much longer," I answered, tenderly caressing her hair as I slowed to a stop before the traffic light. My thoughts wandered back over the events of the previous week as I waited for the light to change. Concern for Karen had been growing daily as she was not responding favorably to the prescription for her sore throat. I had phoned the doctor several days after our office visit, and he had said to call again if she failed to prove shortly.

The next morning Karen awoke crying. I was alarmed when I saw the glands under her jaw puffy and swollen, and immediately phone our family doctor. With dismay, I heard the answering service relay that it was his day off.

Hanging up the phone with tears of helplessness and fear, I longed to have the reassuring presence of my husband, George, but he was out of town on a business conference.

Dialing a familiar number, I called my friend, Esther, and told her that I sensed something was seriously wrong with Karen. My voice was choked with emotion as I wondered what I should do. Ester recommended I call her children's pediatrician. I called right away and was relieved to be given an immediate appointment.

It's probably nothing serious," I tried to reassure myself, staring blankly at the traffic light.

The light changed. My foot automatically pressed down on the pedal. The fear of uncertainty began to well up within me. "Please Lord, help us!" I implored.

I didn't know yet how specifically and totally God was going to answer. We were about to begin an interaction with heaven and earth – an interaction we could not have believed possible. God was going to show us His intimate, personal involvement in every detail of our lives through the painful, tragic days which lay ahead.

Parking near the doctor's office, I helped Karen out of the car. We checked in and waited to be paged for the appointment.

A nurse led us through the hall to an examining room where she asked me questions about Karen's medical history. "I need to take a blood sample now, Karen," she announced kindly. "it will hurt just a little."

Karen winced, but stood bravely as her finger was pricked and squeezed for a few drops of blood. None of us realized what secret those drops would reveal.

After the doctor examined Karen, he left the room to check the results of the blood test. I held my precious, little daughter on my lap, waiting. I hoped he would have an answer which would help her. The door to the examining room was closed, but I could hear voices in the hall as the doctor and nurse conversed. "This is serious!" the doctor said. "Have Mrs. Colflesh come to my office."

Fear twisted within me. In a few minutes a nurse came to the room to tell me that the doctor wanted to see me. While she stayed with Karen, I hurried to the office. Both the unfamiliar doctor and his assistant were waiting. He asked me to sit down.

"We are very concerned about Karen's condition," the doctor began. "You must take her to the hospital right away for further testing. I have called Dr. DeLamerens, who will see you there."

Tears of bewilderment and fright burned my eyes. I felt the blood drain from my face. "Wha ... wha ... what do you think she has?" I asked shakily. It was an awful moment as I waited for him to answer. Inwardly, I cried, "Oh God, help!" I could feel my very being start to crumble in the uncertainty of the crisis.

"We think she may have leukemia," he said, quietly.

"Leukemia!" The word sounded foreign to my ears. My mind could not grasp it. Finally, the word registered and I realized what the doctor said.

"Leukemia! They suspect leukemia!" I didn't crumble. Unexpectedly, I felt a surge of inner strength and a calmness settle over me. God was answering my cry for help and His loving arms were holding me together.

I learned later that even at that moment my friend Myrna was reading the morning newspaper and came upon an article concerning childhood leukemia. As she read, tears welled up within her and she stopped to pray,

Not realizing even then that she was helping to lighten my desperate situation.

Still pale, but feeling God's peace, I walked back to the examining room to get Karen. I calmly told her we were going to the hospital.

"Oh, no!" she cried. "I want to go home."

"It's all right," I assured her. "The doctors want to do some tests to find out how to make you feel better." "Okay, Mommy," Karen agreed. "Let's go." I was unfamiliar with the area and asked the nurse how to find the hospital. "It's just a few miles away," the nurse said, drawing a map for me.

The doctor saw us to the door. The enormity of the situation was so great that I mentally stepped back to look; my husband was out of town, I was at an unfamiliar doctor's office about to go to an unfamiliar hospital and my daughter was suspected to have leukemia!

"This was certainly a dramatic first visit!" I said to the doctor with a hint of a smile. It was one way of dealing with the pressure.

I helped Karen into the car and valiantly drove away. We rode in silence, wondering what awaited us. I found the map confusing and lost my way. Karen started to groan with pain. A sickening knot tightened in my middle and a numbness of emotion swept over me. I continued driving, hoping to find a familiar landmark.

My thoughts tossed to and fro on the doctor's words. "This just can't be real!" I reasoned to myself. Karen has always been so healthy and vivacious, so energetic that we claimed she was built on springs. It must be a mistake. "Be my strength, Lord," I cried as the anxiety mounted within me.

Turning from one road to another, I somehow found a sign that pointed to the hospital where I was to take my precious passenger. Driving into the parking lot, I noticed the front sign: "Variety Children's Hospital, the Hospital with a Heart." I appreciated the kindly sentiment and was relieved to have found my way.

Inside, the receptionist directed us to Dr. DeLamerens' office. Karen ached and was weak. I held her as we waited for the doctor to see us.

"May I use your phone?" I asked the doctor's secretary.

"Certainly," she said, moving the phone toward me. I called George's office. His conference was scheduled to be over, but he hadn't yet returned to the office.

I explained to his secretary that I was at the hospital. "Please have George call me at this number as soon as he gets in," I said.

Next I called home. Our sixteen-year-old son, Michael, answered the phone. I told him, "Karen is in the hospital for tests. I don't know how long we'll be here but I'll try and get home to fix dinner."

"Don't worry about it, " he answered. "I can take care of dinner."

"If Daddy calls, have him call me here. And tell Chris where we are when he gets home from school." Christopher, my eleven-year-old, had a later school shift than Mike did.

We continued waiting. I read several children's books to Karen, hoping to keep her mind off the pain.

I had been informed that Dr. DeLamerens was a pediatrician who specialized in hematology (the study of blood and its diseases) and oncology (the study of tumors). I was hoping we could see him soon. Finally, the doctor stepped out of a small office where he had been examining a patient. He was short with dark, wavy hair and an olive complexion. He spoke with a slight accent as he asked for Karen.

I was impressed with his kind smile and warm handshake as he greeted us.

Doctor DeLamerens displayed tenderness toward Karen as he examined her carefully. When he finished, he told me that he wanted to admit her to the hospital. I was to go to the admissions office. Karen would be assigned a room upstairs on West Ward and he would see us there shortly.

Again we waited, this time for our turn at the admissions desk. I fumbled through my wallet to find our insurance card and other necessary information. After many forms were filled out, I signed each one. Karen was then assigned room 220 West.

We were escorted to our room by a young aide. Inside, a small hospital bed was made up with fresh, white sheets. It was in the corner beside a two-seater couch and a table with a phone. A large, curtained window faced the front of the hospital. A television set was mounted in the wall.

Sinking onto the couch, I realized how tired I felt. Neither Karen nor I had eaten lunch and it was now late afternoon. It had been a long day already.

An attractive, young nurse with short, red hair came into the room. She introduced herself as Geri Van Wezel and brought Karen a hospital kit. She took Karen's temperature and blood pressure and showed her how the nurse's call button and the television control worked. "Feel free to ask me any questions you may have," she offered kindly. "I'll be back in a few minutes."

While Geri was gone I called George's office again. He was still not there. I wondered how he would react to the terrible news.

Karen experimented with the television controls. "Come with me now, Karen," Geri said when she returned. "The doctor is going to give you some tests."

I watched as Karen was taken to a small room at the other end of the hallway. Leaning against the door frame and gazing into space, I suddenly saw George walking along the corridor. I ran to meet him. We embraced and held each other tightly.

"How did you know?" I asked.

"The doctor paged me at the conference, and I left right away."

We walked into Karen's room and sat waiting in quiet disbelief. We could hear Karen screaming through the hall door. George reached out his hand to mine. "Let's pray," he urged.

He closed his eyes. "Merciful Father, our lives and the lives of our children are in your hands. We know you are a loving Father and that you love Karen even more than we do. We relinquish our little daughter to your protection and care. We take our hands off her and give her to you. Do with her according to your will and purposes in her life. In Jesus' name we pray. Amen."

I opened my eyes, wet with tears, and smiled at George. I felt relieved. He was here with me now.

Geri carried Karen into the room. "You have a brave little girl here," she said. "We just gave Karen a bone marrow test and a spinal tap."

"That was the worst test I've ever had!" Karen said, wiping the tears from her eyes. Geri placed her gently on the bed.

"I love you, my little sweetheart," George said, taking Karen up in his arms.

"I love you, too, Daddy."

"How about a 'Karen sandwich'?" I said, as I put my arms around the two of them. With Karen in the middle, we hugged and kissed.

7

I'll stay here while you go home and get what you need," George offered.

The hospital allowed me to be with Karen in her room around the clock. It was a private mother-child unit, and the couch folded out to make a bed.

I drove home to pack clothes for the two of us. Mike and Chris met me at the car. "How's Karen?" they asked in unison.

I looked at our two handsome sons. Mike stood tall with a bronze tan on his well-shaped body. His dark hair and eyes were a contrast to Christopher's fairer complexion and auburn hair. Chris' big, brown eyes looked at me questioningly, waiting for an answer. Both boys dearly loved their little sister.

"We don't have the results of the tests yet," I answered. "I'm going to stay at the hospital with her. She doesn't feel very well."

I fixed a light dinner and packed. Chris drew a get well card for me to take back to Karen. "Dad will be home later," I told the boys as I got back in the car. I'll see you tomorrow."

When I arrived at the hospital, Karen was picking at her dinner and watching television. George and I walked out to the hallway and leaned against the wall by Karen's room. The nursing supervisor saw us and came over to talk. She spoke kindly and urged George and me to keep communications open between us. "Share your feelings freely with one another. Many times a child's serious illness can have devastating effects on a home and marriage," she advised.

We told her we hoped Karen didn't have leukemia. Dr. DeLamerens would give us the results of the test tomorrow.

Later, George read Karen a story and left for the night.

I helped Karen with her pajamas and made my bed.

"I hurt all over," Karen moaned.

"Try to lie down and sleep," I encouraged her.

"I can't! It hurts too much!" she cried.

I was concerned about her increasing pain. The evening nurse came into the room to settle her patient. She introduced herself as Belle. She tried to lay Karen flat but stopped when Karen suddenly screamed in pain.

Belle gathered extra pillows to prop her in a semi-sitting position. "Now Karen, you're going to have to be quiet and go to sleep," Belle said with kind but firm authority. Then she left.

I lay on my bed and flipped through my Bible. "Oh Lord, what is your word to us?" I prayed. "What is your direction? What can we hold to?" I turned to the Psalms and my eyes fell on Psalm 57. I read: "O God, have pity, for I am trusting you!" My eyes filled with tears. I felt so helpless, so in need of pity. I knew my trust had to be in Him; Where else could I go? Who else could I turn to? I continued reading:

> "I will hide beneath the shadow of your wings until this storm is past. I will cry to the God of heaven who does such wonders for me. He will send down help from heaven to save me, because of his love and his faithfulness . . . .
>
> "O, God, my heart is quiet and confident . . . . Be exalted, 0 God, above the heavens. May your glory shine throughout the earth. (Psalms 57:2,3, 7, 11, TLB)

When I finished reading I *knew* God had spoken! He showed me we would be protected from the blast of the storm. He would be our deliverer. His love and faithfulness were constant, and we could have peace and confidence in Him. He even promised that He would bring glory out of this whole situation!

As the events of Karen's illness unfolded, we realized the prophetic nature of this message to us. In the days to come we were to see God leading us through this Psalm step-by-step.

With Psalm 57 as my prayer, I closed my eyes and slept. I awoke quickly, however, when Karen cried out in pain. Belle came into the room. She tried to make Karen's bed position comfortable.

"Keep the bed up," Karen cried.

"You'll sleep better with it down," Belle answered.

"I can't lie down flat."

"Here, let me help you."

"Ow, ouch! Stop! Don't!" Karen screamed. "I have to sit up."

Karen began crying and with each breath got louder. Belle spoke firmly, telling her she couldn't be so noisy because there were other children sleeping. Karen told her she had to be noisy. Belle continued to talk in an effort to calm her and keep her mind off the pain.

As Karen quieted, I heard Belle say softly, "Jesus will help you, Karen. He loves you."

I was moved as I heard Karen answer, even out of her pain. "I know," she said, "and He loves you too, Belle."

I thought back on Karen's early perception of spiritual things and how she had prayed for Jesus to be her Savior at the young age of three. I remembered how she heartily sang "Jesus Loves Me" as she walked through the house, and talked of Jesus so naturally that George remarked that she sounded like a little evangelist. She knew she could trust her Friend to help her now.

The rising sun began to filter light through the hospital window. It had been a short night. I looked over at Karen. She was finally sleeping. I got up and dressed quietly. Belle came in the room to check her patient before she went off duty. I thanked her for last night's care.

"This morning, the doctor will tell us the results of the test on Karen," I told her. "We're trusting in the Lord."

Belle took my hands and broke into tears. "It's so good to see you loving and trusting Jesus." She backed out of the door and closed it gently.

I stood quietly, watching Belle leave. "I'm not going to jump to conclusions," I reasoned, attempting to reassure myself. "It hasn't been confirmed that Karen has leukemia."

The doctor had suggested that the massive white blood count could possibly be the result of an extensive infection. There was still hope that the suspicion about leukemia was wrong.

George met me downstairs in the hospital in Dr. DeLamerens' office, for our early morning appointment. We held hands, silently hoping this terrible scare would be groundless. Soon we were ushered into the doctor's office. He rose from behind his large desk and greeted us with a warm handshake.

"Won't you please sit down," he offered, pointing to several chairs across the desk from him.

"We have completed the results on your daughter's bone marrow test," the doctor began. George and I leaned forward in our chairs. "She has leukemia."

Too numb to react, we continued to listen closely. The exact type of cancer was named acute myelomonocytic leukemia. It was an unusual form for a younger child.

11

"But we have cause for hope," the doctor said kindly.

"And we will provide the latest proven medicine available. There is more learned each day." He continued talking, showing us charts of chemotherapy treatment and statistics of remission results.

We left the office quietly. The truth slowly began to penetrate my mind. Now it was confirmed. *Karen really had leukemia!* She could even die! I staggered under the force of the blow, overwhelmed.

All the fear and anguish of the last twenty-four hours climaxed with thundering force, rushing forward like a huge wave about to engulf me.

"Help, Lord!" my heart screamed out. "This is more than I can bear."

George and I stumbled into the chapel down the hallway from the doctor's office. Behind the closed doors we burst into tears.

As we cried, what had loomed before us as a wave of terror gradually diminished to a gentle spray. Our precious Savior had held up His hand and rebuked the impact of destruction. He brought us into the shelter of His peace and took upon himself the burden of pain which we could not carry.

True to what God promised in Psalm 57, we were hidden beneath the shadow of His wings. The storm was blowing and raging outside, but we found we weren't in it. We were aware that we could step into the storm at any time, but we chose to stay nestled in safety, close against the great, loving heart of God.

I wanted to learn all I could about this disease which had burst upon our family so unwelcomed; it was so sudden and so all-encompassing. What I read was not encouraging. Medical science did not know how a person

12

contracted leukemia. Of all the various kinds of leukemia, Karen's type had the least effective treatment and the least percentage of remission. I could find no hope for a cure.

I closed the books, dismayed. "Lord," I prayed, "Karen's leukemia is no surprise to you. I know you didn't give it to her. Sickness and disease are not of you; but you did allow this to come upon her, for nothing can happen outside of your purpose and plan for us. I know there is no hope for Karen's life apart from a miraculous healing from you. Perhaps, Lord, you have chosen the 'impossible' to show forth your glory.

"Lord, when I think of it, there is no hope for any of us apart from you. Life is so very fragile, and so very precious. Oh Lord," I sobbed, "Karen's life is so precious to us. Please, loving Father, restore her!"

Later at home, I prepared myself to share the news of Karen's diagnosis to Chris. George had already told Mike.

"Honey," I started, but the impact of what I had to tell him about his little sister was too much. My voice broke and I choked out the words between sobs, "Karen has leukemia!"

We held each other and cried. Finally Chris said firmly, "God better not let her die or ..." and he thought of the worst threat he could make to protect his sister, "or I won't love Him anymore!"

I regained my composure, feeling God's peace. I explained to Chris that our heavenly Father's love was with us even in the midst of this terrible circumstance. We could trust Him to do the best for all of us no matter what happened.

"I'm sorry, Mom," Chris said." I didn't mean what I said."

"Let's pray," I said, taking Chris's hand. I committed ourselves and Karen to the Lord and asked for His strengthening. As I prayed, I felt the heaviness lift.

We realized that God was ministering to each member of the family, keeping us in His strength and bearing the heavy burden with us. As God was our strength in emotional pain, He was Karen's strength in physical pain. Her body ached, her lips were swollen and ulcerated, the needles which the medical professionals put into her hurt and the chemotherapy burned as it entered her veins. George and I prayed with Karen that God would enable her to endure it.

As the days progressed, we became familiar with the hospital routine. Mr. Angulo would signal the beginning of the day. Before the sun was up, he would walk along the hallway whistling, burst into our room and flick on the light with a cheery; "Good morning, Karen. How's my little friend today?"

He was the "blood man" from the laboratory. Daily he came to draw blood. Sometimes he took the blood from a vein in Karen's arm, but usually he only had to prick her finger to obtain a few drops.

Karen would fuss, but Mr. Angulo continued to talk in a friendly way to reassure her. He worked quickly, making up the blood slides with the equipment in his carrying case.

"You're a good girl, Karen," he exclaimed as he put a bandage on her finger. As he left the room and turned off the light, Karen and I would turn over for a few more minutes of rest.

Soon the hallway was busy with the sounds of men washing and polishing the floor followed shortly after by the clank and clatter of the food cart arriving. In a few minutes, an attractive nurse's aide-nicknamed "Sam" would bring Karen's breakfast to the room.

Karen didn't want to wake up so early. She especially didn't like the idea of being bathed from a basin and having her bed changed first thing. "Go away, Sam. I'm not awake yet," Karen would protest. "I don't need a bath, either. I'm not even dirty."

Sometimes Karen would talk Sam out of her schedule, and sometimes Sam would persuade Karen out of hers. As it turned out, Karen's bed was always changed at some point in the day, and she was usually bathed. Karen did succeed, however, in skipping baths every once in a while since, as she said, she "really wasn't dirty."

Next Margarete, the cleaning lady, came to mop the floor and tidy the room. After several days she asked me in her broken English if my husband and I were Christians.

"Yes, we are," I answered.

"I thought so," she replied. "I could tell by your look of peace. I am, too!" She cheered us by humming songs of praise as she worked.

I helped Karen with breakfast and read her the menu selections for the following day. She circled the food choices she wanted.

Sam would take Karen's temperature and blood pressure, and Geri would check the intravenous (i.v.) solution and add medicines. If the solution chamber got low, the Ivac machine signaled with a shrill, steady beep. Karen quickly learned the button to push to stop the beep, and then alerted the nurse with the call bell.

Shortly after breakfast Dr. DeLamerens and his team, Dr. Escalon and Dr. Pefkarou, made their morning rounds to see their patients. The doctors came in the room and stood around Karen's bed, visiting with her as

15

they made their examination. Her medicine was adjusted and prescribed at this time as needed.

Karen learned she didn't have a choice as to what was being done to her, but she soon realized how to make the most of it. One of her most enlivening challenges was medicine time. She did not like taking her medicine. To her it tasted bad and it hurt the sores which had developed on her mouth and lips.

When the nurse arrived with the medicine tray, Karen stalled. She would carry on a running conversation with the nurse about how awful the medicine tasted, and would use other persuasive arguments. Everyone was amazed at Karen's extensive vocabulary and her undaunted stubbornness.

Finally, when the nurse was exhausted, Karen would accept the medicine, drinking it with theatrical gasps and gags. "Quick! Quick! A coke!" she cried dramatically, grabbing it to wash away the taste of the medicine.

We came to understand that it was normal for children in the hospital to feel stubborn and cranky, so we were pleased that, all-in-all, Karen realized the need to be obedient and thoughtful. We told her how proud we were that she was doing so well.

Dr. DeLamerens encouraged us with the report that he saw Karen as uncomplaining and cooperative and that we as parents were an inspiration to him. We knew, however, that any inspiration we gave came directly from the Lord and that He was the source of our strength as well as of Karen's.

Occasionally, I would take a break from the room and walk through the hallway of West. As I walked, I realized how unaware I had been of the different world that existed inside a hospital. I had not known its pulse and heartbeat, its routine and business, its loneliness and isolation until we were thrust into its midst.

Yet in this separate world God chose to enact a living drama. He expressed himself by producing trust, patience, love and hope, blessing us abundantly with His presence and allowing it to spill over into the lives of all who came into contact with our precious daughter, Karen.

2
Strong Deliverer

Three days after Karen entered the hospital, it was my 38th birthday. "How can I think about my birthday at a time like this?" I despaired. "I'm going to ignore it."

But God seemed to say, "Other things are important, too, Trudy, both your needs and those of your family. I want you to keep a balance. Rely on me to make this possible."

I knew that God was right. I was glad when three friends arranged to take me to a "birthday breakfast" at the hospital cafeteria. As we ate and talked, the encouragement of my friends strengthened me.

George came to the hospital after work. He brought a gift for Karen to present to me. The two of them had discussed earlier what Karen decided to give me for my birthday. I opened the gift-wrapped package with delight to find a new watch. Several months before, Karen had dropped my watch and it stopped working. A new one was just what I needed.

"Thank you, honey, for such a nice gift," I kissed her tenderly.

Later, George said to me, "The best gift Karen could give any of us was time."

Chris and Mike stayed with Karen while George and I went out for a birthday dinner. We were trying to be brave, attempting to maintain a somewhat normal life style, but neither of us was very hungry. We left the half-eaten food on our plates and returned to the hospital.

"When can I go home,?" Karen asked a few days later. "What's wrong with me?" Karen was ready to finish her treatment and get on with life as she knew it, free and happy. In the hospital she was confined by her i.v. cord and the isolation of her room. Her body pains and the nausea from chemotherapy subdued her activity and spirit. "I want to be well, Mommy," she pleaded.

"It's going to take some time, Karen," I said, trying to reassure her. "You have a problem with your blood and it's not working right. It's called leukemia." I went on to explain about red and white blood cells as I drew her pictures to illustrate what was happening to her. I told her we were praying that God would heal her and that He would use the doctors and medicine to help.

Karen's condition was improving with the chemotherapy treatment. Her white blood count was brought under control and she no longer had severe joint pains. There was an undesirable side effect, however: The platelets, a vital blood ingredient which prevents internal bleeding, were being drastically reduced. As a result, Karen was given quantities of blood platelets intravenously.

The blood fed slowly into Karen's system. My heart filled with gratitude for those who were willing to contribute a vital part of themselves for another's need. I laid my hands on the blood pack and asked God to bless the donors as they had blessed us.

"And make this blood, flowing through Karen's system,

as the precious blood of Jesus, cleansing and healing her. Cover her now, Lord," I prayed, "with the blood of Jesus and protect her from evil."

While Karen watched a television show, I sat down with paper and pencil. "Lord, what is the direction we're to take? What are to be our guidelines and support in this crisis?"

I jotted down what came to my mind:

Keep your eyes on Jesus
We walk by faith, not by sight
Karen belongs to God
Let God bear the burden
All things work together for good to those who
      love God
Give thanks in all things
Rest in God's love under the shadow of His
      wings
Let God bear the burden

Even as I wrote, the Lord was gathering together the Body of Christ, His people, to help. The news spread to churches and fellowships throughout the city. Karen had leukemia!

Church bulletins carried her name on their prayer lists. Sunday school classes and children in Christian schools were praying for Karen. It blessed us to learn that even the congregation of a Jewish synagogue was praying.

Friends telephoned the Oral Roberts prayer tower, Pat Robertson's "700 Club" and Charles and Frances Hunter, asking for healing prayer. Others wrote to friends throughout the country requesting prayer support. Priests in a Catholic monastery were told of Karen and began to pray for her.

I heard a song on the Christian radio station: "Lord,

Listen to Your Children Praying." I knew there were hundreds and even thousands who had now joined us in prayer for Karen. "Lord," I implored, "listen to your children praying!"

Over the door to the hospital were words from the Bible: "And a little child shall lead them" (Isa. 11:6).

"Father," I prayed, "there is such an outpouring of love from all over the country and throughout the different fellowships in the city. Is it possible that you plan here for *Karen* to be the little child who leads others closer to you and to each other?"

As God called our Christian friends to minister to us, we opened ourselves and our situation to them in order to receive spiritual and material help. We trusted God to direct the actions, prayers and counsel of His people to our best interest. It was to become a learning and growing experience for us all.

Several friends brought the following Scripture to our attention:

> Is any sick among you? let him call for the elders of the church, and let them pray over him, anointing him with oil in the name of the Lord; And the prayer of faith shall save the sick, and the Lord shall raise him up; and if he have committed sins, they shall be forgiven him. (James 5:14, 15 KJV)

We believed that we should ask the elders of our church to anoint Karen with oil as the Scripture verse said. We phoned our pastor, Rev. Reed, and asked his approval, appreciating his positive reply.

That evening, three elders came to the hospital. They washed their hands and put on the full-length hospital

22

gowns before entering the room. Karen was on "reverse isolation" to protect her from any germs we might pass on.

The elders, George and I gathered at the foot of Karen's bed. One of the elders held the bottle of oil as he began to pray. "Oh, Lord, we humbly come before you, realizing your might and power and our insignificance apart from you. But because of your precious Son Jesus Christ, who shed His blood on the cross for each of us, we have the privilege of coming directly to your throne of grace and speaking our needs to you.

"You have said in your Word, Lord, that we are to anoint the sick with oil, and we come believing your promise of healing."

As he continued in prayer, I became aware of the powerful presence of the Holy Spirit. I knew that God was pleased with our obedience and our act of faith.

The elders moved toward Karen. They each put oil on their fingers and placed their hands on her head. As they prayed for her healing, the presence of God's Spirit was so strong that one of the men began to weep. It was a precious moment and we knew God was working.

The Body of Christ ministered to us and supported us in many ways. Out of love and concern we received gifts, flowers, cards and food. Our church members, friends from Aglow (a Christian women's fellowship in which I was active), and neighbors touched our hearts with their generosity as, night after night, they brought meals for the family. We were wisely advised to maintain physical strength, and having meals provided made it easier.

The directions for the next step we were to take in dealing with Karen's illness came through our friend Patty.

"Have you anointed Karen's room with oil?" Patty

asked me on the phone. "This thought came to me to share with you."

George and I perceived this as important. He wanted me to take care of it, so I bought a bottle of olive oil and asked the Lord to bless it for His use. I explained to Karen what I was doing and began anointing the room.

"In the name of the Father, Son and Holy Spirit," I prayed as I touched the top and sides of the door to room 220 West, "we anoint and claim this room for Jesus Christ and His purpose." I touched the four corners of the room, the windows, the doors and the objects in it. Then I continued, "Satan, we bind you and command all evil spirits to leave this room by the blood and power of Jesus. We lift up the name of Jesus, for He alone is Lord.

"And now, Jesus," I prayed, "bless all who enter this room. Let them be aware of your presence and peace."

"I liked that, Mommy," Karen said.

I felt good about it, too. Who knew what heartache and suffering was experienced in this room, or what despair, fear or gloom had lingered on from previous times?

During the course of Karen's illness, we were admitted at least once to every one of the seven rooms on West. I anointed each room with oil and prayed. It seems God planned this placement so every room in the unit would be anointed for peace in the name of Jesus.

Karen continued her attempt at independence over the inevitable routine, especially when it came time for her to take her medicine. Alan, one of the evening nurses, was elected to bring the medicine since he, of all the nurses, did the best job of getting Karen to take it.

Alan had a friendly, gentle personality. He was studying to be a doctor and he loved children. He was one of Karen's favorites. At medicine time he came into the room, put the tray of pills and liquids on the table, and sat down to visit.

The two of them discussed many subjects, but Karen especially liked to talk about animals. Alan told about the pets in his apartment and Karen shared her love of animals, particularly dogs and horses.

They laughed and joked together. Karen liked his gentle teasing and good fun. "When I'm better, Alan," Karen said, "I'll come to your apartment and take care of your pets and fix your dinner. I'm real good at making peanut-butter-and-jelly sandwiches."

"That's a terrific offer," Alan laughed. "I'll think about it, but right now it's time to take your medicine."

"Okay," Karen responded cheerfully, and quickly swallowed the necessary medications.

It was pleasing to see Karen's cooperation and I complimented her as we settled in for the night. Lying next to her on my fold-out bed, I reflected on the events of the past few weeks. Things had come upon us so quickly. My heart began to ache. I turned my head to look at our little girl, once so vibrant with life and enthusiasm, now confined to a hospital bed with a vicious disease. Warm, silent tears flowed from the corners of my eyes, rolled down my cheeks and dropped upon the pillow.

Wiping the tears, I had almost fallen asleep when suddenly I was startled to alertness! My blood ran cold! In my mind was a picture of Karen lying in a coffin.

"Oh no!" I cried aloud. I envisioned myself with others standing around Karen: We were praying for her resurrection from the dead! My whole body felt faint as I whispered, "Oh, Lord, instead of healing Karen, are you going to let her die and then raise her back to life to show forth your glory?"

As terrifying as the thought seemed, I knew it was

possible if it was God's plan. I had heard of such things happening before, but to think it might have to be Karen that we had to pray a resurrection prayer for was more than I could bear. Fighting against fear, I tried to sleep.

When Karen awoke the next morning, she was grumpy and wanted no part of the medicine routine. She relented to take her pills, eye drops and mouth rinse, but only after much persuasion on the nurse's part. When the next round of medicine came Karen was not only stubborn but to my surprise, she was openly belligerent. After an arduous battle she took the medicine and the exhausted nurse left.

"Karen," I chided, "I am not at all pleased to see you behave like this. It is very important for you to be obedient to the nurses. They are giving you the medicine that Dr. DeLamerens tells them to give you. You know we are asking God to show the doctors what medicine is right to help you. We are trusting God to do what is best, and He is in charge of your medicine."

Karen realized that what I said was true but she didn't want to hear it. "It's really important for you to pray with me and ask Jesus to give you the power to take your medicine," I told her.

"I don't want to," Karen complained.

I was surprised. Always before she was willing to ask Jesus for His strength to do the things she couldn't. "Maybe it will be better tomorrow," I thought.

It wasn't. Early the next morning, Laurie came to the room with Karen's medicine.

"Good morning, Karen," she said pleasantly.

Karen opened her eyes and started screaming. "Get out of here! Go away!"

Laurie came closer, and Karen started kicking at her

and yelling. Shaken, Laurie backed off. "I'll be back later," she said.

I jumped out of bed. "Karen," I reprimanded her. "I'm not going to allow you to behave like that. You need to ask for help. Jesus is the only one who can help you do what you have to do."

"Don't say that name!" she yelled, putting her hands over her ears.

I told George about the difficult morning when he came to visit. We did some tests to see if we could get Karen to talk about Jesus. We played a game and asked her identify different things in her room. After pointing to a few things, George walked over to a picture of Jesus we had hung on the wall.

"Who's this?" George asked.

"You know," Karen replied, evading the question.

"I want to hear you say who this is."

"I don't want to say it."

Later we tried another test. Karen always enjoyed reading out loud to us. We gave her several books to read, one about Jesus. When she started the book about Jesus, she read everything except the word "Jesus." We pointed to His name and said, "What does this word say?"

"I'm not going to say," Karen answered.

George and I went out in the hall to discuss this strange turn of events. "I wonder why she won't say 'Jesus'?" George wondered.

"I know this sounds weird," I said, "but I've heard of situations like this where the cause has been oppression from the enemy, Satan. The Bible says that "we fight against evil, unseen beings." (Eph. 6:12)

My thoughts went to our recent anointing of both the room and Karen with oil. I knew the Lord had directed us to do these acts. Perhaps through them the enemy had been uncovered and was now compelled to reveal himself. God would have to show us the next step.

"I don't like it at all. What do you think we should do?" George said.

"Maybe Victor and Sara Mueller could help," I suggested.

Just the previous month I had met Victor and Sara, a caring Christian couple whom the Lord was using in a deliverance ministry against the forces of evil. I had seen them pray with people, releasing them from many enemy bondages by the power of the Holy Spirit.

George said to give them a call. I phoned Victor, explaining the situation. He agreed that Karen's attitude sounded serious and needed prayer. He asked us to join him in fasting and arranged to meet us the following day.

We met with the Muellers in the hospital chapel before going to Karen's room. Sara's dark hair and eyes reflected her Cuban heritage. Victor had a trim beard that matched his brown hair. They were a tall, handsome couple with a look of compassion and an air of Godly authority.

We sat in the back of the chapel and prayed together for a long time. The Muellers led George and me in taking authority in Jesus' name over any work of the enemy in our own lives as well as in the lives of our ancestors, where Satan's destructive work may have begun and been passed down, from generation to generation, through ancestral curses. Victor explained that this was an important step toward bringing Karen into freedom.

When we finished praying, the four of us went upstairs to Karen's room. After washing and putting on our gowns, we walked in to greet Karen. When she saw Victor, Karen fearfully covered her head with the sheet. "Go away!" she cried.

Victor knelt beside Karen's bed. "Hello, Karen."

"Something stinks," Karen impudently remarked as she peeked out.

We knew Karen was not acting normally and we prayed for the Lord's protection and guidance. Sensing the enemy's presence, Victor began to speak directly to him. "Satan, you're a liar. You have no claims on this child. Karen belongs to the Lord Jesus Christ. She has been bought with the precious blood of Jesus, and she is His! (I Cor. 6:20; 7:23)

We cut her free now from all inroads the enemy has made through ancestral lines and we sever those bondages and break those curses in the mighty name of Jesus." Karen began to cry and cough, and slowly took the sheet off her head.

We were so involved in our prayer of spiritual warfare that we jumped with surprise when the door opened and a nurse cheerfully brought in Karen's dinner. Moving around the room with silly smiles on our faces, we made small talk until she left.

Victor advised George on the importance of having the fullness of the Holy Spirit in the Christian life, especially when doing battle against Satan. George was open to receive all that God wanted to give him so, with Karen and me looking on, Sara and Victor placed their hands on George's shoulder as he stood at the foot of his daughter's bed and prayed; asking Jesus to baptize him in the Holy Spirit!

The words, "ben anae," came to George's lips and he spoke them out. We perceived it as evidence that Jesus had answered our prayers and given him a heavenly language (Acts 2:4) .

As our friends left, they encouraged us to hold on to the victory that Jesus had given Karen, remembering that

Satan is defeated by the word of our testimony and by the blood of the Lamb. (Rev. 12:11) The Lord showed us proof of His victory that very evening as Karen again began to say the wonderful name of Jesus!

That night, I fell asleep proclaiming God's victory over Satan. Early the next morning I awoke suddenly. It was 4:00 A.M. I quietly walked over to Karen's bed and touched her gently, praying in the Spirit. After a while I laid back down but continued interceding for Karen.

Mr. Angulo entered the room on his early morning rounds. He came to draw Karen's blood for the usual daily analysis. "Karen, Karen, wake up my little friend," he said as he switched on the lights. "Good morning, Karen. Let me have your finger to get some blood."

I lay in my bed wondering how Karen would react. Instead of her recent crying and fussing, she pleasantly stuck out her finger.

"Thank you, Karen, "Mr. Angulo said as he quickly finished. "Have a nice day."

"You're welcome. Have a nice day yourself," Karen replied sleepily.

I was thrilled at Karen's changed attitude and told her so. Karen woke up enough to answer, "Well, the poor man. He has to listen to screaming kids all day. Somebody needs to be nice."

I smiled with joy as Karen rolled over to catch a little more sleep.

In a few minutes, Laurie came with Karen's 6:00 A.M. medicine. She was braced for a difficult, trying period. To Laurie's delight, Karen woke and pleasantly took all her medicine.

After the nurse left, I prayed aloud, "Thank you, Jesus, for giving Karen the power to take her medicine." Karen smiled her approval.

After breakfast, I phoned Sara to tell her about Karen's new behavior and peace. Sara rejoiced with me. Karen was quietly watching Sesame Street on television while we talked. When I hung up, I watched some of the show with her. The puppets talked about having three wishes.

"What would you wish for, Karen?" I asked.

"Jesus," she replied without a moment's hesitation.

I lovingly looked at my daughter. She was truly set free!

"You don't have to wish for Jesus," I said. "He's always with you and He will never leave you."

"I know. Jesus is my best friend. He protects me."

"Thank you, Jesus, for the victory," I gratefully whispered.

God was giving us the abundant reassurance of His victory. Our friends Velma Frank and Ruth Brothers came to the hospital that morning to visit Karen. They noticed a more peaceful countenance on Karen, and remarked about how much better she looked, especially her eyes.

Almost overnight Karen's lips, which were badly swollen due to the chemotherapy, returned to normal. Even the medical staff remarked on how good she looked. The doctors were pleased. Her mouth sores and lips healed enough so that Karen could start on another round of chemotherapy for which the hospital staff was waiting.

George wanted Karen to show appreciation for what the Lord accomplished so he typed a prayer for her to read aloud. She read it sweetly, thanking Jesus for her deliverance and healing. George anointed Karen with oil and asked God to forgive us for anything we or our ancestors may have done to open us to the spiritual attack from which we were delivered. He expressed to the Lord that he would take more responsibility in displaying God's love in our home, and that we would put Him first in all we did. My heart was filled with gratitude for God's work in George as well as in Karen.

The following morning was Sunday. Since Karen felt much better, I left for church to meet the family. As I drove, I sang aloud, "Let God Arise and His Enemies Be Scattered. "

I had not been to church since Karen's sudden illness, My eyes filled with tears as we sang "How Firm a Foundation." Every word ministered deeply to my heart:

How firm a foundation, ye saints of the Lord
Is laid for your faith in His excellent word
What more can He say than to you He hath said
To you who for refuge to Jesus have fled?

Fear not, I am with thee, 0 be not dismayed
For I am thy God and will still give thee aid
I'll strengthen thee, help thee, and cause thee to stand
Upheld by My gracious, omnipotent hand.

When through the deep waters I call thee to go
The rivers of sorrow shall not overflow
For I will be with thee thy trials to bless
And sanctify to thee thy deepest distress.

When through fiery trials thy pathway shall lie
My grace all sufficient shall be thy supply
The flames shall not hurt thee, I only design
Thy dross to consume and thy gold to refine.

What promise and hope these words gave me! How good it was to be together in worship again. Part of our pastor's prayer was from Psalm 103: "As a father pities his children, so the Lord pities those who fear Him." As he prayed, I felt my heavenly Father's arm tenderly comfort me and I realized His compassion. Both the pastor and our family knew those words were prayed specifically for us this morning. I was refreshed and encouraged.

God's greatest encouragement that day, however, came in a very personal way through our friend Ruth. After church she came rushing up to us exclaiming, "George! Trudy! Guess what?"

"What?" we both asked simultaneously.

"I was praying this morning and asked the Lord to give me a specific Bible verse for your family concerning Karen. 'Zephaniah 3:15' popped into my head. I disregarded it, however, waiting for a more familiar sounding verse. I wasn't even sure there was a Zephaniah, but the word persisted, so I checked the index of my Bible and looked it up. There is such a book. Take a look at what it says!" Ruth held out her Bible.

Our hearts thrilled as we read God's personal promise to us for Karen:

> The Lord has taken away the judgments against you, he has cast out your enemies. The King of Israel, the Lord, is in your midst; you shall fear evil no more. (Zeph. 3:15, RSV)

The words of the hymn we had sung earlier ran through my mind: "What more can He say than to you He hath said, to you who for refuge to Jesus have fled!"

3
Encourager

George, Chris and I took our boat for an evening sail while Mike volunteered to keep Karen company in the hospital. Our family had enjoyed sailing for many years. When we moved to Miami, Florida we saw the Lord's guidance in an opportunity to buy a Catalina 27, and we named out new boat "God-Send" in honor of what God had done. Now we were especially grateful to have this means of relaxing.

The balmy, night air was refreshing and soothing. The sparkling lights of downtown Miami were pleasant to observe from the bay and we reflected on the wonderful promise from Zephaniah 3:15 which we were given earlier in the day. It was restful to be away from the hospital and we considered sailing longer but felt an inner nudge to return to the dock.

Within an hour of docking the boat, we pulled into the hospital parking lot. As we walked down the corridor of West, we saw Geri running toward the supply room.

"Oh, good, you're back!" she called out hastily as she saw us approach. "The sore on Karen's tongue started to bleed and we're working to stop it now."

I hurried into Karen's room. Huddled around Karen

were the nursing supervisor, two resident doctors and another nurse. I couldn't see Karen but I heard her fearfully crying for me.

"Here I am, Karen," I called.

The nurses moved aside, revealing our daughter. I was shocked at what I saw! Blood was everywhere! It covered Karen's face and gown, and most of the bed. The closest I could get to her was the foot of the bed.

I put my hands on her feet to calm her, trying to remain calm myself. "It's okay, Karen. Daddy and Mommy are here. You be helpful to the doctors."

I prayed softly, "Thank you, Jesus, for the victory. Thank you, Lord, that you are in control and that Karen belongs to you. Satan, in the name of Jesus get your hands off Karen!"

I continued to hold Karen's feet, praying silently in the Spirit. Within a few minutes, the doctors brought the bleeding under control, and we all relaxed from the crisis. After Karen and the bed were cleaned and changed, we learned more about what happened.

Mike and Karen had been watching television when Karen fell asleep. Apparently Karen knocked the scab off the sore on her tongue and, while she was asleep, a steady stream of blood flowed from her mouth. Karen coughed, and Mike looked at her and saw blood everywhere. He quickly rang the nurse bell and woke Karen. When all the people ran into her room and she saw the blood, she was frightened and began to cry for me. It was at that very moment we arrived.

God's perfect timing brought us from the ocean to Karen's bedside at the precisely needed time. We saw clearly, too, Satan's attempt to frighten us out of the victory that the Lord had given us. Truly, the King of Israel was in our midst and we were to fear evil no more!

"Maybe Karen should pray for the baptism in the Holy Spirit," George said one evening. "She should have the power of the Spirit within her just as we have. It will enable her to fight Satan."

"That sounds like a good idea, honey," I replied, remembering the recent crisis. "I don't think she's too young, either. The Lord promises to give the Holy Spirit to all who are His, and Karen certainly belongs to Him (Acts 2:38, 39)."

That evening I shared with Karen how Jesus promised to send the Holy Spirit to all His disciples as a constant Companion, Helper, Comforter and Strength. We were to ask Jesus to baptize us with the Holy Spirit and we would receive power to witness about Jesus and to do battle against our enemy, Satan (Luke 11:13; John 14:16f; John 1:33; Acts 1:5). I asked her if she would like to pray for the baptism in the Holy Spirit.

"Sure, Mommy," she replied.

I asked her to repeat after me: "Dear Lord Jesus, please forgive me for all of my sins. I open my heart to you and ask you to be Lord of my life. Please baptize me in the Holy Spirit. Amen."

I laid my hands on Karen's head and prayed aloud, thanking Jesus that He was the Baptizer and that He heard and answered her prayer. I then prayed in tongues and encouraged Karen to join me in her own language from the Lord. I asked Karen if she had different-sounding words going through her head that she could speak out. "If not," I explained, "just open your mouth and make sounds that are not English, and the Holy Spirit will form words from the sound."

"I have some words," she said, somewhat shyly. "But I don't want to say them out loud right now."

"That's all right, honey," I said happily. "And thank you, Jesus, for filling Karen with the Holy Spirit."

The second series of chemotherapy treatments was now finished, Karen's mouth sores were healing and, apart from being weak, she seemed to be fine. It was too soon yet to tell if the medicine had brought about remission.

The doctors talked of letting Karen go home as soon as her platelet supply built up. They wanted to keep her under observation because of the danger of internal bleeding; she would receive a platelet transfusion, if necessary.

While we waited, Karen felt healthy enough to enjoy her many new friends among the nurses and aides. One night before bedtime Karen said, "Let's play a trick on Geri." She explained her plan. I was to pull my sofa bed out. Karen would get under my covers and turn her head to the wall so just her brown hair showed. Next I was to put a stuffed animal under Karen's covers, ring for Geri and then hide in the bathroom.

"That sounds like fun, Karen." Pulling out my bed and making it ready, I prepared for my part in the adventure.

With eager anticipation, Karen got out of her bed and moved the i.v. machine so her attached cord would reach. She crawled into my bed, ready for Geri. I rang the call bell and lunged for the bathroom.

"What do you want, Karen?" Geri said, entering the room. Seeing Karen's joke, she played along with the fun. "Mrs. Colflesh," she cried. "Mrs. Colflesh, I can't find Karen. She's gone and there's just a stuffed animal in her bed."

With that, Karen sat up in my bed, laughing with glee. I came out of hiding, and Geri acted surprised. We all had a good laugh together.

Karen also had fun with nurse Emmy. When Karen first met Emmy she was wearing a green hospital surgical outfit and, being heavy-set, Karen told me that she "looked like a big, green leaf."

Emmy had a good sense of humor and jokingly told Karen she would squirt her with a syringe full of water if she didn't take her medicine. That gave Karen an idea, and she asked me to bring her water pistol from home.

The next day, when Emmy walked in the room, Karen said, "I have a surprise for you." She pulled her water pistol out from under the covers and squirted Emmy. Grinning, Emmy came back in a few minutes, and squirted Karen from a syringe. They both laughed at each other's exploits.

Each day we hoped Karen's platelet report would indicate enough of an increase for us to go home. The Fourth of July holiday came while we were still waiting. I remembered happier days, such as the year before when our family went for an evening sail and watched the fireworks display from the water.

There was no activity on West. The other patients had all gone home. Only one child besides Karen was there; a little, three-year-old black boy from the Bahamas named Shevago. I walked restlessly around the quiet halls but returned to the room shortly and sat looking out the window. I was lonely.

"Hello, may I come it?" A cheery voice broke the silence. I turned to see a lovely Cuban lady standing at the door.

"Oh, yes. Please do," I said.

She introduced herself as Aurora Aragon and held a gift out to Karen. While Karen played with the toy, Aurora shared that she spent several months on West when her son was diagnosed with leukemia. She was happy to tell me that he was in remission now and for the past several years was doing very well.

"The first few months are the hardest," she explained with sincere understanding. "I know what it's like to be in the hospital on a holiday. That's why I came." I was glad she was there. I knew she truly understood.

Aurora's visit lifted my spirits. Geri, Karen and I made plans for an evening celebration. George and the boys arrived and soon it was dark. Shevago was brought into Karen's room, and Chris, Mike and I went out on the lawn beneath Karen's window. While those in the room watched, we lit sparklers, whirled our arms and ran in circles attempting to make an interesting fireworks display for Karen and Shevago. To conclude the evening's activities, we gathered in Karen's room where Geri made fresh popcorn for everyone.

The big celebration for us, however, came three days later. For the first time since we entered the hospital five weeks before, Karen was allowed to go home! It was a special day. It was the seventh month, the seventh day and the seventy-seventh year: 7/7/77. God uses the number seven in the Bible to express a perfect completion. We saw God choosing that day for Karen's discharge to encourage and show us that He is in control of the circumstances and that His timing is perfect.

We were to realize later that God would again use the number seven to reinforce His plan for Karen. It, too, would involve a celebration and a home going.

George and I helped Karen pack her suitcase, and we carried armloads of stuffed animals and toys into the car to go home. Chris hung the American flag and strung rows of brightly-colored pennants from the house to the yard before we arrived. The flag and the pennants flapped a happy hello in the breeze as George and I drove into the driveway with our precious Karen.

Karen was grateful to be home. No longer was she confined to one room, attached to an i.v. machine, required to take medicine, have blood drawn and maintain a hospital routine. Now she could dress in her own clothes, sit with her family to eat and sleep in her own bed.

Even though she was still weak, Karen especially enjoyed being outside. She climbed to her favorite perch in the backyard tree and sat on the limb, dangling her feet.

"Look, Mommy," she called out.

"I see!" I responded with a happy heart.

Dr. DeLamerens scheduled us to return to the hospital out-patient clinic four days after Karen was discharged so that her blood condition could be checked.

I woke Karen the morning of clinic. She turned over with a groan. "I don't feel well. My head aches," she complained. Her legs were covered with red spots.

"Oh, no!" I cried in dismay. My heart sank. I had seen spots like these before on Karen. They were the result of her platelets being too low, and it was serious.

Holding Karen on my lap at the clinic, she gratefully rested against me waiting our turn. She had already gone through the routine weighing, measuring and having a blood sample drawn from her finger. The doctor would see us shortly to tell us the results.

Soon we were in the examining room with Dr. DeLamerens. "How would you like to visit your friends upstairs on West again, Karen?" he asked. "You will need a platelet transfusion to help you feel better."

"Okay," Karen responded, wearily. She knew she needed something.

I checked Karen in at the admissions office. Just four days before, Karen was going home. Now we were back. "Maybe this will be a short hospital visit," I tried to encourage myself. I didn't realize what lay ahead. It turned out to be the longest and most harrowing stay of all.

Before we admitted ourselves to West, Karen wanted to visit the hospital's gift shop. From time to time, the nurses would buy a candy treat from the shop for Karen, and she wanted to go there herself before she was once again confined to her room. After pointing out all the gifts she thought would be nice for her sometime, we reluctantly took the elevator to West.

Dr. DeLamerens asked George and me to meet in his office. He told us that the recent chemotherapy treatment which Karen had received had not been effective in bringing her into remission. I remembered we were told that 75 percent of leukemia patients usually respond by the second course of chemotherapy. This had been Karen's second.

He went on to say that Karen's type of leukemia did not respond well to medicine, but he was going to administer a third series of chemotherapy treatments as soon as her blood platelets improved. Perhaps this treatment would be effective.

The doctor had never given us false hope on Karen's condition. He also had not given us a time schedule on her life expectancy. We had not been able to bring ourselves to ask, before. Now I heard George phrase the dreaded question.

"How long do you think she has to live?"

"Maybe weeks, maybe a few months," he responded, tenderly. "No one knows for sure."

"You know, Lord. *You* know," I prayed silently. "Thank you that we're all in the palm of your hand."

The next day, the words of the song "Great Is Thy Faithfulness" ran through my mind. I held on to them for strength.

I left the hospital for a few hours to go home. While there, the phone rang. It was a counselor from Pat Robertson's "The 700 Club." We were supporting members of his evangelical television outreach program, and it was a routine, yearly call to express appreciation.

The lady asked if we had any special prayer needs. "Oh, yes!" I exclaimed, and I told her about Karen.

"God has no coincidences," she said. "Let's pray. Lord you prayed, 'Thy will be done on earth as in heaven.' There is no sickness in heaven, and we know it is not God's will for sickness on earth."

She prayed concerning our faith to believe in Karen's healing. She said, "The faith you need is from Jesus, who is within us. Therefore, you already have the faith that is necessary."

The radio was tuned to our favorite Christian station. Inspirational music played softly in the background. As I thanked the counselor for her prayer and hung up the phone, my attention was drawn to the melody and words on the radio:

What a friend we have in Jesus, all our sins and grief's to bear. What a privilege to carry everything to God in prayer. Have we trials

43

and temptations? Is there sorrow anywhere?
We should never be discouraged: Take it to
the Lord in prayer.

I broke into tears, feeling the presence and comfort of
our precious Savior, Jesus. Truly His faithfulness was
great!

Mickey Jordan, a vivacious, Christian woman with a
ministry of healing and evangelism, was visiting the area.
George and I attended our friend's prayer meeting where
she was speaking.

"Do you think we should invite Mickey to the
hospital?" I asked, after hearing her message.

"I don't know. Let me think about it," George replied.

When the meeting was over, George drove me back to
the hospital. He came in to say good night to Karen.

Since the onset of her illness, he had prayed with her
nightly. As he prayed this evening, George asked Jesus to
make His presence known to Karen.

I tucked her in bed, and we talked about the Lord. "I
still wonder what 'ben anae' means, Mommy ," she said,
remembering her father's words in tongues the day he was
baptized in the Holy Spirit. She had asked me this several
times before.

"God will have to give us the interpretation, honey,
because I don't know what it means." As I was talking,
Karen held up her hand for me to stop.

"Wait, God's talking!" Her eyes got big as she listened.
"Mommy, God just told me 'ben anae' means 'Son of
God!'"

I *knew* God had spoken to her. He had made His
presence real, just as George asked in his prayer. Karen

was filled with uninhibited joy and praise. With her face beaming, she lifted her hands to the Lord and worshiped Him. After we rejoiced together, I phoned George to share the exciting news.

Early the next morning George telephoned from home. He asked me to find out if Mickey Jordan could come and pray with Karen. It was exactly what I was waiting to hear. I quickly contacted Mickey at my friend's house. She prayed concerning God's will in the matter, and felt His confirmation to come.

As Mickey entered the room, Karen threw the sheet over her head.

"Oh no. Here we go again," I thought.

George arrived soon after, and Karen brought herself out from under the covers. Her stubbornness showed through, however, for the entire time Mickey was there, Karen refused to talk.

Karen did nod her head in affirmation when asked if she would like to be anointed with oil. Mickey anointed not only Karen, but her bed, the sheets, the pillow, her stuffed animals and the air around her bed. She bound Satan and rebuked him in the name of Jesus. She also rebuked the leukemia.

Mickey laid hands on Karen's head and body and prayed for Jesus to heal her completely. She asked Jesus to transfuse Karen's blood and restore it to wholeness.

We all felt the presence of the Lord and His anointing. Something broke loose within me as Mickey prayed, and my faith went from hope in Karen's healing to assurance of it.

The next morning the doctors came into Karen's room, talking excitedly. The results of her blood test showed such improvement that she could start her third series of chemotherapy treatments right away. I praised God as I saw His answer to our prayers.

The news of more chemotherapy, however, was not so exciting to Karen. The first few days of each treatment she became nauseated and vomited. The only help I could give was to hold her hand, rub her back and hold the pan for her. Yet even while she was groaning, her good nature prevailed. After one extensive period of vomiting, Karen observed the amount in the pan. "Wow. Let me ring for the nurse and tell her how many c.c.'s I threw up this time!"

With each round of chemotherapy treatments, we prayed, remembering Mark 16:18: "If they drink any deadly thing, it will not hurt them." We knew that, as helpful as chemotherapy could be, it was still extremely toxic to the body. We asked the Lord to protect Karen from its harmful side effects.

The hospital staff soon learned that Karen had been readmitted. One of her favorite visitors was Carol Drozdowicz, the day-nursing supervisor. Carol would pop her head into the room each day to say hello.

Karen learned from her that the hospital had a "special closet," full of games and gifts. At least once a week, Carol brought something from the closet for Karen. Between those times Karen liked to dream about the closet's contents and she looked forward to the next surprise.

We frequently played games, many of them coming from the "special closet." It was difficult for Karen to do activities that called for coloring or cutting, since she was restricted by the i.v. board taped to her wrist and hand. The board was used to help prevent the i.v. needle from pulling out.

To our dismay, an i.v. needle only lasted several days.

As the vein weakened, allowing i.v. solution to escape, Karen's hand often swelled. Sometimes it took an entire day for the swelling to go down, enabling her to use her hand again.

Karen's other wrist would be used for a new needle and another vein had to be found to restart the i.v. A special i.v. nurse would examine Karen's hand. "Get a good vein," Karen nervously advised. She knew that if it was not good the first time, the nurse would have to try again.

Karen would grip my hand tightly and turn her face away as the nurse inserted the needle. "Is there a blood return?" she would cry out. She knew the procedure well. If the answer was "yes," the ordeal was over for a few more days.

The Lord continued to guide us in our direction for Karen. Almost every evening, George read to her from a Bible storybook. One night, he read Jesus' teachings about prayer. The Lord spoke to us through it. We were not to give up, but to ask, to keep on asking and to persevere in prayer for Karen.

God also brought to our attention the concept of being thankful in all things. "Rejoice always . . . give thanks in all circumstances (1 Thess. 5:16,18ff); Rejoice in the Lord always; again I will say, Rejoice" (Phil. 4:4)."

Karen and I often sang a lively tune together from the Philippians verse. I realized the Lord hadn't said to rejoice only when things were good or when we felt like it, but to rejoice *always*. He also said to give thanks in *all* circumstances, not just in those we liked.

With these thoughts in mind, I talked with Karen about a different way I was going to pray. I told her it would sound unusual but we could pray this way because we could trust God absolutely. He was in control of all things.

"Lord," I prayed. "We know you are good and you are sovereign over all things, including evil. Therefore, we are trusting you and choose to be thankful, even in these painful, confusing circumstances.

"So thank you, Father," I prayed, "that Karen has a fever, that she doesn't feel well, that she is here in the hospital, and that . . ." I found it harder to say it, but concluded, ". . . that she has leukemia."

My mind screamed "this is ridiculous," but a strange sense of joy welled up within my spirit. I found that God was enabling me to truly give thanks in all things.

We were acknowledging that our loving Father will take care of us in every situation and that our hearts are to be thankful, even when the circumstances are terrible.

We found that Mike and Chris also needed to learn the lesson of thankfulness. My extended stay with Karen at the hospital had a wearing effect on them. They were becoming short-tempered with each other. I made an effort to have dinner at home and we discussed the family situation.

George and I tried to help them realize that they, too, as well as we and Karen, were in spiritual warfare against Satan. Instead of letting the enemy provoke them into fighting each other, they should use the defense of being thankful in all circumstances and not be tricked into being angry with each other.

That evening after dinner I returned to the hospital while George, Mike and Chris went sailing. Several hours later, they arrived at the hospital bubbling over with an exciting story to tell.

As they sailed, George and the boys decided to explore a new section of the bay. Without warning, they ran aground on a sandbar. After trying all the usual procedures for freeing the boat, it still held fast to the sand. To make matters worse, the tide was going out and the water was becoming more and more shallow.

"Daddy, remember what you told us at dinner about being thankful for everything?" Chris spoke up. "Why don't we thank God right now for this situation?"

George gulped and said weakly, "Good idea, Chris. I'd like for *you* to pray."

Chris climbed to the bow of the boat and stood on the deck with his arms stretched toward heaven in the darkness. "Thank you, God," he prayed, "that we are grounded out here in Biscayne Bay at ten o'clock at night ...." He paused to look around, then continued praying, "And with no help in sight."

As Chris said, "Amen," it was as if an invisible hand from heaven reached down. The boat suddenly swung around, freeing itself from the sandbar, and sailed away!

Everyone sat in stunned silence for a long time. Finally, in deep respect, Mike said, "Gee, Dad, God sure teaches His lessons in a dramatic way!"

God continued to encourage our trust in Him. I turned on the radio to listen to some Christian music. The first words I heard were, "Trust Him, He'll never leave you. Trust Him because He loves you."

"I love you, too, Father, and I *do* trust you," I prayed. "Show us what we are to do next for our precious Karen."

We knew we were to have a prayer meeting "to pray in one accord" for Karen (Matt. 18:19). It seemed that now was the time. The hospital gave us permission to use their chapel. We invited our friends and explained our desire to pray in unity. We wanted to thank God for the healing He had already given Karen and to ask Him to complete it.

Karen had a fever of 104 degrees all day of the scheduled meeting. George and I lingered with concern in her room. I could see she was weak and listless. Hilda Puente, the nurse on duty, assured us not to worry and said she would keep a close watch on Karen. She knew where to reach us if we were needed.

"By the way," she asked George. "How do you run a prayer meeting like this one?"

"I don't know," George laughed, breaking the heaviness. "I've never been to one."

It was a blessing to see our friends gathered together on behalf of Karen. As I looked at the group, I realized that it was not the usual gathering of Christians. Even though it was a small group, it was composed of Protestants, Catholics and a Messianic Jew.

I thought again of the Scripture over the hospital door: "A little child shall lead them." My heart warmed as I saw the Holy Spirit bringing His people together in unity through Karen.

George opened the meeting with prayer. We shared the amazing events God was doing in Karen's life, read Scripture and prayed fervently for Karen's healing. We stood, joined hands and sang, "We are one in the Spirit; we are one in the Lord."

God's presence was so real and personal. We experienced a oneness of the Spirit.

One friend prayed, thanking God that He was going to use Karen to reach "hundreds of thousands for His Glory." As I heard her words, my spirit thrilled within me in confirmation. My mind was awed at the concept. I thought again of Psalm 57, God's promise to us at the beginning of Karen's illness: "I will give thanks to thee, 0 Lord, among the peoples; I will sing praises to thee among the nations" (v. 9, RSV).

At the conclusion of the prayers we hugged each other goodbye in Christian love. Warmed and encouraged, George and I went upstairs to Karen's room.

As we turned the corner to West, we were surprised to see Karen sitting on a blanket in the hallway with several of the children.

"Trudy! George!" Hilda called, running to greet us.

"You'll never believe what happened!" She shared with us a most exciting story.

Hilda was sitting on the edge of Karen's bed visiting, when, suddenly, Karen's breathing became labored. She began turning bluish-gray from lack of oxygen. Hilda went into action immediately. She ran for an oxygen mask, had the doctor called and ran back to Karen's room.

Hilda observed Karen for just a moment before administering oxygen. "Before my very eyes," Hilda exclaimed, "just like that" (snapping her fingers), "Karen's color and breathing returned to normal. She put her feet over the edge of the bed and asked if she could go out in the hall to play. I figured this happened about the same time the prayer meeting began. That must have been some prayer meeting!"

"Yes, it was!" we said, with wonder and gratitude.

Even though Karen's temperature was now under control and she felt better, she was becoming irritable with the prolonged confinement. She did not like it when I left to go home or on errands and she wanted me to be with her all the time. Even when I stepped out to the hallway, the buzzer would go off from Karen's room. "I want Mommy!" she called out.

"I'll be in shortly," I answered.

We felt it was important not to allow Karen to be overly demanding even though she was sick. When I had to be gone, I told her in a loving, yet firm manner when I would be back. "I'll give you a call as soon as I get home," I promised, placing the phone beside her so she could reach it easily.

We had taught Karen at home how to answer the

phone. I chuckled when I called her at the hospital and she answered, "Hello, Colfleshes; Karen speaking."

Karen learned to dial the outside line at the hospital and then our number. She was free to call home whenever she wanted. Usually she called to check on my progress and to see how much longer it would be until I returned.

Once, while I was home, Karen's i.v. needle had to be changed. To Karen's distress, I wasn't there.

"Call Mommy and tell her to get over here right away!" she cried.

The nurse kindly phoned me but told Karen they couldn't delay putting in the new needle. I reassured Karen as best I could over the phone. I prayed that she would be brave and that she would know that Jesus was with her. I talked until the needle was in and was glad we could at least be together by phone.

George and I talked to Karen about her demands on my being with her. We asked why she was acting that way. She said she was afraid when I was gone. We shared with her how, even if Mommy or Daddy were gone, Jesus was with her always. He would give her the power to do what she had to do, and He would take away her fear.

We looked up different Bible verses that would encourage Karen. I wrote them out on construction paper to hang on the wall. Karen helped me with one by tracing over my light pencil letters with a red crayon.

"I can do everything God asks me to do with the help of Christ who gives me the strength and power (Phil. 4:13, TLB)," she wrote. We hung it in a prominent spot on the wall.

We also hung two other posters: "The Lord has said, 'I will never fail you nor forsake you . . . The Lord is my helper. I will not be afraid (Heb. 13:5, 6)," and "Fear not, for I am with you, be not dismayed, for I am your God; I will strengthen you, I will help you, I will uphold you with my victorious right hand (Isa. 41: 10, RSV)."

These words of comfort and strength would be sorely needed in the crisis which was just ahead.

4
Mighty God

For several weeks, Karen had the symptoms of a cold. She was continually given antibiotics, but there was no improvement. The cold settled in her throat and each day she became more congested and her voice more hoarse.

An X-ray of Karen's throat was ordered by Dr. DeLamerens. The results showed that her air passage was swollen. The doctors were not sure if it was congestion from a cold or a rare, but possibly cancerous, growth on her larynx. We prayed for the Lord to give the doctors wisdom and direction.

Dr. Escalon called me to his office to advise me on Karen's condition. I mentioned that Karen complained that her throat was itching. Apparently, this information provided the wisdom for which we had prayed because he immediately ordered a bone marrow test and a fourth series of chemotherapy treatments to be started on Karen.

He explained that the chemotherapy would work against the swelling in Karen's throat if it were cancerous. I sensed a race against time between the swelling and chemotherapy.

55

Was it possible that Karen's life was about to be snuffed out?

"Yea, though I walk through the valley of the shadow of death, I will fear no evil" (Ps. 23:4, KJV). This valley was a frightening place in which to walk. I forced myself to trust in Jesus so I would not be overwhelmed by the circumstances.

When the bone marrow test was completed, the doctor reported the results to George and me. Our hearts sank. After sixty days in the hospital, and after three series of chemotherapy, there was no sign of any remission. The bone marrow was still 100 percent cancerous. Since Karen had not responded to the chemotherapy thus far, the likelihood of her going into remission was now even less.

"I'm sorry," the doctor said, as he reported the test results.

"It's in God's hands," George said bravely.

God's peace must have been on our faces because, as the doctor looked at us, he said, "You do realize that her condition is serious?"

"Yes," we assured him. How well we knew Karen's condition was serious.

"Do you think Karen is stable enough for Trudy and me to go out to dinner?" George asked. "You see, this is our sixteenth wedding anniversary."

"That would be a good break for you both," the doctor answered. "Enjoy yourselves and try to relax."

We did enjoy our dinner. However, we didn't relax away from the hospital any more than we did while we were there. We were learning to walk in the peace of the Lord and not by the circumstance. In His peace was our rest.

An oxygen tent and equipment were ordered for

Karen's room to ease her breathing. The see-through tent was set up over her bed and attached to a large machine. She was to stay under the tent day and night. Karen didn't like the idea, however, and didn't want the tent. She tried to persuade us to take it away but finally resigned herself to the new intruder to her freedom.

The hissing of the oxygen and the noise of the water pump woke me during the night. I looked at Karen. Her small body lay beneath the tent. Her chest was rising and falling with labored breathing. "Oh, God," I cried. "What's happening? What is your plan for Karen?" I watched with concern as the nurse checked Karen throughout the night.

Early that morning, I called my friend Esther. "Can you come to the hospital?" I choked out. I fought hard to hold back the tears.

"I'll be right over," Esther said.

We met downstairs in the chapel. Esther knew what I was feeling. She comforted me with the comfort the Lord had given her when her own daughter's life once hung in the balance. She shared her faith, a faith that was refined out of suffering and shaped by a loving Father.

Esther encouraged me to trust God's wisdom and plan for Karen, even if His purpose didn't include healing. It was hard to receive that, although I sensed I must hear it. We prayed together and, through tears, I again released Karen to God's purpose for her life. As we finished praying, we asked for guardian angels to surround and protect Karen.

Karen must have realized how serious her condition was. While George was reading her a story, she confided to him, "I'm glad you're my daddy, and I'm probably not going to die." His heart melted as he held her in his arms.

That night, our doctors consulted a surgeon to examine Karen and consider emergency procedures if her throat should swell shut. The surgeon agreed to sleep in one of the empty rooms on West so he would be immediately available in case of a crisis. I shuddered as a complete tray for a tracheotomy was brought into Karen's room and left there in waiting.

George and I continued to pray. We asked the Lord to send His angels to guard Karen from all danger.

The nurses and I checked Karen's condition constantly throughout the night. To my relief, Karen's breathing became progressively less labored and, by morning, seemed normal.

Karen was sent for another X-ray early that morning for a look at her throat. The radiologist sent us the good news, "Whatever you're doing, keep it up! The growth is reducing and Karen's throat is opening!"

Karen improved so greatly that I felt free to go to my Aglow meeting that week. A friend passed me a note during the worship. It read, "I was praying for Karen this weekend, and the Lord gave me a vision of two huge guardian angels, as tall as the ceiling, standing by Karen's bed. One was at her head and the other at her feet. They had their swords drawn and were protecting her from the spirit of death."

I wept with joy at God's goodness and raised my hands in praise to our mighty God!

I shared this exciting vision with our doctors the next day as they made their morning visit to examine Karen. They all agreed that something special had happened. They seemed grateful that we looked beyond their ability to minister to Karen, as good as it was, and drew our strength from the Lord.

Mighty God

I read Psalm 33:18-22, which expressed our situation exactly:

> Behold, the eye of the Lord is on those who fear him, on those who hope in his steadfast love, *that he may deliver their soul from death,* and keep them alive in famine.

> Our soul waits for the Lord; he is our help and shield. Yea, our heart is glad in him, because we trust in his holy name. Let thy steadfast love, 0 Lord, be upon us, even as we hope in thee.
> (RSV, italics added)

It was exciting for George and me to see how the Lord brought people to minister to Karen. My brother Jim Patterson, a Presbyterian minister in California, and his wife, made plans for a special visit to Florida. Karen was thrilled that her Uncle Jim and Aunt Margie were coming. Her breathing was normal enough to be allowed out from under the oxygen tent. The chemotherapy series was finished and the i.v. discontinued. Without the cord attaching her to the Ivac machine, Karen could wear her clothes. She enjoyed being dressed and out of bed. Her only restriction was that she had to stay in her room in reverse isolation.

We planned a popcorn party to welcome Jim and Margie. Karen wanted Shevago, the little boy from the Bahamas, to come, too. The nurses on duty that night were also invited to attend.

Jim and Margie arrived at our house and we talked excitedly, telling them all that the Lord had done. We ate a quick dinner and drove to the hospital where Karen eagerly waited. Karen's voice was still hoarse, but she told her aunt and uncle the things she had been doing.

"Well, it's time for the party, now," Karen said. She rang the buzzer and Hilda brought in the popcorn popper. Karen poured the beverage while we popped the corn. Shevago and the nurses joined us for a fun time of refreshments.

The nurses left to fulfill their responsibilities and Shevago stayed. Two months ago, when he came to the hospital alone, he wouldn't talk to anyone. Now he smiled and joined the conversation.

Jim asked us to share what we had seen the Lord doing in our lives and what we wanted Him to do now. "I want the Lord to finish healing me so I can go home," Karen said.

We sang joyful Scripture songs, clapping our hands to the rhythm. Shevago smiled and clapped along. Jim read from the Bible. As he read Psalm 6, the words of verse two stood out to me concerning Karen: "Be gracious to me, 0 Lord, for I am languishing; 0 Lord, heal me, for my bones are troubled" (Ps. 6:2, RSV).

Then came the moment I was waiting for. We gathered around Karen to pray. I knew the Lord would speak His thoughts through Jim. "My beloved children," I heard Jim's voice prophesy. "'I have loved you with an everlasting love. Although you do not understand what I am doing now; some day you will know. Be assured of my love and that all I do is done in love.' "

The Lord spoke more words of comfort and reassurance through Jim, but I kept waiting to hear something specific about Karen's recovery. Then the words came: " 'Because you have given Karen to me, I am giving her back to you.'"

60

"*I am giving her back*," He had said. "Oh Father!" I exclaimed. My heart thrilled with wonder and rejoicing.

I thought again of the words I had just read in a devotional book. "For *this hour* I, the Lord, have prepared thy heart and in my kindness I will not let thee fail." I realized our faith in Karen's healing was not dependent on us alone. Our loving Father developed the faith we had and He would be faithful to maintain it. It gave me great comfort to trust God's sovereignty and to know He would not let us fail Him.

Our Lord continued to increase our faith and trust in Him to the place where we were fully prepared for the unknown coming battle. Before the storm hit, we had a time of calm and encouragement. We took Jim and Margie sailing on the last day of their visit. The sun and the gentle breezes delighted us as the boat glided effortlessly through the water. I returned to the hospital refreshed and relaxed.

Many people came to visit and pray. Many more sent cards and letters.

"This one's from Mrs. Wright!" Karen exclaimed as she opened an envelope. Mrs. Wright, a dear, elderly lady from our church, carried out a ministry of writing to the sick, the shut-in and those away from home in school or service. At least once a week she had been faithfully sending cards to the hospital. Karen learned to recognize her elderly script before she opened the card, and, although they had never met, they were becoming good friends.

One of the letters that came contained an appeal for money for Bibles. Karen read it with interest and told me she wanted to give her money to provide a Bible. At that point she had about six dollars saved at home. "How much do you want to give, honey?" I asked

"All of it," she replied.

Nurse Lisa came in while Karen was reading the letter, and Karen asked her if she wanted to give some money for Bibles. Karen explained all about it, and Lisa said she would like to contribute too. She gave us five dollars to send in with Karen's money.

George wrote a note with the money and explained the circumstances. We were touched when, a few weeks later the founder of Bibles for the World, Rochunga Pudaite, wrote Karen a personal letter of thanks and encouragement.

Giving Bibles became a real interest of Karen's, and she kept a "Bible bank" on her bedside table for contributions. One day, she drew a picture of herself in bed with the oxygen tent behind it. She had a smile on her face and beside her was a huge guardian angel.

"Mommy," she said, "would you please print the words 'Trust in the Lord and give Bibles,' beside my picture?"

As encouraging as our friends were with their prayers, visits and cards, the days were growing long. I was anxious to go home. After Karen's throat opened, her condition remained basically the same, continuous slight nausea, low fever and an imbalanced blood picture. She could not be released until these conditions improved.

As we waited, I filled some of the time by reading the Psalms aloud to Karen. She related to Psalm 6, especially verse 6: "I am weary with my moaning ...." (RSV).

While I read, I noticed Karen moving her lips as though she were talking quietly. "Mommy," she said, "my stomach was really hurting so I prayed in tongues about it, and it's gone!"

We rejoiced as I finished reading Psalm 6:

Depart from me, all you workers of evil; for the Lord heard the sound of my weeping. The Lord has heard my supplications; the Lord accepts my prayer. All my enemies shall be ashamed and sorely troubled; they shall turn back, and be put to shame in a moment. (Ps. 6:8-10, RSV)

The next morning I awoke to another day of waiting. The blood picture was the same: No improvement; no going home.

"How long, Oh, Lord? How long?,' I cried.

The sky was overcast. I felt as gloomy as the day. Karen was watching Captain Kangaroo on television, and I left the room to wander around the halls. I found myself in front of the chapel doors and thought I might find relief by sitting in its serene environment.

The doors were usually kept locked, and I had to make arrangements to get the key when I planned to go to the chapel. "Perhaps they're not locked today," I thought. "Besides, I don't want to ask at the desk for the key with these tears in my eyes."

I pushed against the doors, hoping they would open to a welcome place of refuge. They held firm against my push. It was more than I could take. The tears started to roll down my cheeks, and I leaned against the wall.

But the Lord had "heard the sound of my weeping" (Ps. 6). A lady I knew from the finance office came walking down the hall at that very moment. She saw my distress and said, kindly, "Trudy, I'll get the key for you."

She opened the door and placed a reassuring hand on my shoulder. In the quiet, filtered, blue light of the chapel, I felt free to cry. I knelt before my Lord and poured my heart out to Him.

"Lord," I sobbed. "I relinquish Karen to you and to your glory and to your plans for her life. Do with her as you will."

After a while I looked up and saw three words printed on the blackboard, "Pray for Kelly." My heart went out to the hands who, in hope, perhaps with tears, had written those words. I did pray for Kelly, and for Shevago and Anthony and for all of the other children on West as well as those throughout the hospital. I again asked the Lord's blessing on this hospital and all who worked in it.

I left the chapel feeling better. The mail had arrived when I got to Karen's room, and there was a letter for me. When I opened it, I knew God had timed it to arrive at that hour. My friend wrote, "Let not your hearts be troubled, neither let them be afraid" (John 14:27, RSV) and "Faith is the assurance of things hoped for, the conviction of things not seen" (Heb. 11:1, RSV).

"Thank you, Father," I prayed, "for your constant presence and reassurance."

Our church called a special meeting to pray for Karen and for another member of the congregation who had cancer. It warmed our hearts to feel their prayer support.

"Surely, Lord, you will act soon," I thought, but Karen did not improve. Her throat became congested again and her voice even more hoarse. The doctors ordered the oxygen tent again and only permitted her out from under it for short periods of time.

Karen asked if she could have a popcorn party. Holiday, the head nurse, said, "So sorry, Karen. Not until your throat is better."

The chief surgeon was called in to look at Karen's throat. He said it appeared that she had a large ulcer. It was too risky to put an instrument down her throat for a better look because of the danger of her hemorrhaging due to her low platelet count.

George and I felt restless about Karen's condition. It was as if she were "on hold" and we were to do something next. We wondered if we should call the Muellers.

"I don't know what we're to do," I said. "Let's ask the Lord to have Victor call us if he is to minister to Karen again."

While George was with Karen, I did some errands and stopped at home for a quick sandwich. The phone rang as I sat down to eat. To my delight, it was Victor!

"I was looking up a number in my phone book to call somebody concerning our meeting tonight," he explained. "I came across your number and thought I would give you a quick call to see how your little girl is."

"Oh, Victor, I'm so glad!" I said, and told him about George's and my conversation and of Karen's condition.

"Come to our prayer meeting tonight, and we'll lay hands on you in proxy for Karen," Victor said. "Then we will see what the Lord would have us do further."

I enjoyed the fellowship of prayer and praise at the Muellers. Toward the end of the meeting, we prayed for specific needs. I sat in a chair in the center of the circle, and everyone gathered around and laid hands on me and prayed for Karen. I felt the power and anointing of the Lord flow from their hands into me as we prayed for God's healing hand on Karen.

The Lord gave Sara a vision as she laid hands on me. "I saw Karen full of joy," she related. "She was adorned with flowers around her head and was wearing a beautiful, white dress. She was laughing and happy."

I looked at Sara, "Was your picture of Karen here or in heaven?"

"I don't know," Sara answered.

I returned to the hospital, laid hands on Karen and prayed. Already, unknown to us, the Lord had called several friends to start fasting for Karen.

The next day began like any other. We didn't know the Lord had chosen it as Karen's "day of resurrection."

Breakfast was served. I took a shower and folded up my bed. Sam bathed Karen and changed her sheets. Margarete washed the floor and emptied the waste basket. The doctors made their rounds and examined Karen. Holiday Jones, the head nurse, brought in the medicine and stayed for a while to visit. She usually had Saturday off, but she agreed to work not only that day, but to stay a double shift. "I must be crazy'" she said, "but here I am."

"How about a popcorn party tonight, Holiday?" Karen asked.

"Not yet, Karen," she replied. "But I promise you when your throat is better we will have a popcorn party."

"Oh good!" exclaimed Karen.

Karen was quiet for a moment and then she said, "Hey, Holiday, do you know why the little boy took a stick of gum along with him on the train ride?"

"No."

"Because," said Karen with a grin, "he wanted to chew, chew, chew."

"Oh, no," we both groaned as Karen giggled.

After lunch, Karen and I played a game on the floor of her room. "I feel tired, Mommy," Karen said as she crawled back under her oxygen tent.

"While you rest,, Karen, I have to do some errands. Let me see if Holiday has time to read to you."

It was a slow day on West. Holiday was happy to spend some time with Karen. "Bye, Mommy ," Karen said.

"I'll see you soon, honey," I answered.

Mighty God

I stopped at the grocery store on the way home. I felt restless as I waited in line. I sensed that it was important for me to leave quickly.

I finally checked through the line and drove home. "Hi, Mike," I said as I walked in.

"Hi, Mom," he answered. "The hospital called and wants you to call right back."

"It's probably Karen calling to see when I'll return," I chuckled as I dialed the familiar number.

To my surprise, Mrs. Quintiliani, the nursing supervisor, picked up the phone on West. "Trudy," she said, her voice sounding urgent, "Karen has taken a terrible turn for the worse. Can you come back right away? It's very serious!"

"But ... but ... how could that be?" I stammered. "What happened?"

"Her throat closed up and she couldn't breathe. The doctors are working on her now. Please be careful driving here," she answered.

I hung up the phone in disbelief. "Lord," I prayed, "what do I do now?" George was out of town at a Boy Scout event and wasn't due back until late that night.

"Call for prayer," the Lord answered. "Yes!" I thought. I knew urgent prayer was more important than my immediate presence at the hospital.

I quickly explained to Mike the need for prayer. I dialed a pastor friend, Jerry Claus. "Karen needs prayer," I choked out.

"I'm glad you caught me," he said. "I was just going out the door on business for a few days." He reassured me that he and his wife would pray right away.

"And one more thing, Jerry," my voice strained. "When Karen first got sick, the Lord showed me a vision for her resurrection from the dead. If I get to

67

the hospital and Karen's dead, what do I do?"

"All you can do is pray. God will bring about the results He desires. We'll support you in prayer, Trudy. God be with you."

I called Victor and got through right away. (Often his phone was busy for hours.) I quickly told him the situation, and also the thought of the resurrection prayer. "You know, that idea went through my head before you mentioned it," Victor replied. "Do you want us to meet you at the hospital?"

"I don't know. Let me call you from there if I need you."

"Okay," he said. "We'll be praying."

I wanted to get to the hospital but felt I should also give Velma a quick call. "I don't even know if Karen's still alive," I cried. Velma comforted me with a prayer for God's strengthening. I ran to the car and drove off.

As I turned onto the freeway toward the hospital, a cloud of despair enveloped me. I began to imagine that Karen was dead. "No! I can't allow this! Jesus!" I prayed. "Karen is in your hands and my hope is in you."

I concentrated on driving, but prayed out loud in the Spirit all the way to the hospital. I received strength from the Lord as I prayed.

Mrs. Quintiliana met me in the parking lot. She was just leaving her shift. "I was worried when you didn't get here right away," she said.

"I called for prayer. Is Karen still alive?"

"Yes!" she answered. "We've moved her to intensive care."

Dr. DeLamerens met me in the hallway of West. He told me the doctors had put a small tube down Karen's throat to make a passageway for air.

We hurried to the intensive care unit (I.C.U.). To my surprise, I saw Victor and Sara walking toward us. Victor said that the minute we hung up the phone he felt the Lord urging him to go right away to the hospital. His car wasn't working so he started to call someone for a ride. The phone rang again before he could dial. The friend calling had come right over and taken them to the hospital.

The doctor asked them to wait as he took me into I.C.U. I rushed to the side of Karen's bed. Her eyes were wide open and she looked frightened. A tube was sticking out of her mouth and a doctor was wrapping tape around her head to secure the tube.

Another doctor was attaching small disks to Karen's chest, hooking her onto a heart monitor. Another machine monitored her breathing.

I knelt down beside Karen's bed and took her hand. "It's okay, Karen," I spoke reassuringly. "Mommy's here, but most important, *Jesus* is here. Everything is going to be all right because He is here protecting you."

As I spoke I heard a voice speaking softly, "The Lord is my shepherd; I shall not want. He maketh me to lie down in green pastures: ... He restoreth my soul ..." (Ps. 23:1-3, KJV).

I looked into the face of a beautiful lady standing at the head of Karen's bed. "Lord," I breathed, "thank you for having someone here to bring your words of life to Karen."

I thanked her for being there and she introduced herself as Ella Flagg, the supervisor of respiratory therapy.

I asked her if my two friends could come in for prayer. She said she would call them.

Holding Karen's hand, I prayed as Victor and Sara came into the unit. I wanted them to lay hands on Karen too, but they were asked to stay behind a short screen at the foot of Karen's bed. There were several staff

TOO PRECIOUS TO DIE

members still working on Karen.

Victor was tall enough to see over the screen. I felt reassured as I saw him. They were both reading Scripture, praying and rebuking Satan.

As Victor prayed, he rebuked the spirit of weak heart beat, irregular breathing and death. He told me later that he saw the results of his prayers registering on Karen's machines. Her heart responded with a firm beat and her breathing became regular.

Victor claimed each of the thirty-nine stripes of Christ for Karen's healing. I could hear Victor praying, "Jesus, your word says that by your stripes we are healed [Isa. 53:5]. We claim stripe one for Karen in the name of Jesus, stripe two in the name of Jesus, stripe three . . . ."

Sara rebuked the spirit of leukemia in the name of Jesus. Karen raised half-way on her bed in a coughing fit. Her tongue forced its way out from under the tape. She grabbed the oxygen tube that was attached to her mouth and pulled it off.

"If only Victor and Sara were allowed closer to Karen," I prayed.

"Here," the doctor said to Victor, "hold her feet." The doctor hurried to replace the oxygen tube.

The Muellers moved forward and held her feet. They smiled at me and prayed. I continued to hold Karen's hand. She became calm.

Karen was exhausted and fell soundly asleep. Holiday was assigned I.C.U duty so that Karen would have a familiar nurse.

Victor, Sara and I were invited to wait in the nursing office across the hall. As I walked out of I.C.U., I saw Velma. We embraced. She said the Lord told her to come.

I phoned George at the scout camp, but no one

answered. "Lord," I prayed, "please send George home early."

Miss Kristen, the evening supervisor, kindly brought us coffee. As we waited, the story of God's mighty power and miraculous timing began to unfold.

After I left the hospital, Holiday stayed in Karen's room to read to her. After several stories, she said, "Karen, how about taking a rest now? If you need me just ring the buzzer."

Holiday walked toward the door. She heard a loud slapping sound and turned. Karen sat straight up in bed, throwing the oxygen tent over her head with both hands, and choked out the words, "I can't breathe."

Holiday ran to get the emergency cart that was across the hall. As she put the oxygen mask on Karen's face, Karen fell back on the bed. Holiday checked Karen's wrist and found no pulse. "Call Dr. Heart," Holiday shouted to the ward secretary. ("Dr. Heart" was a code name for patient heart stoppage. The call brings the resident doctors and the respiratory department to the needed room immediately.)

"Call Dr. DeLamerens and call the blood bank, too," Holiday called as she worked to resuscitate Karen. To Holiday's relief, Karen's heart started beating again.

The medical teams arrived quickly. "Her breathing's impaired," Holiday said. The decision was made that Karen needed a clear air passage immediately. A tracheotomy was ruled out as too dangerous, so a small plastic tube down her airway was considered. Even the tube could cause internal bleeding, and there was doubt it would go down the swollen throat.

"This child has terminal cancer. Perhaps it would be best and kindest to do nothing," someone commented.

"No! This child is special and her parents are special. We must do all we can," someone answered.

71

Ella, the lady I had met in I.C.U., held Karen's head as the resident doctor struggled with the small tube and the intricate procedure of carefully inserting it down Karen's throat.

"It's not going in!" the doctor exclaimed, exasperated.

"Her heart has stopped!" Holiday cried. "There's no pulse! She's not breathing!"

Ella, with her hands on both sides of Karen's head, silently prayed, "Lord, what is your will for this child?"

"My will is *life!*" came the sure response.

"Oh, Lord, give her life!" Ella blurted.

Immediately, the tube glided smoothly down Karen's throat. The air passage was opened. "One . . . two . . . three ..." Holiday counted as she felt Karen's pulse return. "I've got a beat!" she exclaimed.

"Praise your name, Jesus," Ella sighed. Her eye caught the poster on Karen's wall:

> Fear not, for I am with you. Do not be dismayed. I am your God. I will strengthen you; I will help you; I will uphold you with my victorious right hand. (Isa. 41:10)

"Oh, Lord," Ella said. "This little girl knows you and loves you. Thank you for letting me be your voice and hands."

God had used Ella's prayer that day to do what I had never wanted to face - a prayer of resurrection. I thought, with relief, that it was behind me now.

Holiday joined us in the nurse's office for a break. "Karen is still sleeping," she said. "You know," she continued, "this was really an unusual experience for me. The whole time during the crisis with Karen, I felt as though Someone was guiding me. I was already starting to get what the doctors wanted before they asked and I was doing what needed to be done before they spoke. It must have been God directing me."

"It was!" we exclaimed. We praised Him and rejoiced. The Lord filled us with an exhilaration as we spoke words of faith, read the Scriptures and prayed. God's deep inner peace filled the room, and we laughed and sang.

Miss Kristen stopped in to ask if everything was all right. She seemed surprised to see us smiling; surely God's peace passes understanding!

Ella stopped by the office. "I'm a Christian, too," she smiled. "And filled with the Spirit. I praise God for what He did for Karen." We shared that we, too, believed in the power of the Holy Spirit. We rejoiced together in our mighty God.

A portable X-ray machine was taken to I.C.U. for a picture of Karen's throat. The doctor who inserted the tiny tube examined the X-ray. He later told us that when he saw it he realized that her throat was so swollen it was a miracle the tube went through and there was no hemorrhaging . "I could never do it again," he said.

I tried once more to reach George, but still there was no answer. As I hung up, the phone rang.

"Trudy," I heard my friend Carol Slayden say. "What's going on? I've been thinking about Karen all day. I haven't been able to do anything but pray for her. I tried to reach you in Karen's room, and they switched me over here."

"Oh, Carol!" I rejoiced. "I'm so glad you called."

I shared with her what had happened. She said she would continue to pray and would call others to do the same.

Ella returned to the office. "Mrs. Colflesh," she said. "Karen's awake and wants you." I crossed the hall to I.C.U., washed my hands, put on a gown and walked over to Karen's bed. I was so happy to see her. The sparkle in her eyes, though weak, revealed that she was equally happy.

Karen could not talk because of the tube in her mouth and throat, and the tape binding her mouth. I hugged and kissed her and sat down on the bed to reassure her of Jesus' presence and power.

"Karen, we're going to have to figure out a plan for you to call me when you want to." I collected a piece of paper, pencil and tape from the nurse's desk and wrote: *I want Mommy*. I showed it to Karen and taped it on the head of her bed. "Anytime you want me, just point to the paper and someone will come get me," I said. "I'm not allowed to stay in here with you like I was in your room," I explained. "But I'll be just across the hall in the nurse's office or over on West."

While I talked to Karen, Alex, the blood technician, came in to draw blood. (Karen had once played kickball in the hall of West with Alex, and they had had fun teasing each other.) Now it was serious. Alex kept track of the oxygen in Karen's blood so the doctors would know how to regulate her oxygen intake. "You're a good girl," Alex said, patting Karen reassuringly.

One of the I.C.U. nurses came over to me. She looked familiar; she had worked on West several times since we had been there.

"Mrs. Colflesh," she said. "As I walked into the hospital this afternoon before my shift, I saw the biggest, prettiest yellow butterfly darting and flitting among the flowers. For some reason my thoughts immediately went to Karen as I watched."

"A butterfly!" I thought. "How appropriate and beautiful. A symbol of resurrection and new life." I smiled and said, "Thank you for sharing that."

Telling Karen I would be back soon, I walked out to the hall; Hilda came running over from West.

"George is coming," she shouted. "I was looking out the window and saw him walk through the parking lot. I wanted to catch him before he got to Karen's room."

My heart leaped. It was hours before he was expected. "Oh, thank you, Father," I prayed. I ran to the elevator to meet George as he stepped out, still in his scout uniform, and I knew he had come straight from camp.

He looked surprised to see the Muellers standing in the hallway behind me. I put my arms around him and we all walked back to the nurse's office, explaining the crisis on the way.

"You know," George said, "I was sitting at the conference feeling more and more restless until, finally, I excused myself and left for the hospital."

George and I went in to see Karen. Later we all sat in the nurse's office and reviewed the split-second timing of the High Commander of Heaven: Holiday being in the room at the right moment, the Lord directing her every move working with the doctors, Ella praying for life, the tube being inserted smoothly, Victor and Sara being given an immediate ride to the hospital, the Lord bringing them to Karen's bed for spiritual warfare and now George coming back early from the conference.

"I just opened my Bible to the Psalms," Victor said, "and God drew my attention to Psalm 6. Listen to what it says." He read:

Be gracious to me, O Lord, for I am
languishing; O Lord, heal me, for my bones are
troubled ....
Turn, O Lord, save my life; deliver me for the
sake of thy steadfast love.

For in death there is no remembrance of thee;
in Sheol who can give thee praise?
The Lord has heard my supplication; the Lord
accepts my prayer.
All my enemies shall be ashamed and sorely
troubled; they shall turn back, and be put to
shame in a moment. (Isa. 6:2, 4, 5, 9, 10, RSV)

"How true!" we exclaimed. George and I went to see
Karen again. Sara Mueller called home to check on her
children.

When we came back to the office, Sara said excitedly,
"Listen to this. I had a message to contact a friend. When I
called her, she said she had been praying for Victor and
me. She wondered where we were because the Lord gave
her a vision of a long, low white building, which she didn't
realize was Variety Children's Hospital.

"Over this building," Sara continued, "she saw heavy,
thick, black clouds. And now for the exciting part!" she
exclaimed. "There were hosts of angels with their swords
drawn! They were fighting through the darkness to bring
God's answers to our prayer!"

We knew that our Mighty God had directed the battle
thus far. He would continue to command and show us His
mighty power over the enemy.

5
Miracle Worker

Dr. DeLamerens came to the nurse's office where we were waiting for him. "Karen's heartbeat and respiration are doing well," he reported. "She is getting an amazingly good percent of oxygen in her blood. More platelets were rushed here from the blood bank and we are giving her a transfusion now."

"What are platelets?" Victor asked.

The doctor explained that they were a necessary part of the blood to prevent internal bleeding. Since the insertion of the tube in Karen's throat caused irritation of the ulcer, it was vital to keep the platelet level as high as possible. Karen's level was greatly below normal.

"How many platelets should Karen have?" Victor asked?

"It would be good if she had sixty - or seventy - thousand," the doctor answered.

"I mean, how many should she *really* have?" Victor continued.

Dr. DeLamerens smiled and said, "What I'd really like to see is 100,000 platelets."

"Good," said Victor. As Dr. DeLamerens was leaving, Victor told him confidently, "We're going to pray and ask God to give Karen 100,000 platelets - or as many more as He would like to throw in!"

I gulped as I heard Victor. Karen hadn't had that high a platelet count since she became sick. But we all agreed that we should ask God in faith for 100,000 platelets for Karen. We bowed our heads and Victor prayed. The entire matter was in God's hands.

Velma asked to see George and me a few minutes before she left. We walked to West and went into Karen's now vacated room. It looked like a whirlwind had gone through. Papers were on the floor, emergency equipment was scattered around, chairs were pushed out of the way and the bed was removed.

Hilda helped us straighten things. After she left, Velma talked. She reminded us that God desires to have first place always in the hearts of those whom He loves and, as difficult as it is, He requires us to put everything and everyone on the altar of sacrifice to Him.

"Your faith is being tried to the limits," Velma continued. "But God is faithful and will not allow you to be burdened with more than you can bear."

She prayed with us before she left. We thanked her for her support and asked her to stop by our home to tell the boys what was happening.

Then George and I walked back to the nurse's office. I realized it was late and no one had eaten. "Perhaps you'd better go home and eat some dinner," I told the Muellers.

"I believe the Lord wants us to fast," Victor said. "Neither Sara nor I have eaten since breakfast. We just haven't been hungry."

George said, "I haven't eaten since breakfast, either."

"Neither have I," I responded.

Ella stood in the doorway and heard our conversation

about fasting. "I believe the Lord is calling me to fast for Karen, too!" she said. We realized that God had called all of us into a fast for victory over this spiritual battle.

George and I went into the I.C.U. Karen was dozing but her eyes lit up when she saw us. I brought along my tape recorder and played a tape of Scripture set to music. I had played this tape often in Karen's room on West. The air around her filled with God's Word as we listened to the softly playing music.

Holiday came into the room. "It's time for suctioning," she said.

Karen shook her head no and grabbed my hand.

"I know you don't like it, Karen," said Holiday, kindly, "but we have to keep your tube cleaned out."

She opened a package which contained a small tube and attached one end to the suction machine. Then she opened a package which contained one sterile glove and carefully put it on, keeping her hand surgically clean. With her gloved hand, she took the tube and cautiously slid it through the passage way, down the length of Karen's throat.

It was extremely uncomfortable and caused Karen to gag and cough. "The coughing is good, Karen. It helps bring up the phlegm," Holiday said.

The amount of blood that came up with the phlegm aroused my concern but Holiday said, "That's not unusual. It should decrease as time goes on."

It was difficult to stand there without gagging, myself. After the procedure was over, I left for the office again.

As I went out the door, the doctor who had inserted Karen's tube went in to examine her and to speak with George.

A few minutes later, George came out of I.C.U. looking pale and asked Victor if he would pray for him. We all joined hands and Victor prayed a prayer of reassurance and again thanked God for the victory.

We hugged the Muellers goodnight and thanked them for coming. "Keep praising God" they encouraged us as they left.

Holiday found us so she could say goodnight. "This is a day I'll never forget," she said. "I knew it was God's plan for me to be here today."

"Yes," we agreed, and thanked her for all she did.

The hospital let us stay in Karen's room overnight. An extra fold-out bed was brought in for George. We lay there, overwhelmed with the events of the day.

My faith that God would heal Karen literally stretched in all directions, enlarging enough to cover the situation. It must have been similar to how Peter felt as he stepped out of the boat to walk on the water toward Jesus, even though he knew it was impossible for the water to support him.

We were also in an "impossible" situation. Karen's life was critical. Our hoping it was different would not change the situation.

I was out of the boat of any medical hope, yet I was standing on water. I knew this was only possible by faith in Jesus. I focused my vision intently on Him. I concentrated. "Jesus ... Jesus ... Jesus," I called as I drifted off to sleep.

George didn't tell me until several days later, that the doctor told him he didn't expect Karen to live through the night. I was unaware of the extra burden on George as I fell asleep.

I was startled awake as the telephone rang. It was I.C.U. Karen wanted me, so I put on my robe and went down the hall. I sat beside Karen and sleepily held her hand. After a while I suggested that we both try and get some sleep. I realized this was hard for Karen. The lights, machines and constant activity of the I.C.U., in addition to the discomfort caused by the tube in her throat, made it difficult for her to rest. She agreed, however, to try to sleep.

I'll be in your room on West, honey. You have the nurse call me whenever you want me." Karen had me paged two more times that night, but I didn't mind at all.

George and I got up early and dressed. We sat in Karen's room, grateful for her good night in I.C.U. We sipped a cup of hot tea as our only breakfast since we started fasting. It tasted good.

Dr. DeLamerens popped his head through the door. He had a broad smile. "You tell the Reverend he's got his miracle" he exclaimed.

"What do you mean?" we asked.

"I just got the morning report on Karen's blood work. She not only has the 100,000 platelets you prayed for, she has 105,000!"

We were stunned and overjoyed. Surely God's hand was on Karen! We hurried to I.C.U. to tell her the good news. Alex had just finished another blood test.

"This is great!" he shouted. "The oxygen level in Karen's blood has returned to normal!"

All over the hospital the staff became electric with the progressively good news of Karen's improvement. One of Karen's nurses stopped me in the hall. She said she went to church that morning especially to pray for Karen. Holiday, and other staff members, called to hear of Karen's progress. Many reported that they were praying for her.

Ella told us that her church was also praying. She had heard the exciting reports. "Karen is just what this hospital needs," she said. "I've been praying that we'd all see a miracle. We're in need of encouragement and of seeing God's hand here."

I returned to I.C.U. Karen was vigorously waving a note back and forth in the air to get someone's attention. "Let me see the note, Karen," I said, walking to her bed.

"I want Mommy - NOW!" it read. I chuckled. That wasn't exactly the note I had written. One of the nurses had added the *NOW* to the note to better express Karen's way of saying it.

I reassured Karen that I could stay with her for most of the day. Sitting in a chair by her bed, I showed her the note pad I brought with me.

"This will help you communicate," I said as I wrote different words on each page: "Cold"; "Toilet"; "Book."

"You can point to the word which tells what you need," I continued. I was glad that Karen was a good reader and learned, to my amazement, that she was a good speller as well.

She took the pad and pen and started printing the letters. "Healing for ..." As I watched I read aloud what she wrote. I wondered what she would say. "Healing for Goos," she finished.

"Goos?" I asked, not understanding.

Karen shook her head no and printed "Goas."

"Goas?" I questioned.

Frustrated, Karen printed, "Geos."

"Geos?" I asked. Tears came to her eyes as she shook her head again.

Then she had another idea. She pointed toward the bed where a ten-year-old Cuban-American boy lay. He had both an arm and a leg in a cast and a tube coming out of his throat.

Earlier, Karen was told about the other children in the I.C.U. room. This boy had been in a car accident. His name was Gus.

This time tears came to my eyes. I realized what Karen was asking. She wanted to pray for the Lord to heal Gus.

"I understand, honey!" I exclaimed.

Karen was relieved. We joined hands and asked for Gus to be healed. Surely our prayer went straight to the heart of God. We especially rejoiced when we saw Gus discharged from the hospital many weeks later, well on the way to recovery.

Since Karen could spell, I wrote the alphabet on a page of the note pad. When she wanted to communicate, she would point to the letters, and I wrote her message for her.

It amazed me that she would spell complete sentences rather than just key words. She pointed, "I want to see a book," instead of simply, "book."

Karen had a storybook about the Battle of Jericho. I read it to her several times that day and explained how we, like Joshua of old, needed to shout the victory *before* we saw the walls fall down. We could trust that God had already given us the victory of opening her throat. We were to claim and shout that victory even before it could be felt by Karen or seen by the doctors. This was a big step of faith for all of us. George joined us as we prayed a prayer of thanksgiving to God for bringing Karen through this crisis and for opening her throat.

Karen took the pad and pointed as I wrote out her message: "I want to eat." Her eyes looked very sad as I told her she couldn't eat until the tube was out. I knew she received fluid through her i.v., but it didn't help her stomach feel better. I told her that Daddy and I weren't eating, either. We were fasting, or "fashioning" as Karen used to call it. Several times a day Karen would point to spell out "eat" or "drink." I knew she was very uncomfortable.

"Lord, what can I do?" I asked.

He reminded me of His words in Scripture: "I am the bread of life; he who comes to me shall not hunger, and he who believes in me shall never thirst" (John 6:35, RSV); "Whoever drinks of the water that I shall give him will never thirst; the water that I shall give him will become in him a spring of water welling up to eternal life" (John 4: 14, RSV).

I read these Scriptures to Karen and prayed, "Lord, be to Karen her bread of life and her living water. Fill her full of yourself so that she will not feel hunger or thirst." I realized that she, too, was called to fast and was an active participant in the raging spiritual warfare. Many times during the days that followed, I prayed that the Lord would sustain her physically.

Velma called to give me a direction she had received as she was praying for Karen. She suggested that I go to the hospital chapel and read the same prayer which King Hezekiah had prayed to the Lord in the temple when he was in battle against God's enemy. So that very evening, I knelt on the chapel floor with my Bible open, praying Hezekiah's prayer.

I concluded, "So now, O Lord our God, save us, I beseech thee, from his (the enemy's) hand, that all the kingdoms of the earth may know that thou O Lord art God alone" (2 Kings 19:19, RSV).

"Oh, God," I cried, "show forth your victory so that the world may see your glory and give honor to your name."

I returned to I.C.U. Karen motioned that she wanted to get out of bed. I checked with the nurse, who temporarily disconnected Karen from her monitoring machines. Karen now had freedom to move. A bit shaky, but delighted, Karen got out of bed and walked in as many directions as her i.v. extension would stretch. "Thank you, Lord'" I whispered. "You *are* showing forth your victory."

The next morning, Sam, the nurse's aide, said she was telling a friend last night about Karen's remarkable improvement. "Knowing Karen," she had said, "I won't be surprised if she's up walking around by now."

"That was exactly what she was doing, Sam," I said. "at the very time you were talking to your friend." We both laughed with delight.

Anthony, another child who was on West when we first came to the hospital, but had since left, was rushed back in critical condition. He was temporarily placed in Karen's room while she was in I.C.U. Anthony was in much pain. I prayed that the cards and banners on Karen's walls would help cheer him and his parents.

I was allowed a different, unoccupied room for the night. Celia, a Cuban nurse's aide who loved Karen, came in to help me make the bed.

"Trudy," she said, with a heavy accent. "May I talk with you?"

"Surely," I replied.

"I see how you face Karen's illness and I see your faith," she continued. "I have some needs. Would you pray with me?"

We shared for a few minutes, and then prayed. Afterwards, Celia took my hand. "Thank you," she said. "I feel much better. Before I go, I want you to know Karen taught me to say an English word without an accent."

"What's that?" I asked.

"Well, last week I read to her from her Bible storybook

about David and a giant. When I said his name the way I thought it should be pronounced, Karen squealed with laughter.

" 'No, no!' Karen said. *'This* is the way you say it: So she had me practice until I could say 'Goliath' right."

During the night, Karen called for me only once. It was before she was suctioned. She communicated to the nurses not to start until I was there to hold her hand. As I sat there with Karen, I was relieved that blood was no longer brought up in the process.

Both Karen and I felt rested when morning came. She was given a bath. While her bed was changed, I held her on my lap. She snuggled against me, her hair brushing my cheek. It was full-bodied and thick. (Even when Karen was a baby, she had a full head of hair.) I reached over for the hairbrush.

As I stroked her head, a huge swath of her hair clung to the brush.

"Oh, no!" I gasped in surprise. I knew that chemotherapy could cause hair loss, but I was hoping it wouldn't happen to Karen.

I brushed again, and more hair pulled loose. It was happening, after all. There was nothing one could do to stop it.

"Karen, your hair is thinning," I said. We had already explained to Karen that this could result from chemotherapy, so she would be prepared. She watched as I pulled a handful of hair off the brush. Swath after swath of hair came out as I continued brushing.

"Karen," I said, "I want you to see how you look now so it won't be such a surprise as your hair gets thinner."

I found a mirror and Karen moved it around to look at her head. Quite a bit of hair still framed her face. I was pleased that her appearance didn't seem to bother her.

"I'm going to ask the Lord that when your hair grows back, Karen, He will give you a glorious, radiant crown of hair on your head. You are such a brave little girl and such a good sport for all you have to go through."

Karen cuddled closely to me as I held her and prayed. I knew that God would give her something special. If He had given me a mother's heart overflowing with love and compassion for my little one, I knew His own loving heart contained infinitely more.

I asked Karen if she wanted to do anything special. She pointed to a giant coloring book and crayons she was given. The coloring book was so large that we decided to lay it on the bed. She stood beside it, using the bed as a table.

Karen looked a sight, leaning against the bed as she colored. There were wires leading from her chest; these were taped to a heart-monitoring machine. An i.v. cord was attached to her wrist. A long, flexible oxygen tube was attached to the tube in her mouth. Tape encircled the lower part of her head to keep the tube in place. Shaggy hair stuck out in all directions on her balding head. Her hospital gown, tied at the back, revealed her bottom peeking through.

If the scene wasn't so humorous, it would have been pathetic. Yet, tears of joy were in my eyes because Karen was alive, standing and coloring.

Dr. DeLamerens came into I.C.U. When he saw Karen coloring he too was filled with joy. "She's some little girl!" he said. My smile showed my agreement.

He took me aside and explained his plan. He had contacted the hospital across town and arranged for Karen to have a cobalt treatment on her neck. She would be transported there by ambulance that afternoon.

From the beginning of Karen's illness, George and I

prayed for God to give the doctors wisdom and direction in their decisions. We later found out that the cobalt treatment was considered an heroic measure, an unusual attempt to prolong life. Normally it was not given to a terminally ill child. When we realized this, we were very grateful for our doctor's decision. Even more, we knew that God was in control.

I explained to Karen about the ambulance ride and the cobalt machine, and explained how this would help her throat: The machine was very big and gave off rays like light; she wouldn't feel anything.

Later that morning, Karen took the note pad with the alphabet and tried to spell "machine." She couldn't get close enough to the correct spelling for me to understand. She finally drew a picture of a large rectangle with a small square on top and lines going vertically and horizontally. With God's help I suddenly recognized that the picture was a "big machine."

Karen nodded her head up and down enthusiastically; her eyes shone with delight. "You want me to tell you again about the cobalt machine," I said. She was relieved that I understood.

Dr. Pefkarou, a lovely, young, Greek lady (part of Dr. DeLamerens' team), accompanied Karen and me in the ambulance. She carried along portable oxygen equipment. At one point, Karen was given the oxygen as she struggled to get enough air.

Karen was strapped onto a rolling stretcher which rested on the floor of the ambulance. Dr. Pefkarou and I sat on the seat along with a nurse from I.C.U. In the front of the ambulance were the driver and his assistant.

It was the first time Karen and I had been in an ambulance. It was different to look from the inside out. We drove through a residential area. Someone was washing his car, another was mowing the grass, someone else was walking their dog. The scenes seemed somehow unreal.

"How strange," I thought, "to be doing such ordinary things. Life is so much more important!" I had not been outside the hospital since Karen's crisis and had forgotten that normal activities had gone on for others even though mine had come to a screeching halt.

The radiologist at Mt. Sinai Hospital skillfully marked an area of Karen's neck for treatment. He told me the initial reaction from the cobalt would be further swelling of Karen's throat but that within two days her throat should begin to open further. The tube would maintain an air passage during this time. He would schedule another treatment if this one showed results.

In a protected area of the room I watched Karen on a television screen. She was rolled under the huge cobalt machine. She was able to hear me through a microphone, and I talked to reassure her. I reminded her to not move a muscle until the treatment was finished. The doctor counted aloud so she would know how long to hold still. When it was over we all complimented her on how well she did.

It was good to be sitting as we rode back to the hospital, for I was weak from my fast. Karen must have felt weak, too.

I brought along the story of the Battle of Jericho. Asking Karen if she would like me to read, she nodded yes. So, with the doctor, nurse and attendants a captive audience, all heard the wonderful story of Joshua's faith and obedience and of the victory given by God to the Israelites.

Afterwards, I said to Dr. Pefkarou, "Karen's swollen throat is like the walls of Jericho. We're trusting in the victory that her throat will be open even before we see it happen."

"We'll know soon," she replied, glad for my faith.

After Karen settled in I.C.U. again, I took time to read to myself from the Bible. Since Karen's crisis, I often thought of the testing given to Abraham concerning his son, Isaac. Turning to Genesis 22, I read God's words to Abraham: "Take your son, your only son Isaac, whom you love, and go to the land of Moriah, and offer him there as a burnt offering ..." (verse 2, RSV).

I reflected on the words: "Your only son . . . whom you love ...." I thought of Karen, my only daughter, whom I loved. Hot tears rolled down my cheeks. Inside, I felt I was ripping. Was I still holding on to Karen?

"Oh, God," I cried. "It's so hard to relinquish my daughter, my only daughter, whom I love. But my desire is to be obedient to you. Loving Father, I place Karen on the altar before you. I do not hold on to her life. I freely offer her to you to do with as you propose."

There was no guarantee of a happy ending, as when God returned Isaac to Abraham. I knew I was walking by faith. The water still felt firm under my feet, but it wasn't easy!

A message that my friend Carol called was left at the hospital desk. I telephoned her from Karen's room on West. As we talked, I told Carol that I had just read the story of Abraham and Isaac. "Relinquishment seems to be a gradual process," I thought aloud. "But at some point it must be finished; unless, of course, we take back what we relinquished. "

"Will you pray with me, Carol," I continued, "and see if the Lord shows you anything else I need to surrender concerning Karen?"

We prayed. Pouring my heart out to my heavenly

Father, I gave Karen to Him. I wanted Him to know that I was truly letting go. As I finished, a nurse interrupted to request information. I asked Carol to wait for a moment.

"Trudy," Carol exclaimed when I picked up the phone, "while you were gone the Lord showed me a wonderful vision! I saw Karen in a beautiful, white-satin dress. She was happy, smiling. She was held out by a pair of hands that were offering her to someone.

"Then I saw Jesus reach out and receive her with joy. He held Karen to himself for a few minutes. Then He laid her back down in her bed very gently and lovingly."

"Oh, Carol," I cried. "I *did* give Karen to the Lord, and He has given her back!"

I telephoned George with the exciting news of Carol's vision. "Now we have a 'twice-given' daughter," he said. "The Lord has given Karen to us again!"

The evening food cart rattled past as I leaned against the counter of the nurse's station on West. I wondered how long the Lord wanted me to fast; it was now the end of the third day. A nurse interrupted my thoughts.

"Trudy," she said. "We have an extra turkey dinner here. Would you like it?" I knew the Lord had lifted the fast. That turkey was the best I ever ate!

While Karen was in I.C.U. I read Bible verses to her on healing:

> Surely he has borne our griefs and carried our sorrows he was wounded for our transgressions, he was bruised for our iniquities; upon him was the chastisement that made us whole, and with his stripes we are healed. (Isa. 53:4, 5, RSV)

And the faith which is through Jesus has given the man this perfect health in the presence of you all. (Acts 3:16, RSV)

He himself bore our sins in his body on the tree, that we might die to sin and live to righteousness. By his wounds you have been healed. (1 Pet. 2:24, RSV)

Beloved, I pray that all may go well with you and that you may be in health. (3 John 2, RSV)

Then they cried to the Lord in their trouble, and he delivered them from their distress . . . . he sent forth his word, and healed them, and delivered them from destruction. (Ps. 107:13, 20, RSV)

Bless the Lord, O my soul, and forget not all his benefits, who forgives all your iniquity, who heals all your diseases. (Ps. 103:2, 3, RSV)

That evening they brought to him [Jesus] many who were possessed with demons; and he cast out the spirits with a word, and healed all who were sick. (Matt. 8:16, RSV)

"Karen," I said as I turned to Mark 5:25. "Here is the story of the woman with the flow of blood who touched Jesus' garment and was healed. Remember how you read that paragraph to me?"

I thought back to when Karen was first sick, how she surprised me by reading all those words. Her favorite part of the story was the ending which I now read: "Daughter, your faith has made you well; go in peace, and be healed of your disease" (Mark 5:34, RSV).

Karen identified with the woman who was made well

by Jesus' touch. She also liked the concept of Jesus calling her daughter. She and I had discussed the idea earlier, and understood that those who loved Jesus were His sons and daughters. It thrilled my heart when Karen looked at me and said, "Then that means that even though you're my mommy, you're also my sister with Jesus because we're both His daughters."

"That's right, honey," I said, amazed at her perception.

Karen's first cobalt treatment showed positive results, so the decision was made to continue with a second dose. It was hoped that this treatment would open her throat. Karen and I again traveled by ambulance to Mt. Sinai Hospital where she was given another cobalt exposure.

The next day, Carol came to the hospital. She was allowed in I.C.U. briefly and brought Karen a set of cute hand puppets. Karen liked the present but turned to continue the television program she had been watching.

Carol chuckled when she saw that Karen was watching the show "Emergency", "as if she didn't have enough of ambulances, hospitals, and I.C.U. rooms in real life!" she said.

As she left, Carol said, "The Lord gave me Psalm 93 for you today." In the Psalm I realized that God was telling me nothing happens outside of His rule and decree; He is robed in strength and majesty. He reigns!

I was grateful to have the reassurance. That night the doctor talked to George and me. "We cannot leave the tube in Karen's throat much longer. It will cause too much irritation and perhaps internal bleeding.

"We need to assure an air passage, however. Since her blood picture looks good, we feel we should perform a tracheotomy."

They planned to put an incision through Karen's throat to create an air hole, just below the cancerous growth and remove the tube. "She will be much more comfortable," the doctor said, "and, of course, will be able to talk and eat again."

Karen had asked me every day on the note pad when the tube would come out and when she could eat. Even though I didn't like the idea of a hole in her neck, I was assured it would heal easily when the opening was closed. The benefits of eating and talking were obvious.

The operation was scheduled for the next morning, so George and I explained to Karen what was planned. "And just think, Karen," I said, "you'll be able to eat again."

Karen took the note pad and pointed to the letters as I wrote: "Granola bar." "No, Karen," I laughed. "You can't start off with that. It will have to be something softer."

She thought back to several weeks earlier when I brought granola bars to her room for snacks. When the sore developed in her throat, we felt it best that she not eat rough foods. I put the bars away in her closet, completely forgetting about them. Karen hadn't forgotten, however. I was sure she would ask again if it was OK to have one.

George arrived at the hospital early the next morning. We prayed together with Karen before she received her preoperative shot. I especially prayed for the Lord to cover Karen's subconscious mind with the blood of Jesus to protect her while she was under the anesthetic.

We walked through the hallway as they wheeled Karen to the operating room. We waved goodbye as she disappeared through the swinging doors; the sign above them read, "No Admittance."

We waited in the cafeteria over a cup of coffee. It wasn't long before the surgeon who operated on Karen appeared and told us that everything went fine.

We continued to wait until we were told we could see Karen in the recovery room. It was a joy to see Karen's mouth again without the tube and all the tape. She gave a hint of a smile when she saw us.

George and I broke into laughter when the nurses in the recovery room showed us a small chalkboard on which Karen had written a single word. In big, bold, capital letters we read: "EAT."

Karen was moved to her room on West after the operation. Anthony, who had by now occupied the room for several days, was moved to another. His condition had worsened.

Karen knew that Anthony was one of the "regulars" on West although they only saw each other and waved hello once. His mother Judy and I occasionally talked in the hallway.

Karen was glad to get back to her familiar surroundings and all her nurse friends on West. Private duty nurses were hired for twenty-four-hour attention to Karen. A heart monitor, suctioning equipment and oxygen were set up in her room. It looked like a private I.C.U.

Hilda came into Karen's room, smiling. She held something behind her back.

"Guess what I have for you, Karen?" she said. From behind her back, she produced an orange Popsicle which Karen grabbed with glee. She jammed it into her dry mouth. With joy, we watched Karen eat the first morsel of food she had had in a week.

What a week it was! At this time, just the week before, Karen had stopped breathing. But the Lord brought her through; now He ended her seven-day fast with a juicy Popsicle.

The doctors took an X-ray of Karen's throat and

reported the good news. Her air passage had opened to twice the size it had been the week before.

Lisa stopped in to visit as soon as she came on duty.

Karen was already learning to talk. She put her finger over the opening in her throat. "Hi, Lisa," she whispered hoarsely. That evening, George, the boys and I went out for dinner. It was good to be together again with the crises behind us.

Later that night, the parents of Dr. DeLamerens' patients met together in the hospital auditorium. We were told the good news about a financial foundation which was established for his patients. It would pay for 100 percent of the hospital bills incurred after October first, only a month away! What a blessing that was going to be!

Thankfully, our medical insurance paid for 80 percent of Karen's bills. The remaining, steadily-mounting expenses were ours. Karen's stay in I.C.U. cost several thousand dollars for just one week. Now we rejoiced to learn that soon the foundation would cover the entire cost. This truly lifted our financial burden!

After the meeting, I stopped in the hallway to talk to Judy about her son Anthony. He was still critical. I put an arm around her shoulder. I told her about God's power and what He brought us through last week.

"God loves Anthony, you and your husband, Judy. What do you want to ask Him for?"

With tears in her eyes she answered, "I just want my son to stop suffering."

"Are you willing to release Anthony to the Lord for His purposes?" I asked.

Judy nodded. I prayed for God's presence and peace. We placed her son in God's loving arms and asked that he be healed; I prayed as the Lord directed, coming against Satan and bound anything that would interfere with the Lord's perfect plan for Anthony. When finished praying, we sensed His peace.

Judy thanked me and went back into her room.

The phone rang first thing the next morning. I was awake but still lying in bed. I reached over and answered it. Carol was on the line.

"I'm sorry to call you so early," Carol apologized. "But I felt it was important to call you now and not later."

"What's up?" I asked.

"Well, I don't quite understand. But I feel the Lord wants me to encourage you to keep looking to Jesus and not fear."

I thanked her for calling, then dressed and went to the kitchen for coffee. Dr. Pefkarou sat at the nurses' station. "Trudy," she said quietly. "I think you should know that Anthony died this morning."

"Oh, Father," I quietly lifted the prayer of my heart, "Anthony is no longer suffering. You have healed him in a more perfect way than we could even imagine."

"How gracious of the Lord," I reflected, "to wait on receiving Anthony into heaven until his parents released him."

Judy told me later that Anthony talked about being with Jesus, and his passing was peaceful.

I went back into Karen's room. I didn't want to tell her about Anthony but knew I must: Death was a reality she had to deal with. She lived closer to it than most people.

"I have something sad to tell you, Karen." My eyes filled with tears as I said, "Anthony died just a little while ago."

"Oh, Mommy ," Karen cried. "I wish you hadn't told me that."

"I know it's hard, honey." I picked her up and held her on my lap. "But I wanted you to know since you knew
him and prayed for him. Now we need to pray for his family."

I choked out a prayer for God to comfort the family. We both cried. After a while, I said, "Karen, let's talk about heaven, where Anthony is now. Can you tell me what you know?"

"Well, Jesus is there," she replied. "And there's no tears, or hurting or sickness. It's always light; there's no night, or bad people and everyone is happy."

"That's good, Karen. You know a lot about heaven." We talked about Anthony being in heaven and what it must be like for him.

In the days that followed, we were to experience a time of peace and calm, a much-needed relief from the intense warfare for Karen's life. God was bringing us forth into His victory and there was joy ahead.

6
Great Physician

After Karen was returned to her room on West from the Intensive Care Unit, she was assigned special private nurses. One well-meaning nurse, whom we did not know, arrived at the 6:00 A.M. shift. She started buzzing around the room, opening the curtains and chatting cheerfully.

When the nurse was far enough away, Karen motioned for me to come over to her bed. Her rapid hand motions meant "Quick!"

I leaned over Karen. She whispered loudly the well measured, firm words, "Get her out of here!" It was obvious that Karen was regaining her old spunk!

We were glad when a different nurse came the next day. Of all Karen's private duty nurses, her favorite was Lois. Lois was a lovely, calm, middle-aged lady who treated Karen with gentleness and love. She often held Karen in her lap, encouraging her to fall asleep for an afternoon nap. Karen needed this rest but usually would not take it otherwise.

Watching Karen and Lois snuggle, I felt gratitude that our family could share the blessing we had in our daughter Karen with others.

At one point, when Karen was out of the room for a bone marrow test, Lois and I had an opportunity to talk together. I shared how much I was looking forward to being home with Karen again.

Lois looked puzzled. "You do realize the seriousness of Karen's illness and her poor prognosis?" she asked.

"Yes," I replied. "But I can't look at the circumstances. God is in charge of our total situation. I believe He's going to heal her. I *know* He has a special plan for Karen."

"A long time ago, I lost faith in a God who lets little children like Karen suffer and have disease," she shared.

"It's a difficult thing to understand," I answered. "But God didn't do this to Karen. Disease and sickness aren't God's will for us; they are a result of sin in the world. His will for Karen is health. We're praying for a miracle."

I shared how I had met Jesus in a personal way and how He filled me with the Holy Spirit. I wanted Lois to realize that she could know and love God. "He is a loving Father, not cruel. He makes a pathway of victory for us through our suffering."

"Thank you for sharing," Lois said. "If I prayed, I would say I would pray for you. I do wish you both the best."

We received a good report regarding the results of Karen's bone marrow test. We learned she was in three-fourths remission! My heart sang with joy.

The doctors were excited. At last the chemotherapy began to work. They planned to begin a fifth series of chemotherapy treatments that day in hopes of an even greater remission.

"Lord," I prayed. "Is this your plan for healing Karen? To work through the chemotherapy and have her go into total remission, permanently?" I was excited at the prospect of what God would do.

That evening, as I walked into Karen's room, I saw two nurses, the doctor and George. They were all wearing white isolation gowns and were standing around Karen's bed. It appeared as though they were examining Karen and were discussing something important.

Concerned, I hurried to the bed, I surveyed the group of gowned figures. To my surprise, Karen was sitting in the middle of the group playing a game of "Mr. Mouth."

"Mr. Mouth" was a modem version of tidily winks. It had a battery-operated "Mouth" that opened and closed as it revolved. It fascinated the staff, and they were enjoying a game with Karen before her chemotherapy shot.

Karen's appetite was stimulated by the medicine and she ate heartily. Just before bedtime, she asked for a bowl of cereal. A few minutes later while George was in the hall, the doctor who treated Karen during her crisis walked past. He had doubted she would live that night when her heart stopped.

"By the way," he said, pausing as he saw George. "How's your little girl?"

"See for yourself," George said with a grin, pushing wide the door to Karen's room. The doctor saw Karen sitting at the side of her bed swinging her feet and eating a bowl of cereal.

"Now, *that's* a miracle!" he exclaimed.

The swelling in Karen's throat continued to recede, permitting her to breathe more easily. There was no longer any need for additional oxygen for her tracheotomy opening. The tube in her neck had been removed and replaced by a smaller one. Her incision was healing well.

The next day, Holiday walked into the room, smiling.

"Remember the popcorn party I promised you, Karen, when you were better?"

Karen remembered.

"Well, today is Shevago's birthday, and we will let him come to your room tonight to have cake and popcorn."

"Oh, boy!" Karen exclaimed. "That will be fun!"

Shevago put on a small gown and washed before he came into Karen's room. We sang "Happy Birthday" as he blew out his four candles. Holiday popped the corn and everyone enjoyed the happy celebration. It helped Shevago, as his parents lived in another country and couldn't be with him.

I went home overnight. The next morning, when I arrived at Karen's door on West, I noticed the "reverse isolation" sign had been taken down.

Karen was disconnected from the monitor machines and the nurse was wheeling them away.

"Look, Mommy!" Karen shouted happily and held up her arm. "They've taken off the i.v. and given me a heparin lock." (A heparin lock kept the i.v. needle in her arm, but it wasn't attached to an i.v. machine with a limiting cord.) "And," she continued, "They've taken out my trach tube, too. I don't need it anymore."

"And this will be the last I'm needed here," announced Lois, with a smile.

Dr. Pefkarou was as excited as I. "Karen is doing so well we have discontinued the intensive care," she said, happily. "And as soon as her chemotherapy course is finished she should be going home."

"Home," I reflected. "How sweet the sound." We had Karen home for only four days in the last three months. It would be so good to all be home again.

Eating was a delight for Karen. Now that she was so much better, she thought she would ask permission to eat some of the things that had been restricted.

"Holiday, do you think I could eat nuts again? I'd really like to have some peanuts."

"That would be okay now, Karen," Holiday replied.

Just then the door opened and Carol, the nursing supervisor, walked in with cards and letters in her hand. "Karen," she said. "You get the strangest mail!" She handed Karen a postcard picture of President Carter with a small bag of peanuts stapled to it!

"Peanuts!" Karen cried out in delight.

God's timing couldn't be more perfect. He cared for even the smallest details of Karen's life, including her desire for peanuts.

I read the card as Karen eagerly cracked the peanut shells and chewed the nuts. "Hi, Karen," it stated. "We are on vacation and thought you might like some peanuts grown near our president's home. Hope you are feeling better. May Jesus bless you."

The card was unsigned and I couldn't figure out who had sent it, but I do know the Lord himself made sure that it *was* sent.

The day after Karen's chemotherapy was finished, I thought she would be discharged. I took the cards, pictures and posters off Karen's wall. She helped pull the adhesive from the back of the cards. We put her games and stuffed animals in bags and lined everything up by the door. All we needed was Dr. DeLamerens' final checkout of Karen before we could go.

Hilda stopped in the room. She noticed the plastic label that she and Karen had made several days before and stuck to the light shade over Karen's bed. "You don't want to forget this, Mrs. Colflesh," she said, pointing to the little label.

I read again what Karen printed on it: "Mommy, I love you."

"This is too special to leave," I said, carefully peeling it off and re-sticking it on my notebook. "I'll always treasure it."

The afternoon wore on and I wondered if we'd get home that day. Dr. DeLamerens was tied up in meetings and promised he would see us later.

As the evening grew later we finally went to bed. Karen and I were disappointed to still be at the hospital. For all the time we had spent there, however, I knew we could wait one more day.

Just as I was about to fall asleep, Dr. DeLamerens quietly opened the door. "May I come in?" he asked. He apologized for not arriving sooner, but said he was sure Karen could be discharged the next day. As I rested my head back on the pillow, I realized that it would be September the seventh. The last time she was discharged, Karen had gone home on the seventh day of July.

"I believe you're showing your special hand in sending Karen home on the seventh day of the month, Lord," I said. "Thank you for choosing your perfect number as a sign of your completion and victory in her life."

We were up early the next morning, eager to leave as soon as the doctors completed their rounds. Karen was officially discharged, we hugged everybody on the hospital staff goodbye, and Holiday helped us carry our belongings to the car.

On the way down in the elevator, Karen said, "It sure would be nice to stop in the gift shop and get a little treat." I agreed with her and checked in my wallet. It was totally empty.

"I'm sorry, Karen," I said. "I don't have any money with me. We'll have to get something later." She was disappointed, but knew that without money, we could buy no candy.

As we opened the car door, Karen's eyes glanced at the car tray on the floor. "Look, Mommy! Money!" she cried with delight.

I had forgotten that the money was there. We counted it and found there was just enough for some candy. We returned to the hospital gift shop where Karen happily bought a candy bar.

"Isn't God good?" she stated, recognizing her treat as His provision.

"He surely is!" I rejoiced.

We turned on the Christian radio station as I drove out of the hospital parking lot. My eyes filled with tears of joy as I heard the musical strains, "To God Be the Glory, Great Things He has Done." Immediately following that song I heard, "He Touched Me and Made Me Whole." Karen and I looked at each other and smiled. We were heading home.

We spent the first few days at home just resting. It was a joy to be there. George and I marveled at Karen's rapidly-regaining strength and praised God for our "twice-given" daughter.

God was so wonderful toward us and did so many mighty things that I wanted to share His marvelous works. I called the president of our local Aglow Fellowship and asked if I could speak briefly at our monthly meeting the coming week. "If it's okay with you," I added, "I'd like to invite Ella, the hospital supervisor of respiratory therapy, to also say a few words."

"Great idea," the president responded. "We'll look forward to hearing you both!"

At the meeting, Ella and I shared the exciting events in Karen's recent crisis. I thanked each of them from my heart for their prayer support and assured them that God was answering.

Ella related her part in the events of the day. She told about the miracle of the tube sliding into Karen's throat. "But there was fear that Karen would hemorrhage to death," she said. "Everyone wanted the parents to know that everything possible was being done, so Karen was rushed to I.C.U., even though we thought she would die.

"But," Ella continued, "everything was being restored in Karen. 'How can it be?' they asked. The monitor said the heart worked normally when just a few minutes before it was not getting any oxygen. The miracle was already taking place.

"We kept waiting for the mother to come. I thought, 'What is this mother going to say? She's been here daily, only spent a little time away and now she's going to return and find her child dead.'

"But when she walked in, she was so calm. I kept looking at her and said to myself, 'What's wrong with this woman? Her child is dying!'

"Then she leaned over the bed and said, 'Karen, Mommy is here; but, most of all, *Jesus* is here. Jesus is in control of this situation right now, Karen. Don't worry about a thing because Jesus is going to make it all right!'

"I tell you, at that moment I reached up and grabbed *Faith,* and I said, 'Lord, you give her back her life. Lord, you heal her, because I'm not going to settle for anything less!' "

As Ella shared, the ladies gave astonished gasps, and occasionally even laughed; however, when Ella finished saying what she told the Lord, they broke out clapping and cheering. Praises to our mighty God punctuated the air. It was an exciting meeting and my heart was full of the joy of the Lord.

Karen became stronger each day and we spent a beautiful time together. It was warm and sunny, and we often went on bike rides, taking a picnic lunch along. One of Karen's favorite stops was to visit a neighbor's puppies. She greatly enjoyed romping and running with them.

We read, played games, laughed and cuddled. Karen's big brothers were especially tender and considerate, demonstrating their love to Karen.

Karen's routine included visiting the outpatient clinic once or twice a week so that the doctors could check her progress and health. At the clinic, we waited with other mothers and children for our turn. Some faces were familiar, since they had been hospitalized on West with us.

I saw Aurora, who so kindly came to visit us on the fourth of July. We chatted as we waited together, and I was happy to see that her son was looking so well. It was encouraging to see all the healthy-looking children who were in various stages of recovery and remission.

One of the ladies from the Jewish women's group, "The United Order of True Sisters," brought me a cup of coffee. This chapter of the order sponsored Dr. DeLamerens' clinic. They were there to help administer the clinic and to cheer patients and their families. These ladies worked hard to raise and share money by paying the clinic expenses, relieving us of an additional burden.

"Bless these wonderful ladies, Lord," I prayed, "for their loving ministry to us."

Karen was weighed and measured and her finger was pricked for a blood sample. It was very important to keep track of her blood picture. Her hemoglobin had been so low on one visit that the doctor considered admitting her to the hospital for a blood transfusion.

"It will give her more energy," he said.

She doesn't seem to lack any," I responded. "Among other things, we've been riding bikes together."

"Well, then, let's see how she looks next week," the doctor said. "You can go home today."

I turned to Karen after the doctors left. "We just squeaked through again, honey."

Each time we went to the clinic we never knew if Karen would be admitted to the hospital or allowed home for another week. After clinic, Karen happily went upstairs to West to say hello. She was happier still that she didn't have to stay there.

She saw Marcie, the ward secretary, and gave her a big hug.

"I've really missed you, Karen," she said. "But I'm glad you're home. I haven't ordered any special chocolate milkshakes or bacon, lettuce and tomato sandwiches for West since you've gone," she chuckled.

The following week I took Karen for her clinic appointment.

"It's time for her next series of chemotherapy," the doctor said, "so I'd like to have Karen admitted. We'll give her a bone marrow test now and a blood transfusion tonight. Tomorrow we will start the chemotherapy."

"Oh, no!" cried Karen. "I want to go home!"

Tears were in my eyes, too. I didn't realize the doctors planned to admit Karen that day. We had both hoped she would go home.

"It's just not right!" I felt. "She's hardly been home at all." I didn't want to see her go through more pain and suffering.

The doctor said, reassuringly, "Your stay this time won't be long at all. You should be home in a week."

Karen was given a new room on West. Before she got

settled, she went to the small kitchen off the hallway. She pulled a paper cup out of the wall container, got a can of soda from under the sink and moved the chair over to reach the ice machine. She filled her cup with ice and Coca-cola. Karen accomplished this with such ease, it was obvious she had done it many times before.

One of Karen's part-time nurses saw me in the hall and stopped to talk. She heard of Karen's remarkable recovery and was glad she was doing so well.

"I've been reading about God moving through the power of His Spirit in people's lives today, just like you've experienced in Karen's. Do you have the baptism in the Holy Spirit and the gift of speaking in tongues?"

"Yes! I have received the baptism in the Holy Spirit and speak in tongues." As we talked, she expressed her desire to have God's power in her life.

"If you want to receive this baptism, God is ready to give it to you," I informed her. "Do you have time now? We could pray about it."

"Why, yes," she said. "I just went off duty. I'd like that."

We went into Karen's room and sat down. I read different Scripture verses aloud to her. The passages referred to the baptism in the Holy Spirit.

"Before you ask Jesus to baptize you in the Holy Spirit," I continued, "it is important for you to invite Him into your heart as your Lord and Savior, and to repent of your sin."

"I've already asked Jesus to take away my sin and to be my Lord and Savior," she said.

"Good!" I responded. "Being baptized in the Holy Spirit will enable you to live the Christian life. We receive this baptism by asking Jesus for it, just as we asked Him for salvation.

I led my nurse friend in prayer and she asked Jesus, simply and beautifully, to baptize her in the Holy Spirit. We were aware of the power and blessing of God.

"Thank you," she said as we finished. "I feel such a great peace."

"Remember," I said as we hugged goodbye, "you can begin to pray in tongues whenever you want. The language God gives to you is a new and deep means of communication, your spirit to God's Spirit. It is part and parcel of having the Holy Spirit in your life."

"I'll try praying that way as I drive home."

"Let me know how it goes," I said as we walked to the hall.

As she left, Dr. DeLamerens came over to speak to me. "You look happy," he commented, noticing the expression on my face. "I have some news that should make you happier still. We just received the results of Karen's bone marrow test and she's in 90 percent remission."

"Ninety percent! That's wonderful!" My face glowed now from the good report as well as from the Holy Spirit. "Thank you, Lord, for your joy," I whispered gratefully.

The next day, Karen started on her sixth course of chemotherapy. She took different medicine this time and we were thankful that it didn't cause a nauseous reaction. I saw my nurse friend and she beamed her reply. "God gave me a new language," she said, "and it's wonderful."

The following Sunday, while the family was at church, I suggested to Karen that we have our own time of worship together. She liked the idea, so we prayed and read the Bible.

I sang a few songs of praise, but Karen could not join me. Her throat was healed from the tracheotomy, but her vocal cords seemed to be damaged from the cancer that had attacked them.

Karen could only speak in a low, hoarse vocal range. I asked the doctors if her voice would return to normal. They didn't seem optimistic.

This condition, however, didn't bother us; we had faith that God would restore her voice in His timing. Without her voice, Karen could not be an evangelist and "sing God's praises to the nations," as He had shown us in Psalm 57:9. Therefore, the matter was in His hands.

Karen's stay in the hospital went smoothly, and as the doctor had expected, we were home again within a week.

Since Karen could not attend school because of the danger of infection, I was directed by Karen's school personnel to make arrangements for a "home-bound teacher."

Mr. Rothra came to our house to teach Karen, and soon they became good friends. Karen thought it was fun to have her own, special teacher.

She started reading the book which her class was working on in first grade. Karen delighted in her work and finished the 130-page reader in three days.

"You will definitely need more advanced reading, Karen," Mr. Rothra stated on his next visit. I quietly worked in the kitchen as Karen and her teacher sat at the dining room table.

The two of them exchanged jokes and stories, and then worked on reading and mathematics. Soon Karen was doing third-grade material and talked Mr. Rothra into teaching her cursive writing.

"You're going to have to stop letting that pencil 'jump' out of your hand," Mr. Rothra warned Karen, "if we're going to get to serious writing." Karen giggled as she thought of her "game" of dropping her pencil to the floor during the lessons.

"See ya later, alligator," Karen called out as she

waved goodbye to her teacher.

It was soon time for our weekly visit to the clinic. As we drove, Karen said, "Jesus talked to me last night."

"What did He say?" I asked.

"He said, 'I am returning your voice.' "

"What wonderful news!" I exclaimed, reaching over to squeeze her hand.

The doctors' faces showed joy as they examined and talked with Karen at the clinic. They were obviously glad that they had attempted "heroic measures" to restore her life.

Karen's blood report showed that everything was returning to normal. Her platelet count was especially high. "That count sounds good enough for you to play on your slip-n-slide," I said. Karen was delighted, since she had not played with her new gift since she received it four months before.

After we finished at clinic, we gathered our things to leave for home. I always brought books and games to use while we waited our turn. Karen put on her favorite hat, a Mickey Mouse cap with a visor. The hat was perfect for covering her almost bald head.

"Let's stop at the ladies' room," I said to Karen before leaving. While I was in the booth, Karen waited for me by the sink.

Two women came into the ladies' room. I heard one say to the other, "Isn't that a cute hat he's wearing?" I really chuckled when I heard Karen very seriously reply, "The *he's* a *she!*"

At home, we set up the slip-n-slide as promised. Chris and Karen had a wonderful time running and throwing themselves on the slippery, wet plastic strip, sliding on their tummies, and jumping up to start all over again.

Great Physician

George arrived from work in time to see the big occasion. He rejoiced with me as we watched our children happily at play. It was very good to laugh. Our hearts were light. God was giving us a brief period of rest and rejoicing before He called us into our most difficult and hardest walk.

7

Sovereign God

The week following Karen's good report at clinic she was scheduled to enter the hospital for another series of chemotherapy treatments. At the hospital, Karen persuaded Dr. Pefkarou to let me come to the testing room so she could hold my hand during the necessary, but dreaded, bone marrow test. Karen promised she would cooperate and hold as still as possible. The doctor must have remembered the first bone marrow test when it took three people to hold Karen down.

Karen held my hand tightly and kept her promise to lie still. We were all glad when the test was over.

The test report caused me concern. There were more cancerous cells in her marrow than before. Her partial remission was failing.

"I thought she would show steady improvement toward total remission," I said to the doctor.

She reported the grim news that Karen's type of leukemia never goes into full remission. The very fact that she was surviving even this long was unusual.

"God," I prayed, "I know *all* things are possible with you." Within a week, Karen's chemotherapy was finished and she was released from the hospital. Our stay at home was short-lived, however. After two days, Karen woke up with a fever.

I called the doctor. He said, "Bring her to the hospital."

Karen's white blood count was very low; the doctor decided to admit her and to immediately start her on antibiotics to counteract serious infection.

The days seemed to drag as we waited for Karen's condition to improve. One week went by, then two. I read the results of Karen's blood test each day, hoping to see improvement; but from what I could interpret, it appeared that more and more cancerous activity was indicated. None of the doctors said anything concerning this to me on their daily rounds.

"I have to know what's going on," I thought, starting toward the door of Karen's room. "Maybe I can find Dr. Pefkarou. "

Half way out the door, I stopped short, realizing, "I don't want to know."

Karen was resting, so I took out my pen and paper. With Thanksgiving just a week away, I needed to quickly compose a letter to include with the Thanksgiving cards we had decided to send. The cover of our card read, "In everything give thanks." There were many things for which we could be thankful, even in the midst of this difficult time.

The next day, after reading Karen's blood report, I just *had* to know what was happening. Nurse Holiday was available, and I asked her if we could talk. We went into an empty room to be alone.

"Karen has gone into relapse," Holiday said, softly. "She no longer has any remission and her condition is very serious."

I was numb.

"I'm so sorry," Holiday said as she put her arm around me and lovingly hugged me.

Unable to respond at first, I finally choked out, "That's only the medical picture you see. There's another side, too."

I walked out of the hospital stunned. "Oh, God!" I cried in distress and prayer. "Oh, God!"

As I grieved over the news of Karen's condition, God posed a question to my heart: "What if I have a ministry for you and your husband that requires going through the death of your child?"

It stopped me cold in my tracks. "Oh, Father, no!" I gasped.

Every feeling and thought within me froze in fear. Yet, even in my incapacity, a small, quiet strength began to radiate from deep within my spirit to permeate my being.

God reminded me of the declaration which George and I had made throughout Karen's illness. From the very beginning, we had prayed, "To your greatest glory . . . ."

Sincerely and honestly we had released Karen to the Lord with "no strings attached." We couldn't add conditions now. My only hope was that "God's greatest glory" would be a miracle of healing.

My body numb, I turned the key in the ignition. Needing someone to talk to, I drove to Velma's, blinking back my tears. Sobbing, I told her what Holiday had said. Velma cried with me.

"Let's pray," she urged, reaching for my hand.

She prayed aloud that I would perceive what God wanted to show me and that He would protect my faith. She concluded with the heartwarming promise from Scripture that God is able to do exceeding abundantly above all that we ask or think (Eph. 3:30, KJV).

Feeling stronger, I phoned George at the office to tell

him about Karen's relapse, asking, "Maybe we should hold our Thanksgiving card?"

"No," he answered. "It's very important that we go ahead in faith and mail it out. No matter what God's plans are for Karen's future, it doesn't invalidate what He's already done."

Psalm 91 became a mainstay to me. I was comforted as I read:

> He who dwells in the shelter of the Most High, who abides in the shadow of the Almighty, will say to the Lord, "My refuge and my fortress; my God, in whom I trust."
>
> For he will deliver you from the snare of the fowler and from the deadly pestilence ["That was leukemia all right," I thought];
>
> he will cover you with his pinions, and under his wings you will find refuge; his faithfulness is a shield and buckler.
>
> You will not fear the terror of the night, nor the arrow that flies by day, nor the pestilence that stalks in darkness, nor the destruction that wastes at noonday.
>
> A thousand may fall at your side, ten thousand at your right hand; but it will not come near you. (Psalm 91:1-7, RSV)

"Lord, what else can we do? What else *should* we do?" I prayed.

The Lord spoke through His Word: "Take the whole armor of God, that you may be able to withstand in the evil day, and having done all, to stand" (Eph. 6:13, RSV). We were to stand in the faith God gave us and keep on God's armor. He would see us through.

118

Attempting to bring Karen back to some level of remission, the doctors prescribed another course of chemotherapy. Karen's blood had responded before. Perhaps it would again.

My body became more weary than it had in the past. The constant running between home and the hospital and the emotional strain was wearing.

Mrs. Quintiliani, the nursing supervisor, saw me rush down the hallway late one afternoon on my way home. She stopped me for a moment to ask how I was holding up. My eyes filled with tears. "It's just so hard to keep going."

Seeing my distress, she placed her arm around me. "We all love you here," she said, comfortingly. "You and your husband are holding up marvelously."

"Thank you," I said, appreciating the solace. "We love you here, too." My spirit was lifted as I drove home thinking of the loving arms and the loving hospital.

A new friend was brought into our lives at this time. Her name was Arlene and she began to have a special prayer concern for Karen. One day, she came to the hospital to visit and to encourage us.

As Arlene stood to leave she asked, "Karen, is there anything you would like me to bring next time I come to visit?"

"Oh, yes!" Karen replied. "Would you please bring me some chocolate chip cookies?"

The next day, Arlene returned with a batch of warm chocolate chip cookies. She also had some hand-drawn pictures and a note from her young son, Jonathan, inviting Karen to come fishing with him as soon as she was able.

Karen and I ate the cookies right away. Arlene declined our offer and said, "The Lord has called me to fast for Karen."

"Thank you, Lord," I silently prayed. "You continually surround us with loving, praying support."

"Trudy," Arlene said quietly, as she stood in the doorway preparing to go. "I want to share something with you that came to me earlier today, but I can't tell you that it's from the Lord. I don't know if it's just me, or if it's from the Lord."

"What is that?" I asked, understanding how she felt about not wanting to presume to be speaking for God.

"Well, this Scripture verse came to my mind," she answered. " 'This is not a sickness unto death but unto the glory of God.' I immediately thought of Karen."

As Arlene left, I pondered on that Scripture. It was spoken by Jesus before He raised Lazarus from the dead (John 11:4).

Was it possible we still had the dreadful possibility of having to pray for Karen's resurrection ahead of us? "Oh, God!" I cried out in fear, "Don't let it go that far!"

The radio was tuned to the Christian station and the song, "He who overcomes shall stand; he who overcomes shall rise; he who overcomes shall reign," was playing.

Hearing the words, I responded, "Yes, Lord. We will stand firm in you. We will overcome; we will conquer all that you allow to be on our pathway."

The day before Thanksgiving, Karen's chemotherapy was finished and she was discharged. She even felt good enough to play me a game of kickball in the hallway before we left the ward.

George called the room while we were packing. "This is really a day to rejoice," he said. "First, Karen is coming home. And second, I've just been offered an interview for a job promotion to New Jersey!"

"Oh, honey!" I exclaimed. I didn't know whether to be happy or upset. If George were accepted for the job, he would become the Council Scout Executive, a position he had worked toward his entire career.

On the other hand, if he took the job, we would be moving and Karen would have to change hospitals. Thoughts of "How do I know what the hospital will be like? Who will the doctors be? How far will we have to drive?" went through my head.

"That's really a biggie," I replied to George, not sounding the least excited.

"Check with Dr. DeLamerens and see what he says. I'll see you at home, honey. I love you."

"Karen's illness should not hold you here," our doctor advised. "She can be treated at other places, too. I would not let her leave, however, until she was well enough to travel." He was extremely reassuring.

But I didn't *feel* very reassured. However, I *did* hear what the Lord was saying to me: *Remember Sarah of old, Trudy. She followed her husband Abraham* into *the wilderness, and I led Abraham.*

"Yes, Lord," I answered. "I know you will not lead us astray. But the whole idea is scary."

I know, He answered. *But you can trust me.*

We had a happy Thanksgiving Day together as a family. George's dad, "Grandpa Colflesh," spent several days with us. After a turkey dinner, Karen got her softball and glove, put on her Mickey Mouse cap and asked, "Who wants to play ball with me?"

"I do," said Grandpa, and the two of them happily went out to the yard to play.

"What a marvelous sight!" I said to George as we watched the two throw a ball back and forth. Running outside with my camera, I exclaimed, "I'll get some pictures. "

Karen tired quickly and soon came back in the house.

Several days later, we made plans to visit Carol. The day we were to go, Carol called to say she didn't feel well and didn't want to expose Karen to any germs. As we talked, Carol told me she had another Scripture verse to give me.

"Let's hear it," I said.

> For God has already given you everything you need . . . . He has given you the whole world to use, and life and even death are your servants. He has given you all of the present and all of the future. All are yours, and you belong to Christ, and Christ is God's. (1 Cor. 3:21-23, TLB)

"The part that really stood out to me," Carol said, "was, 'life and even death are your servants.' "

"I never heard it put quite like that before," I answered. "Thank you for calling."

Even death is a servant of God. For what was God preparing us? How could we make death bow down to us? I didn't know.

"Please, Lord," I cried. "Don't let it come to death!"

I explained to Karen that we wouldn't go to see Carol as we had planned because she was sick.

"I have an idea," Karen suggested. "Let's bake her some cookies to cheer her up."

We talked about what kind of cookie to bake. Karen wanted to make this an exotic procedure; she suggested Chinese fortune cookies (complete with fortunes inside).

But then she thought about her suggestion and said, "No. We don't believe in fortune - we believe in God."

"I have an idea," I said. "Why don't we make cookies and put Bible verses in them - Scripture promises?"

"And instead of *fortune* cookies," Karen chimed in, "we could have *promise* cookies."

So the plan was set. We used a box which contained Bible verses on small paper scrolls. Karen would carefully take a scroll, unwind it and copy the printing on a piece of paper. She got as far as "It is good to give thanks ..." when we realized that the piece of paper was going to be too big to fit in a cookie.

"Karen," I suggested. "Help me with the cookie dough. We'll just put the scrolls right from the box into the cookies. That will work much better and faster."

And it did. We couldn't find a recipe for fortune cookie shells, so we made sugar cookies and pressed each scroll right into the dough.

The cookies turned out fine, and it was fun to break them open to find a Bible promise.

We divided the batch into thirds. We left one part for the family, dropped off another at Carol's for her and her family then drove to Arlene's to bring her family the last third.

Everyone was delighted with the idea and the gift. Karen made friends quickly with Jonathan and, while they played, I visited with Arlene. As we left, we made plans to come again soon so Karen and Jonathan could go fishing together.

George flew to New Jersey for his job interview. Another man had already been interviewed for the position and the choice was to be made after George's visit. We knew that the Lord could easily show us if it was not His purpose for us to move. If George did not receive the job, that clinched it. Up to this point, however, George felt God's leading and direction to accept the interview.

The phone rang that night. It was George. "Guess what, honey? I got the job!"

"That's wonderful," I said. After hanging up, I shared the news with the children.

"Oh, boy," said Karen. "I'll be able to play in the snow again. I'll need a sled, ice skates and skis."

"Not so fast," I laughed. "We have to *get* there first."

Before Karen went to bed, she reviewed her activities for the following day. First, her teacher would be at the house. Next, she would go to the clinic and then, at last, go fishing with Jonathan.

When morning came, to our dismay, Karen felt weak and nauseated. She had to lie on the couch during her school lessons, which her teacher cut short because of her obvious discomfort. After he left, I drove Karen to the hospital for clinic.

"I don't think I can walk very far, Mommy," Karen said, as we pulled into the hospital parking lot. On clinic day the lot was always jammed. Usually an available parking place could only be found at the far end of the lot. We would have a long walk to the clinic.

"Jesus," I prayed aloud. "Please help us find a parking space close to the entrance for Karen."

We drove slowly through the front row of the parking lot. "Look, Karen. Jesus saved a parking space for us right in front of the entrance!" Parking in the space, we thanked God.

I held Karen on my lap as we waited for her blood report from the clinic. Dr. Pefkarou gave me the news; Karen's white blood count had climbed seriously and she would have to be readmitted to the hospital.

124

My heart dropped. I felt weak. Karen didn't seem to mind the news; she felt so sick, she was glad she was going upstairs where she could lie down.

Later that afternoon, I called Arlene to tell her we couldn't come to her house for fishing. Although she didn't know Karen was admitted until I phoned, the Lord had called her to fast again for Karen.

I shared how distressing it was to see Karen's white count rising. She prayed with me, telling Jesus we trusted Him. Then she thanked Him for the situation, knowing that He had everything under His control. She rebuked Satan, asked again for healing and released Karen to God's will.

"We worship you, Jesus. We lift up your Holy name," I agreed in the encouraging prayer.

Karen went through the usual procedure for hospital admittance. We were well acquainted with it by now. The hardest part of the re-entry was starting a new i.v. The nurses knew Karen well and, even though they did their best, Karen squeezed my hand tightly. With tears in her eyes, she cried, "Pray, Mommy. Pray."

George returned from New Jersey late that afternoon. He called from the airport to learn whether we were at home or at the hospital. When he discovered where we were, he came directly to the hospital.

Since it was close to dinner time, George suggested that I drive home with him; then he would bring me back later that evening. Karen was receiving a blood transfusion as we left. She looked pitifully weak and sick as we said goodbye.

On the way home, I asked George to stop at a grocery store so I could buy food for dinner. As he turned the car off, the weight of everything happening all at once hit me, and I broke down and cried.

"Here you just arrived home from being accepted as Scout Executive," I sobbed, "and I don't even have dinner for you."

George put his arm around me and snuggled me closely to him.

"Karen and I wanted to plan a celebration for you," I said, tears rolling down my cheeks. "Now she's back in the hospital, so sick we can't do anything. How long is this going to go on?"

"Oh, God, our Father," George prayed. "It gives us so much pain to see our little daughter ill like this. We ask that you will do what you are going to do in her life; either heal her, Lord, or take her to heaven. We freely give Karen to you to do as you will. In Jesus' name we pray. Amen."

We never did go into the grocery store. Instead, we drove home, got the boys and went to a fast-food restaurant to eat. Later, all of us went to the hospital. Walking into Karen's room, we were overjoyed to see her sitting up and feeling much better.

The next morning, Karen began her ninth course of chemotherapy. Her white count was still rising, but I still hoped that the medicine would subdue it.

"Karen," George said, as he talked to her on the phone. "I won't be able to visit you until after my meeting tonight. But when I come, I'll bring you a surprise."

Karen loved surprises and wondered all day what he would bring. I didn't know either; George had told me he would buy something.

Later, George told me that he had become busy and completely forgot about buying something for Karen. He remembered in the middle of his meeting.

He knew that the stores would be closed by the time his meeting was finished, and he wondered what he could say to Karen; he hated to disappoint her.

His thoughts were interrupted as the chairman of the meeting said, "George, our district chairman wanted to do something special for Karen, so we've bought her this gift." He handed George a big, gift-wrapped package.

When George arrived at the hospital, he had a smile as wide as his face. Karen opened the gift and discovered a cute baby doll that kissed when its arms moved together.

"Oh, boy, Daddy! Thanks!" she yelled gleefully. "Where did it come from?"

"Straight from Jesus," he answered. Then he told her the whole story.

Soon, Karen's chemotherapy was finished. Even though she had a fever, the doctors decided she could be discharged to take antibiotic medicine and to rest at home.

Several times that night, I was up with Karen, giving her medicine to ease her pain. Her head ached severely as a side effect of the particular chemotherapy used this time.

The next morning, her fever was still high. "Karen, if this Tylenol doesn't lower your fever, I'm going to have to sponge you."

"Oh, no," she groaned. She hated to be sponged. There were times in the hospital when her fever reached 104 degrees and the nurses had to sponge her to help lower the temperature quickly. The cool water on her hot body felt miserable, and she would beg for a blanket, crying, "That's enough! That's enough! It feels cold!"

Rubbing Karen's back as she lay in bed, I waited for the Tylenol to take effect. The phone rang. Mickey Jordan, the evangelist who had prayed for Karen last summer, was on the line. She was in town on business and called to ask about Karen. She had heard about some of the mighty things the Lord was doing in Karen's life.

"At present," I said, "Karen's not doing very well."

Mickey advised that I read God's Word aloud to Karen and continually pray that she be protected by the blood of Jesus. "Let us pray right now for Karen," she said.

Mickey prayed so earnestly, I felt the power of the Holy Spirit crackling through the telephone wires and electrifying my whole being. Mickey felt the power, too, and said, "I see the glory of God all over Karen!"

"God bless you, Mickey," I said. "Thank you so much for calling!"

I ran back to Karen's room and told her about the exciting telephone call. Then, laying hands on Karen, I prayed. God made His presence known and we felt His love and power. I didn't have to sponge her, and by the next day, Karen's fever was down to 100 degrees and she improved steadily.

At our next clinic visit, however, I was dismayed to learn that Karen's white blood count had risen sharply. It became apparent that the last course of chemotherapy was not holding the white count under control as it had done in the past.

Even though her count was high, Karen was not admitted to the hospital. We were free to go home. "We'll see you in a couple of days," Dr. DeLamerens said as we waved goodbye.

The following day, when George got home from work, I said, "Honey, let's take the children and buy our Christmas tree tonight. I'm not sure whether or not Karen will be released after clinic tomorrow."

We bought the tree and everyone stayed up late to

decorate it. We didn't know how long Karen would be home, and we wanted her to take part in the family fun.

We had a special tree ornament that looked like Frosty the Snowman. It was Chris' and Karen's favorite bulb, and each year, they argued over who would hang it up. We thought we would solve the problem by letting them take turns hanging it each year.

"It's my turn to hang Frosty," Karen piped up.

"No, it's my turn this year," Chris said, defending his position.

"Well, let's let Karen hang Frosty this year," I said. Chris reluctantly agreed.

My heart ached as I wondered, "I'm not sure Karen will be here next year to hang Frosty." Did I know something deep in my heart that I was not yet able to acknowledge?

Even when Karen was making a Christmas gift for my mother, I felt the possibility it could be a final reminder to her of Karen. Yet, I truly still didn't know what God was going to do. I had no doubt that He *could* heal her, but I also knew that God might have other plans. The only certain thing was that we had to wait patiently as He directed us and gradually revealed His purposes.

8
Man of Sorrows

We bought the Christmas tree early and decorated it. As I had suspected, when I took Karen to clinic the next day, she was admitted to the hospital. Her white blood count had continued to rise sharply, and it was important to start her immediately on more chemotherapy.

First, Karen was given an electrocardiogram to determine if her heart had been damaged by any of the chemotherapy. The medicine the doctors were to use this time was especially strong and could be dangerous if her heart had been affected.

Karen's system could only tolerate a specific amount of this particular medicine because of its strength; but we were hopeful that its use might bring Karen back into remission. It had been given to her just before her last remission. Now the doctors were going to give her the last amount she was allowed.

"I have good news for you, Trudy," Dr. Pefkarou said. "None of the chemotherapy has damaged Karen's heart."

"That's great!" I responded. "We've prayed for Karen each time she's received chemotherapy, asking God not to let it harm her."

Mark 16:18 came to mind: "If they drink any .deadly thing, it will not hurt them ..." (RSV). We claimed this for Karen over the chemotherapy.

"Thank you Lord, for protecting Karen," I prayed.

Although Karen had started chemotherapy, she was allowed to leave her room to attend the annual Christmas party downstairs. It was given for all of Dr. DeLamerens' patients. After the entertainment, Santa Claus walked among the children while they ate refreshments. When he came to Karen, he asked her what she wanted for Christmas.

Karen had already told me she wanted a game called Twister and some other things, but her answer to Santa surprised me. "I'd like a portable television," she answered.

"Karen," I said, "that's a pretty big order."

Santa smiled and looked at me. "We'll see if we can get that for you, Karen." He walked away, saying, "Have a Merry Christmas, children."

Karen's limited energy failed after the cake and ice cream. She asked to return upstairs even before the gifts were handed out.

"I'll wait and get your present for you, Karen," I said. "Daddy will take you back to your room."

When I brought her present upstairs, Karen didn't show much interest. Her stomach was greatly bothering her. She was in so much pain, the doctor ordered a shot of Demerol to ease her. Karen hadn't needed a pain-killer that strong before. This new development caused me to worry.

The next day, Carol visited and invited me out for lunch. Not wanting to leave Karen for long, we went to the hospital cafeteria where we chose a quiet table on the patio. The fresh air and the warmth of the sun felt good.

As we ate, I talked about Karen, my hopes and God's plans. We talked about the Scripture verse which proclaimed, "life and even death are . . . [our] servants."

"I can tell you one thing, Carol," I bravely stated. "I won't give up on Karen's life until she's buried in the ground." Then I added, weakly, "If it should come to that...."

Karen developed ulcerated sores on her bottom and Laurie, the nurse, prepared a tub of warm water for Karen to sit in.

"No! No!" Karen cried. "I don't want to sit in the tub. Leave me alone! I don't want to get out of bed."

"You have to, Karen," I said, gently but firmly. I lifted her out of bed to the floor, encouraging her to walk to the tub.

"I don't want to walk," Karen complained.

"You need to, honey, to keep your legs strong."

Karen resisted our help, but Laurie and I got her to the tub. As we lowered her into the water, it began to overflow. "Oh, no!" I said, jumping back from the splashing water.

Karen stopped struggling and began to giggle. Then we all broke into laughter as Laurie and I grabbed extra towels to catch the running water and sop up what we could.

In a few minutes, Karen decided that was enough tub-sitting. "I want out!" she demanded.

"Wait a few more minutes," I answered.

"Get me out of here!" she yelled.

Just then, my friend Nancy Hedlund poked her head through the door and greeted us with a pleasant, "Hello. May I come in?"

I was glad to see Nancy. I had met her recently through Aglow and wanted to know her better.

With Nancy's arrival, we decided Karen had enough tub-sitting. Laurie left with the tub. I dried Karen off and helped her into a fresh gown and panties and back to bed.

Nancy moved a chair to the bed and spoke with Karen. "I thought you might like to hear some stories, Karen. I used to be a storyteller to other little children, and I'd like to tell you stories, too."

"Okay," said Karen. She rolled over on her side toward Nancy, getting comfortable.

Nancy was quiet for a few minutes, as if she were thinking what to say before she began. "You know, Karen, I can't think of one of my usual stories," she finally said. "But we can still have a story. We'll just make up one and have an adventure of our own."

Just then the Ivac machine beside Karen's bed started to beep a shrill tone. "What's that?" Nancy asked in surprise.

"Oh, don't worry," Karen laughed as she pushed a button to stop the beeping. "That just means my machine needs more solution."

Laurie came into the room and added more i.v. solution to the Ivac. After the machine was taken care of, Nancy continued. "We could have an animal in your story, Karen. Do you have a favorite?"

"Well," Karen answered. "I have two favorite animals. One's a dog and the other's a dolphin."

"Oh, dear," said Nancy. "A story with a dog would be different than a story with a dolphin."

"I have a good idea," said Karen. "Why don't we put them together and make one animal."

"Like a dolphog or a ... a ... dogaphin?" Nancy asked.

"Yes," giggled Karen with delight.

Karen decided she liked the "dogaphin" best. He had the head and legs of a dog and the tail of a dolphin. With Dogaphin decided upon, the adventure story began:

> Dogaphin was strolling along outside of the hospital when he heard someone yelling from the second floor. "Get me out of here! Help, get me out of here!" Curious as to who was calling, Dogaphin disguised himself as a doctor and worked his way up to Karen's room. He found her and asked what was the matter. Karen told him she hurt all over. Dogaphin said he knew a place where Karen could go that had trees with healing in their leaves that would make her well.
>
> Karen said she wanted to go there. So Dogaphin, Karen and Ivac the machine (since it was attached to Karen) started off on their adventure to this wonderful place.

Nancy could see Karen becoming restless with pain, so she ended the first part of the story. She told Karen she would be back the following day for the next segment in the adventures of Dogaphin and Karen.

Walking Nancy to the hall, I thanked her for coming. She told me she was glad she had come, for she had been blessed. Even though she had to do many things in preparation for Christmas, she explained that the Lord spoke to her about coming to the hospital first.

"Trudy," Nancy said as she took my hands. "I know the Lord is with you. From the moment I walked in here, I felt His presence and peace all around you, Karen and this room."

Those words were greatly appreciated, for the days had been wearing and my spirit was low. Nancy came again the following morning. "Guess what, Karen?" Nancy asked. "As I was coming to see you today the Lord told me the name of the place you and Dogaphin are going to on your adventure. It's called 'The City of His Brilliance'!"

"What a beautiful name," I thought. Nancy sat beside Karen's bed and continued the story:

After Karen, Dogaphin and Ivac left the hospital, they came to a mountain. It was called the Mountain of Difficulty and turned out to be a very long, hard climb. Ivac found it especially difficult because he had wheels instead of legs, so he spent a lot of time beeping and complaining.

As they neared the top, they rounded a sharp bend on the path. To their surprise, a big, green, scaly dragon blocked the way. The dragon told them he wasn't going to let them go to the City of His Brilliance, and he breathed fire at them.

But Dogaphin pulled out his Book and told the dragon they weren't going to be afraid of him because, "Greater is he that is in ... (us) than he that is in the world" (1 John 4:4, KJV). With that, the dragon angrily stamped away.

Karen rode Ivac down the other side of the mountain with Dogaphin running beside. When they reached the bottom and rested for the night, Karen asked Dogaphin to tell her again about the City of His Brilliance.

"Oh, it's a wonderful city," said Dogaphin. "It's a beautiful city. It doesn't have a sun or moon or anything else for light. The light comes from the center of the city. Out of the center of the city flows a river of sparkling, crystal-clear water. The river has life in it. On both sides of this river, trees grow. You know, the trees with the leaves that have healing. And Karen fell asleep, dreaming about the wonderful city. "

As the story ended, Dr. Pefkarou came in the room. "Time for your chemotherapy, Karen," she said.

"My hand hurts," Karen told her. The doctor examined the area around the i.v. needle.

"Everything looks okay. Tonight we will take the needle out, after your last dose of medicine."

Once again, Karen was finishing a series of chemo· therapy treatments.

"Will this one be effective?" I wondered. "Maybe tomorrow we can go home - now that she's finished with the medicine." I was encouraged to see Karen looking much stronger since she had received the blood transfusion earlier in the day. It would be good to be home again.

Because it was the Christmas season, many groups of people were coming through the halls. They stopped at Karen's door to sing carols and give her gifts and treats. However, the Lord sent a young man that night to minister especially to Karen.

This special person was tall, with long, flowing hair and gentle, soft, blue eyes. He carried a guitar with peace signs and world-religion symbols pasted on it. When he talked, he spoke quietly. He sang beautifully.

I asked his name and he said, "Gabriel."

"How appropriate," I thought.

Karen told Gabriel that her birthday was coming soon.

"What sign are you under, Karen?" he asked.

As I waited to hear her answer I wondered if she would remember our discussion about how to answer that question.

"I'm under the sign of the cross," Karen said.

I smiled. She had remembered.

"Well, since you're into Jesus, I'll sing you some Jesus songs," Gabriel answered. He sang songs of faith and encouragement. As he sang, I prayed that God would reveal the truth of Jesus to him.

"Don't stop," Karen said. "When you sing, my hand doesn't hurt."

"Thank you, Jesus, for sending Gabriel," I prayed.

That evening, the i.v. needle was removed from Karen's wrist and the board and tape were unwrapped from her hand. But all night, her hand bothered her. When Karen woke in the morning, she gasped, "My hand's all black!"

The sight made me nauseous. The entire inside of her palm was infected. I remembered the doctor saying how difficult it is to control infection with leukemia, and if it should get out of control, the results would be fatal.

The doctor examined Karen's hand and treated and dressed it.

"It's just too much," I thought, fighting back the tears.

At the nurses' station I asked Dr. Pefkarou, "What about Karen's hand?"

"We'll give her a blood transfusion and start her on

antibiotics intravenously," she answered, kindly. "I'm afraid, though, you won't be going home today."

Nancy came later that morning. It was hard for Karen to listen to today's adventure, but it helped keep her mind off the pain in her hand. Nancy and I gently placed Karen's wrapped hand in ours. We prayed for God's healing and asked Him to subdue the pain.

"Karen," Nancy said. "Picture yourself being held and comforted by Jesus, just like in this picture of Jesus tenderly holding a little lamb." She pointed to a card on the wall.

I taped the card to the foot of Karen's bed where she could see it better. "Every time your hand begins to hurt," Nancy continued, "call out to Jesus and know that He is holding you. You can see things in your mind by thinking them, and that way, you can see yourself being held by Jesus."

"This has been a hard day," I said to Nancy as she was leaving. Tears rushed to my eyes.

Nancy hugged me. "Trudy," she said, "I will commit myself to holding Karen, you and your entire family before the Lord."

I didn't realize how drained I was. It was as though a huge weight came off my back as Nancy spoke. The Lord had waited until just this time to send Nancy into our lives. She was fresh in the midst of the battle, ready to help bear the burden. We didn't know it yet, but God called her to have a special place in preparing Karen for the fulfillment of His great plan.

We were greatly encouraged on the following day. Karen was feeling much better and the infection had begun to heal.

While Nancy visited with Karen, Chris and I went on a

whirlwind Christmas-shopping expedition. "Please make our time count, Lord," I prayed. "And let us find what we need."

The ease with which we accomplished everything was delightful. Surely the Lord had gone before us!

When we returned to the hospital, Nancy told us her family and their young adult Christian fellowship were meeting together for a Christmas Eve worship service. Her husband, Ron, and she talked to the group, and if we wanted, they would come to Karen's room to hold the service.

George and I agreed that their coming would be wonderful. The hospital staff consented to the gathering.

Nurse Geri, who had been away at graduate school, came back to work on West during her vacation. She was a favorite of Karen's, so it was a special treat to have her with us. Because Karen was the only one on the ward at this time, she had Geri all to herself.

In preparation for the Christmas Eve gathering, Geri brought the decorated tree from the hall into Karen's room and wrapped a sheet around the base. We put stuffed animals under the branches.

Earlier, George and I had covered Karen's wall and door with Christmas cards which we had saved over the years because they were special. With the sparkly decorated tree and the brightly colored cards, Karen's room was very festive.

My mother flew in from Long Island the afternoon of Christmas Eve. George brought her directly to the hospital where we had a happy reunion.

Mother tried to be brave but later broke down and cried. George put his arms around her to comfort her. She hadn't seen her only granddaughter since last summer, and it was a shock seeing Karen without hair, in pain and very weak.

"I know we can trust the Lord in this whole situation," she said through her tears.

George and I agreed.

When it was time for the Christmas Eve worship service, we turned off the lights in the room and lit the tree. The room glowed with beauty and peace.

Ron, Nancy, their family and friends arrived. Geri helped to bring in extra chairs and got white gowns for everyone to wear after they washed.

We sang Christmas carols accompanied by guitar and Nancy told the familiar, beloved Christmas story of Jesus. We sang again, songs of Scripture and praise. The door was open and the music drifted down the halls.

Parents from other sections of the hospital slowly walked by. Some stayed to listen. Truly, Jesus was "visiting the sick and lonely" through His church that night.

At the end of the singing, everyone gathered around the bed and held hands, joining together in prayer for Karen.

The power and joy of the Lord's presence was so strong that we lifted our voices, singing to the Lord in the Spirit. As the songs quietly ceased, one of the people began to sing in prophecy.

A heavenly tune of beauty, with words from Jesus, spoke to us through the song in verse that rhymed. He was speaking directly to our family with words of encouragement: He said He was with us in our wilderness, giving us His strength.

His words touched my heart. In spite of the circumstances, it was a blessed Christmas Eve.

God expressed His love. His beloved body of believers

ministered to us in His name. Our hearts were warmed, as we continued to feel their goodbye hugs long after they had gone. Karen, too, was touched. As I kissed her goodnight she told me she "prayed with her heart" the whole evening.

After Karen had fallen asleep, George filled her stocking with surprises and hung it near the tree.

"The doctor said he wanted to let Karen go home for Christmas, and overnight, if possible," I said to George. "I'll let you know in the morning what he decides."

When I woke early Christmas morning, I saw Karen's stocking overflowing with candy canes, balloons and toys from George's handiwork. Below the stocking was an unexpected surprise that came while we slept, a bag full of brightly wrapped gifts given to the hospital for the children.

"Merry Christmas, Karen," I sang out, getting up to kiss her. "Look at all the presents."

"Bring my stocking over here," she said, waking quickly. I helped her pull out the assortment of toys, candy and nuts.

"Look, a dolphin," Karen said. She held up a pencil with a dolphin on the end. We both thought of Dogaphin.

Nurse Sam came in and washed Karen, admiring the gifts. I dressed Karen in her pajamas and pink robe, wishing that she could wear the fancy new dress I had just bought for her. But she was limp and in much pain. She didn't need the additional complication of a dress.

"She will wear it for her birthday," I thought.

Dr. DeLamerens made his morning rounds to examine Karen. "Merry Christmas, Karen," he said, as he fondly patted her hand in his. "I am happy to tell you that you may go home on a Christmas pass."

"We'll put her on a heparin lock and hope it holds so Karen won't have to have a new i.v. started when she returns," he said. "I'll send antibiotics for Karen to take orally, and some pain killers."

Karen had a great amount of pain because of her infected hand and sores in her mouth and throat. We tried to cheer her with the gift bag of toys from the hospital. Karen attempted to look at the gifts, but it was hard for her to think about much beside her pain. She was glad to be going home, however. By the time we were released and in the car, she had rebounded somewhat due to the effects of the pain killer.

It was a joy to pull into our driveway again with Karen. It seemed like there should be trumpets blowing and people shouting, "Karen's home! Karen's home!"

Karen must have felt that way too, because she said, "No one is here to greet me."

It was Sunday, and the family was at church. George and I talked earlier on the phone, and he knew we would be home about the same time they would be.

"Don't worry, Karen," I said. "Everyone will be here soon. Do you want to walk into the house?"

"I can't," she cried.

She seemed so weak and frail as I lifted her out of the car, yet my heart thrilled as I carried my precious bundle into our home.

Mother had started the turkey roasting before the family left for church and its delicious aroma filled the air as we entered the door.

I laid Karen on the couch, lit the Christmas tree and turned on Christmas music. We heard a car pull into the driveway. "Daddy's home," Karen said, happily.

Chris burst through the door, followed by Mike, Mother and George. "Merry Christmas!" he shouted.

"Merry Christmas!" I answered as we all greeted each other with hugs and kisses.

It was a happy day. Gifts were given and received lovingly. Taking snapshots was fun, but it was hard for Karen to smile because of her pain.

"Don't worry about smiling, Karen," I said. "I just want your picture."

The doorbell rang, and to our delight, it was Holiday.

She had come over to give Karen a gift.

We invited Holiday for dinner, but she didn't have time to stay. The visit perked up Karen and she sat at the table with us when it was time to eat.

After a bite of turkey and a piece of a roll, however, Karen asked if she could lie down again. I helped her to the couch and gave her another pain killer. Soon, Karen was feeling well enough to play with Chris and some of her toys.

That night, Karen enjoyed being in her own room and bed again. She had a good night's sleep.

Karen would not eat breakfast because she said her throat hurt too much to swallow. She did manage, however, to sip a little milk through a straw.

Soon it was time to gather Karen's things for the return trip to the hospital. As we waved goodbye to the family from the car, none of us knew this had been Karen's last visit home.

At the hospital, we were grateful to discover the heparin lock on Karen's arm had held, and she was easily connected to the i.v. machine.

George brought Mother to the hospital that afternoon.

She relieved me by staying with Karen for several days and nights, giving her much tender love and attention.

Over the days we became more concerned because Karen was not eating. Even soft foods were too difficult for her to swallow. The doctors consulted a nutritional specialist who prepared a special intravenous formula to meet Karen's needs. With the introduction of i.v. feeding, Karen gained more strength and her metabolism balanced again.

After a few days of mother's help, I returned to the hospital to stay with Karen. It was a difficult time for both of us. Her infected hand was healing, but it hurt and itched. The sores on her bottom were irritating and she hated to sit in warm water to treat them. Her throat and mouth caused her a great deal of pain and it was extremely difficult for her to swallow anything.

"It's time to take your medicine," the part-time nurse said cheerfully as she walked into Karen's room.

"I don't want to," groaned Karen.

"You have to," said the nurse.

"Nobody cares about me," Karen complained.

"That's not true, Karen," I said. "It's just that you have to take your medicine to help you."

The nurse was getting Karen's tub ready for her to sit in. "According to your schedule, you're to take your bath now," she said.

Karen resisted, but I helped the nurse get her into the water.

"Nobody cares, nobody cares," she groaned.

Karen was very low that day and needed our constant reassurance that we did indeed care. The discomfort and pain were difficult for her to rise above. She leaned heavily on us for support.

Hearing Karen's complaints, the nurse thought she would take a different approach and snap Karen out of it. My heart sank in dismay as I heard the nurse say, "Okay, Karen, if that's what you say, nobody does care then."

I could tell the words cut through Karen's heart like a knife.

"Don't say that!" Karen screamed.

"Okay," the nurse said. "But I just wanted you to know we're trying to help you."

"Get me out of this tub! You get out of here! I'm not taking my medicine," Karen yelled.

I said to the nurse, "Let me have some time alone with Karen. She can take her medicine later. I'll let you know."

I lifted Karen from the tub, dried her, put her in a hospital gown and helped her back to her bed.

"It's just not fair," Karen sobbed. "It's all a fake. This isn't a Hospital with a Heart. Nobody loves me. Nobody cares. I don't want my medicine. It's not worth it. I just want to go home!"

Karen had reached the lowest point of her long, drawn-out illness. All the frustrations and discouragement of illness and pain heaped themselves upon her at once, and she broke under the weight.

Tears welled in my eyes. "Oh, no, Karen," I cried. "That isn't true. Everything you're doing is worth it. This *is* a Hospital with a Heart and everyone here loves you."

The tears began to roll down my cheeks. "And Karen, I care about you. I love you. I'm so proud of you and how you do such hard things - you take medicine you don't like, you're brave when you have your blood taken or an i.v. put in, you trust God and call upon Him to help you and you know He answers.

"Oh, Karen, I just love you so much," I said with all my heart. "Let me tell you how much I love you. I even loved you before you were born. Daddy and I prayed to have another baby and we asked God to give us a little girl. God even told a friend of mine, while she and I were praying, that He was going to give us a baby. He was talking about *you!*

"Right after that, you began to grow inside me. I was filled with such joy, knowing you were coming. I prayed for you every day and took the best care I could of myself so you would grow healthy and strong.

"When you were born, Daddy and I praised and thanked God for giving us a little daughter. We thought and thought about a special name to give you. At last we decided Karen would be just the right name for you.

"We loved seeing you grow and learning all the important things children learn. You learned so quickly. We were proud of all you did and enjoyed you and loved you each year you grew.

"You're such an important part of our family, Karen. All of us, Chris, Mike, Daddy and I are *so* glad that God gave you to us. You're such a special person. You are so very, very precious and we love you so much. Nothing will ever take away our love for you."

I cried as I talked, and Karen cried as she listened. She knew that I meant what I was saying. She didn't see me cry often, but now I felt like I wanted to cry and cry and cry. How very much I loved Karen!

"Mommy," Karen cried out. "We've got to quit this; we've got to quit this."

"Jesus," I sobbed. "We need you."

A calmness settled over me. "Speak to me, Lord," I implored in my heart. "What are your plans for Karen?"

"It's going to be all right," He answered gently.

I looked at Karen. Her morale was lifting. She seemed

ready to go on again and face the hardships and pain. She knew she was loved and that the love was secure. How good it had felt to pour my heart out and tell her how much I loved her.

I attempted to sing a song of praise to the Lord but my voice was still choked from crying and my heart was still sore. I weakly sang, "The Joy of the Lord Is My Strength."

Again my eyes filled with tears. "It's so hard, Lord."

The door was ajar, and my friend Joan knocked and peeked in. I rose to meet her. She saw my tears, and without a word, came and hugged me. She held me tightly, and as she did I felt the love of Jesus filling me and all my anxieties falling away. "My grace is sufficient," the Lord reassured my heart. "It's going to be all right."

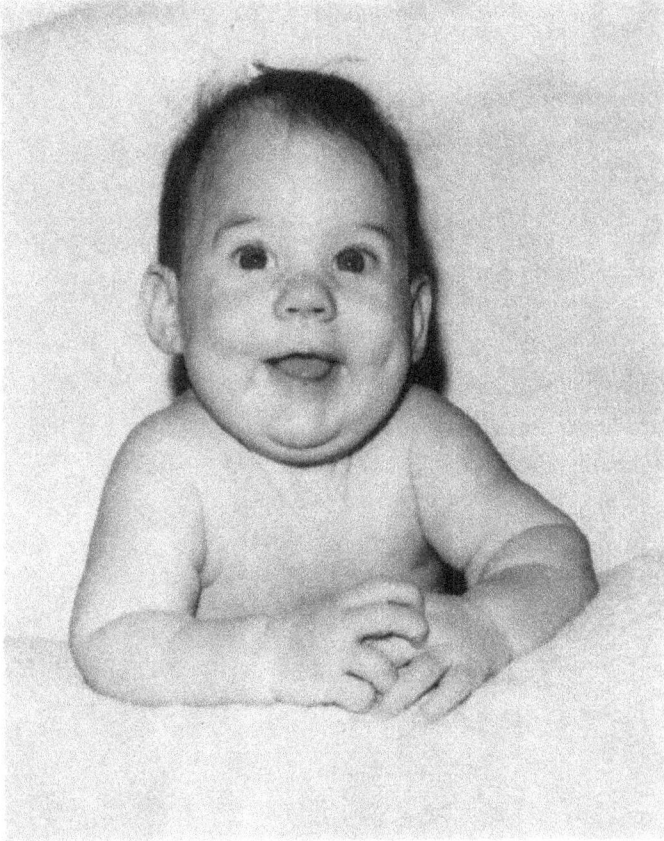

Karen-five months old.

Karen in a field of daisies, age 1 ½ years.

Karen, age 4, in her favorite tree with her brother Chris.

Biscayne Bay
July 1976

Karen, age 5 ½ - swimming with Mommy
in Biscayne Bay

Karen, age 5 ½ - sailing with Daddy
On "GodSend"

Karen, age 6, reading kindergarten book
with marionette on lap

Christopher gets a hug on Karen's 6th birthday

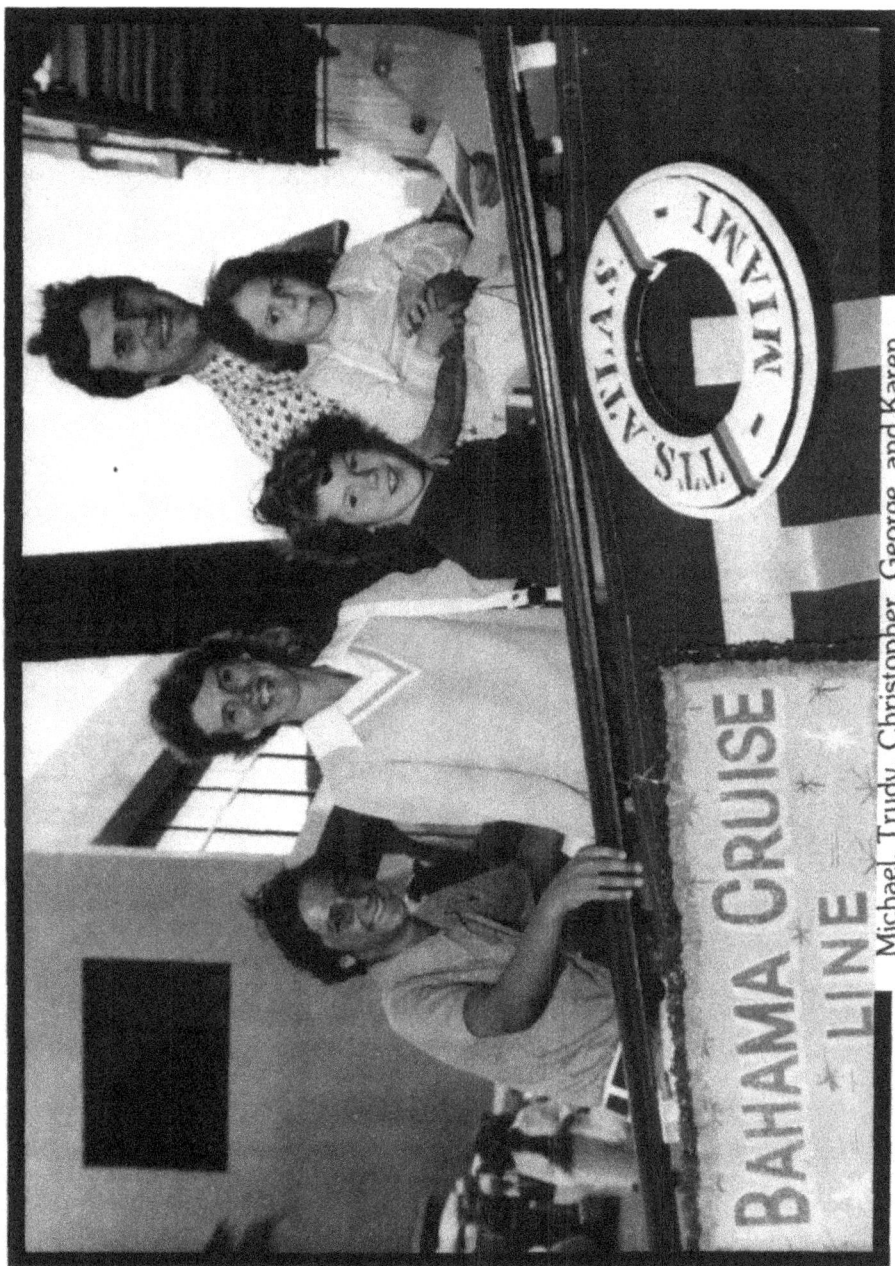

Michael, Trudy, Christopher, George, and Karen.

Karen with Daddy shortly before the crisis
of her heart stopping

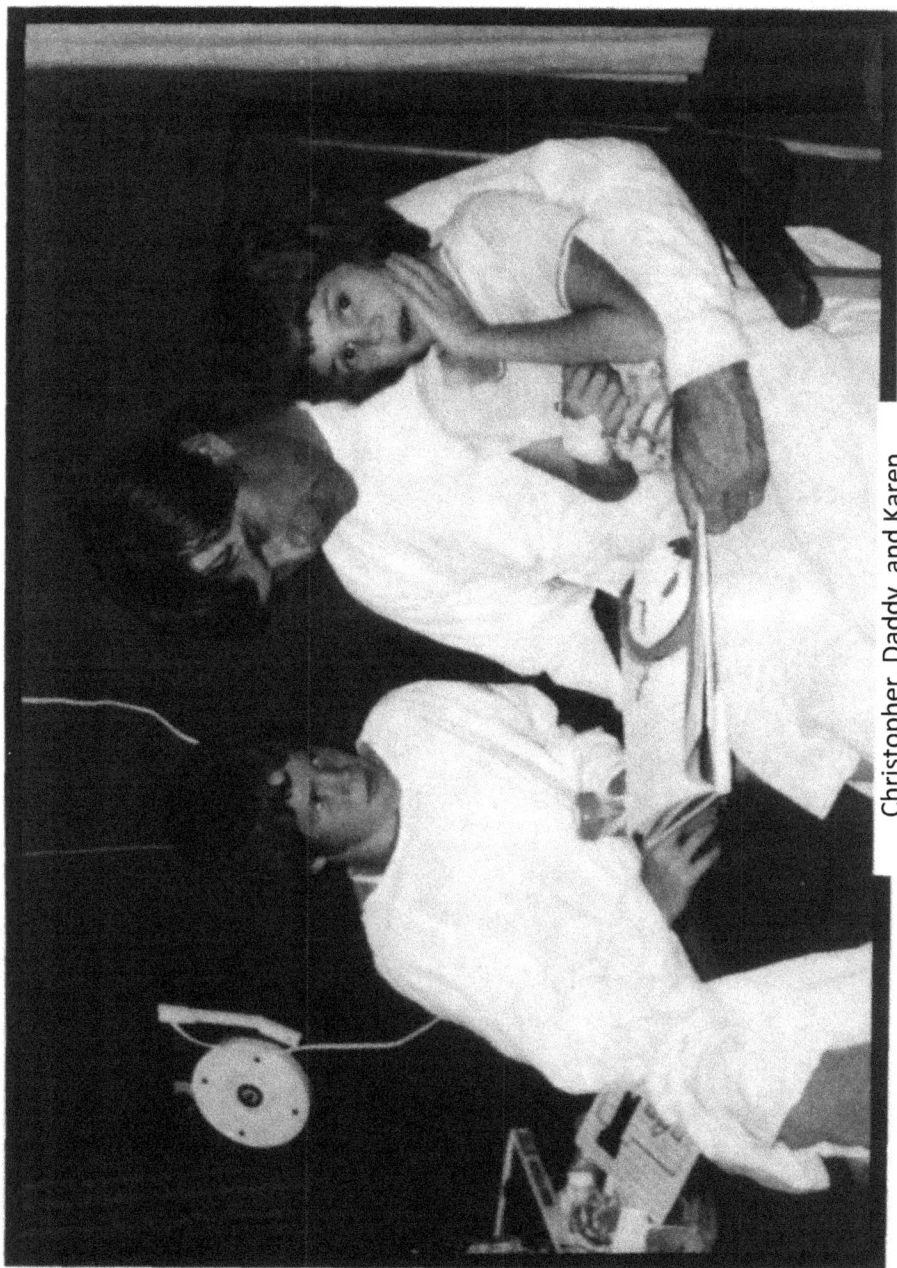

Christopher, Daddy and Karen

Karen on Father's Day – first week in the hospital

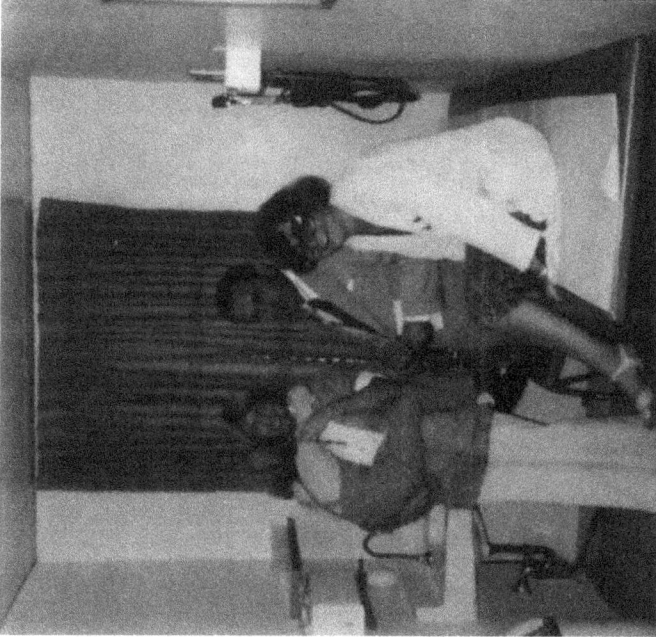

Karen in the hospital examining room
With Nurse Holiday, Dr. DeLamerens
An Dr. Pefkarou

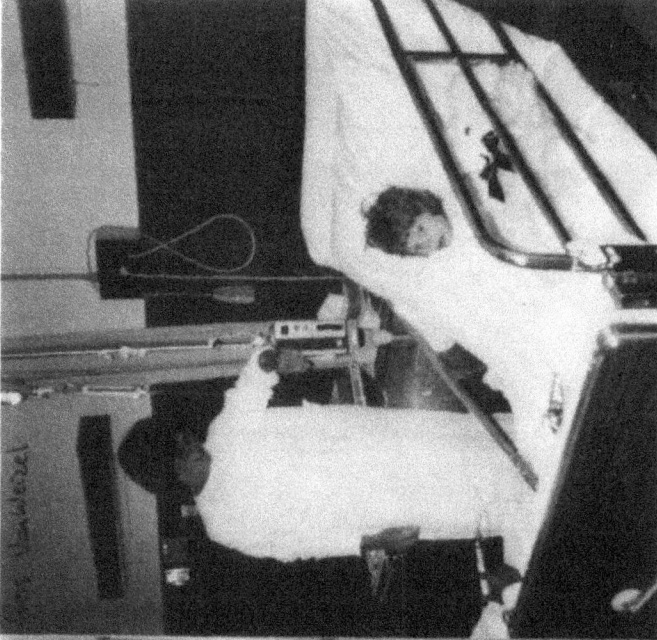

Karen, age 6 ½ - with Nurse Geri first
Week of hospital stay after diagnosis of
Leukemia

Karen after her tracheotomy—happily eating first bite of food in a week.

TRUST
In the Lord
and Bibles
Give

Karen's drawing of herself in the hospital bed beneath her oxygen tent. Beside her she drew a Guardian Angel. She asked for the words to be printed beside the picture

Karen standing beside brightly painted wall
In West, ready to come home from the hospital

Karen wearing her favorite Mickey Mouse hat and shirt

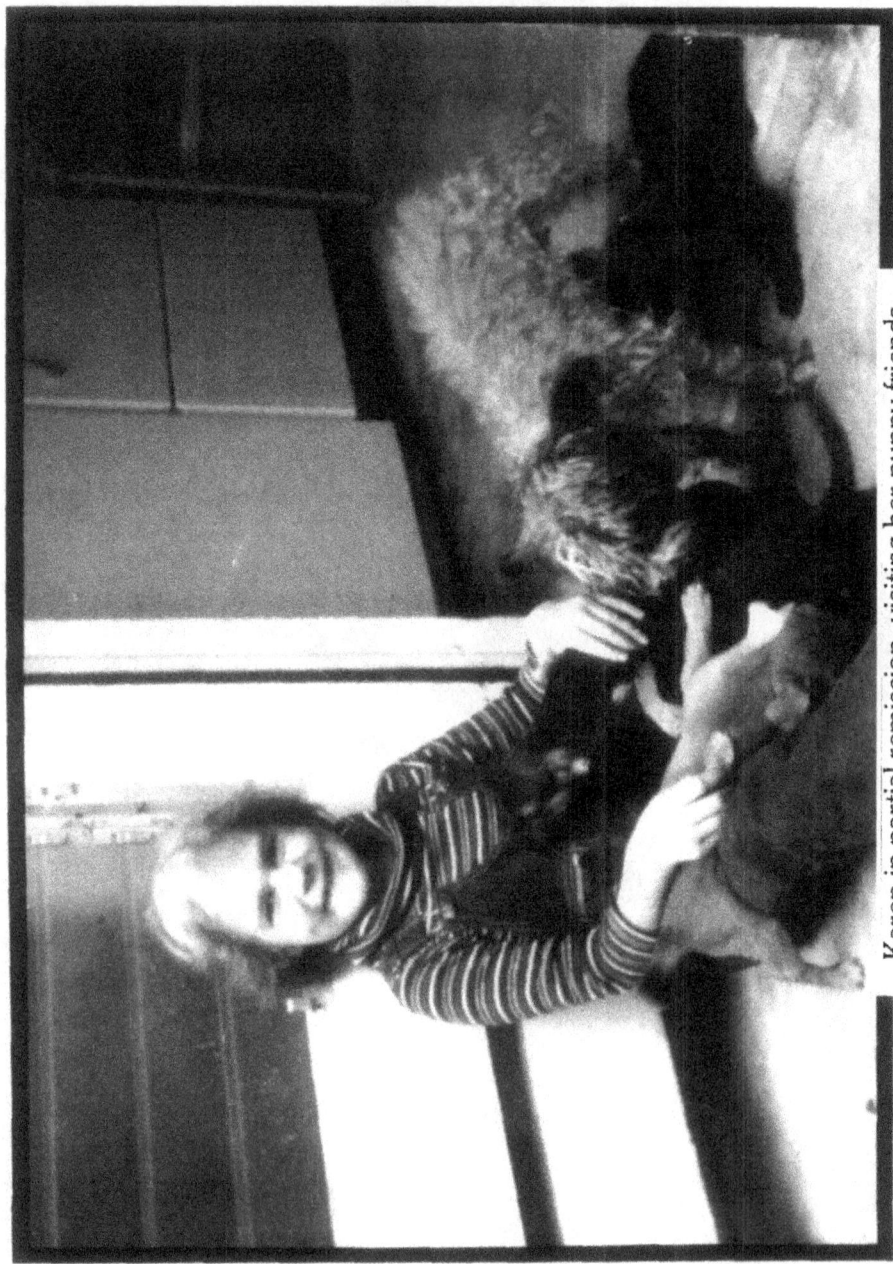

Karen in partial remission, visiting her puppy friends.

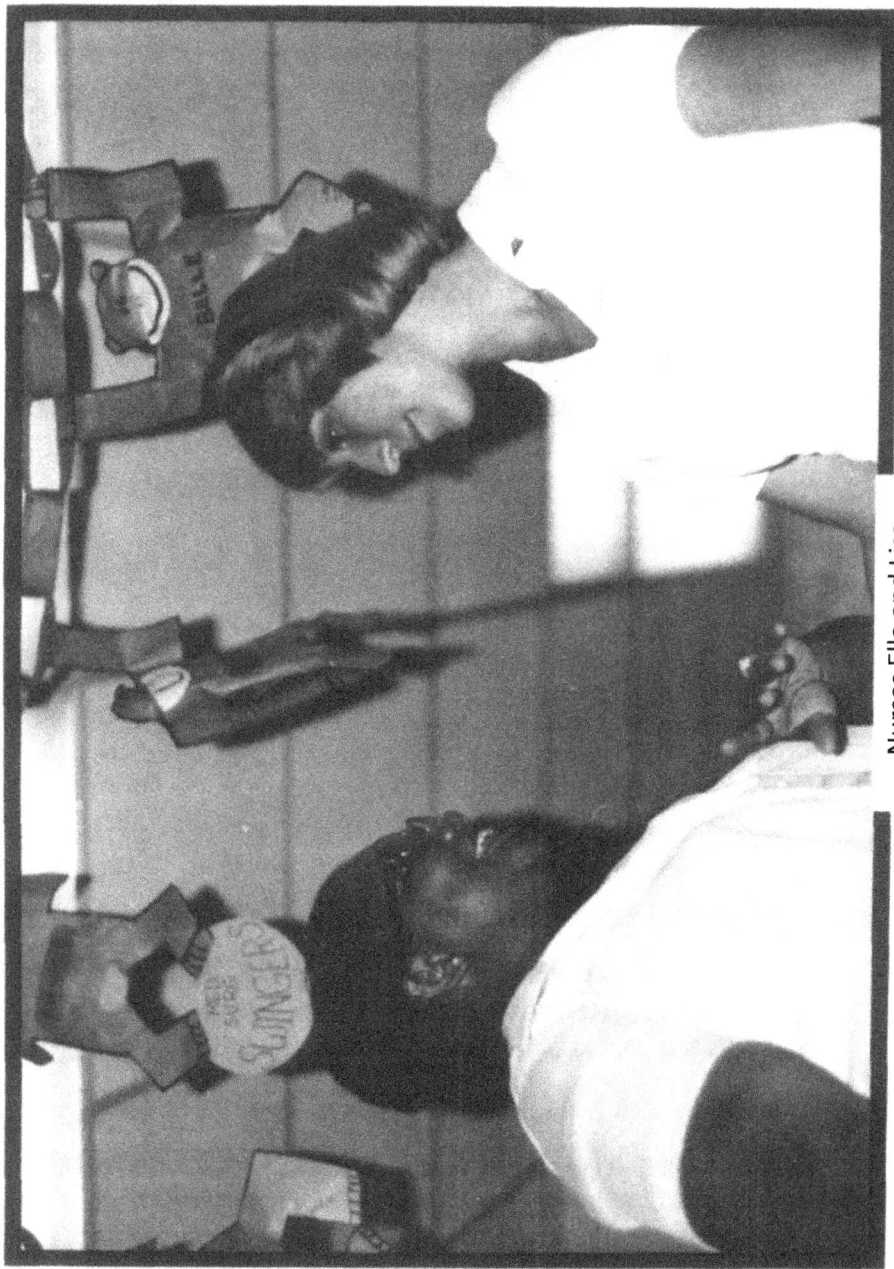

Nurses Ella and Lisa

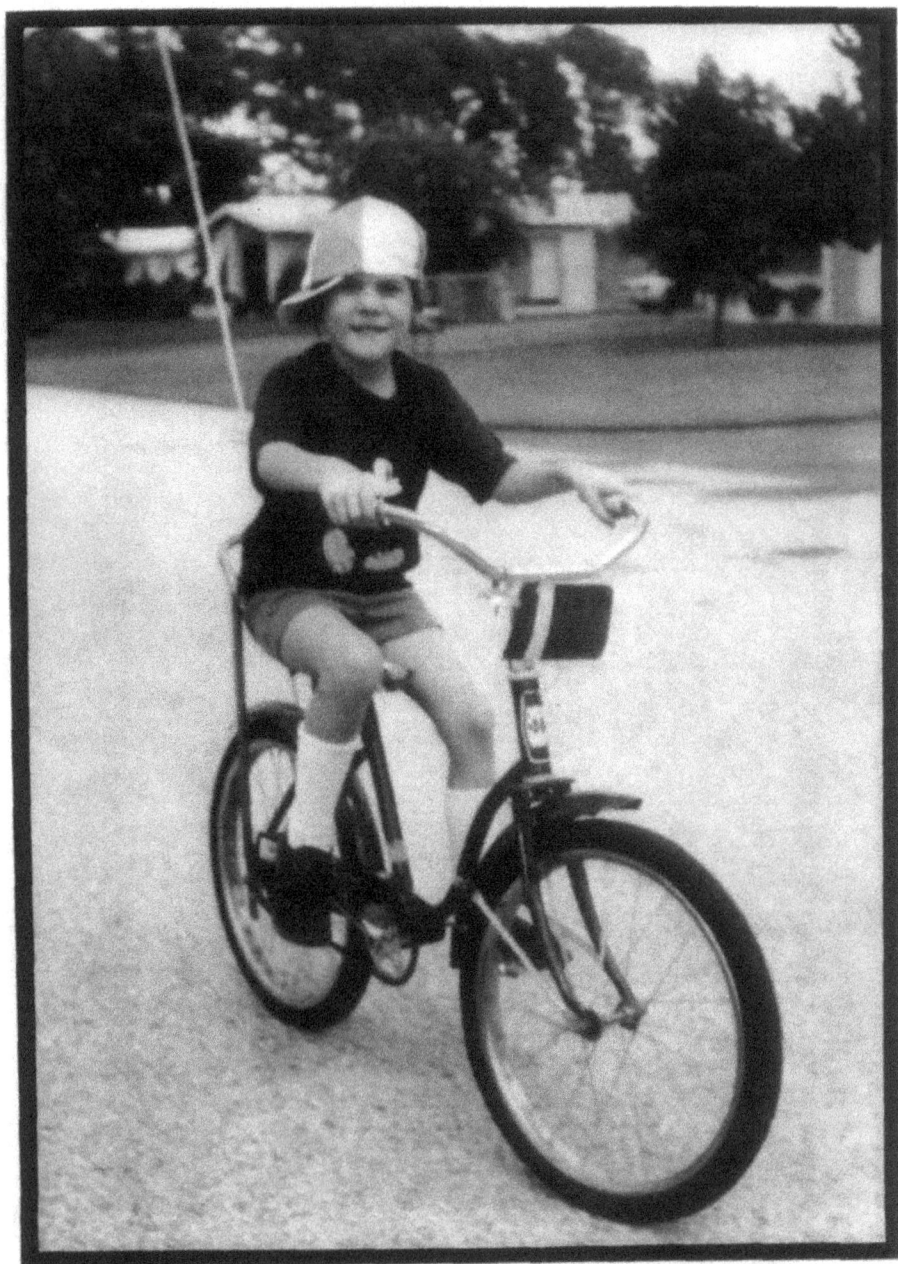

Karen riding her bike during brief
period of partial remission.

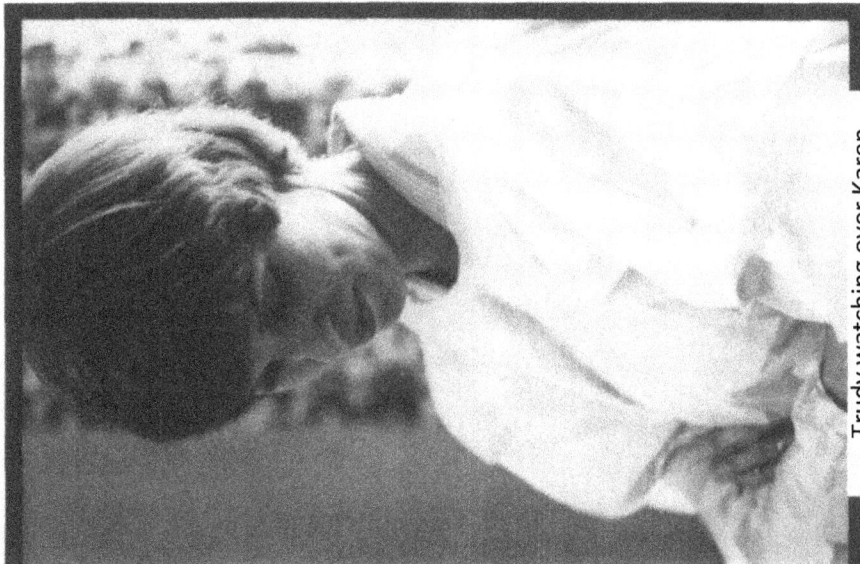

Trudy watching over Karen

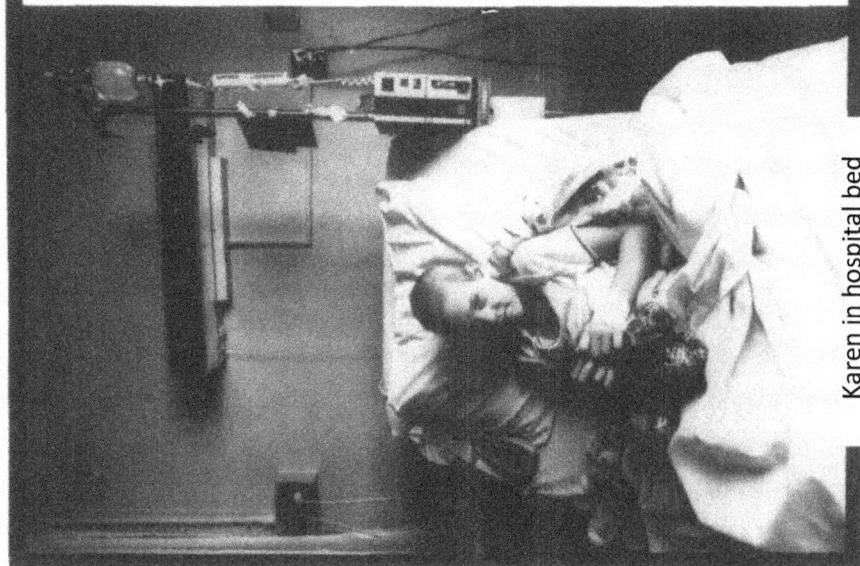

Karen in hospital bed

Karen

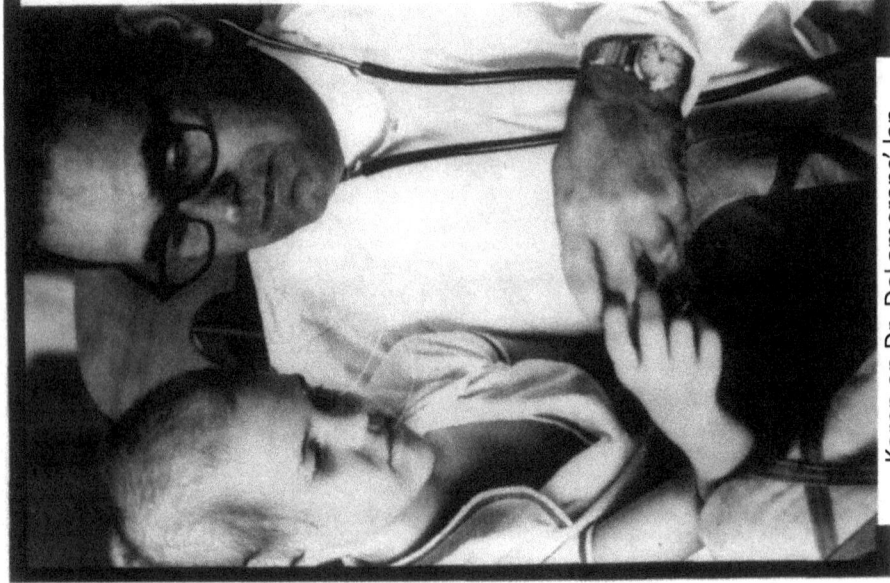

Karen on Dr. DeLamerens' lap

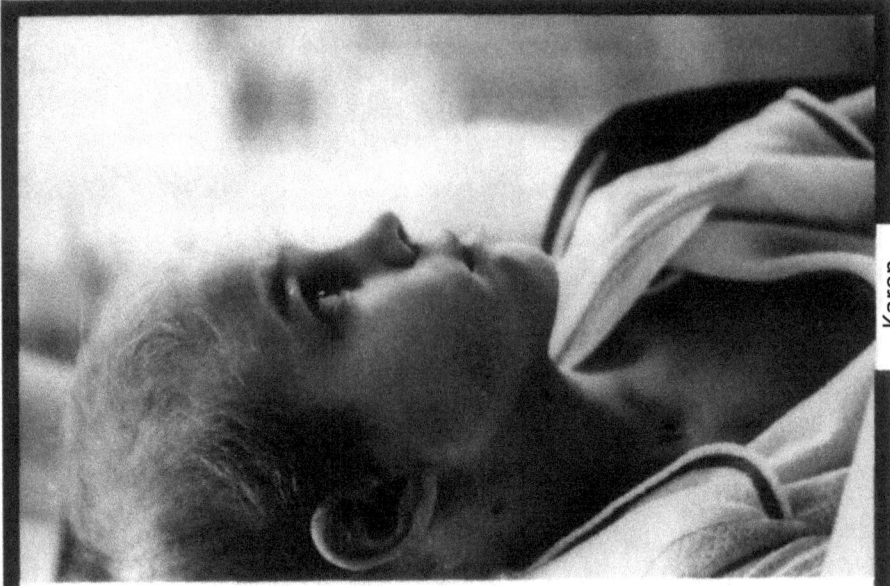

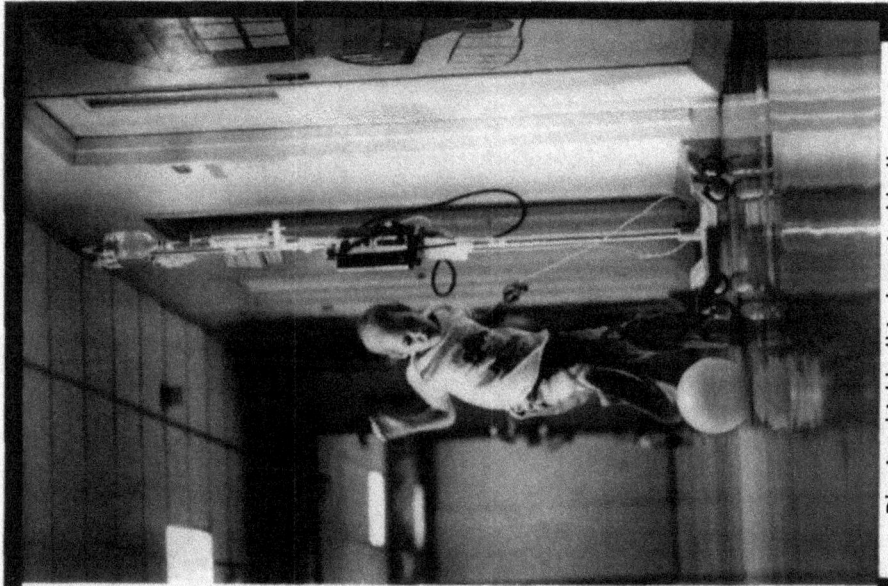
Playing kickball in hospital hallway

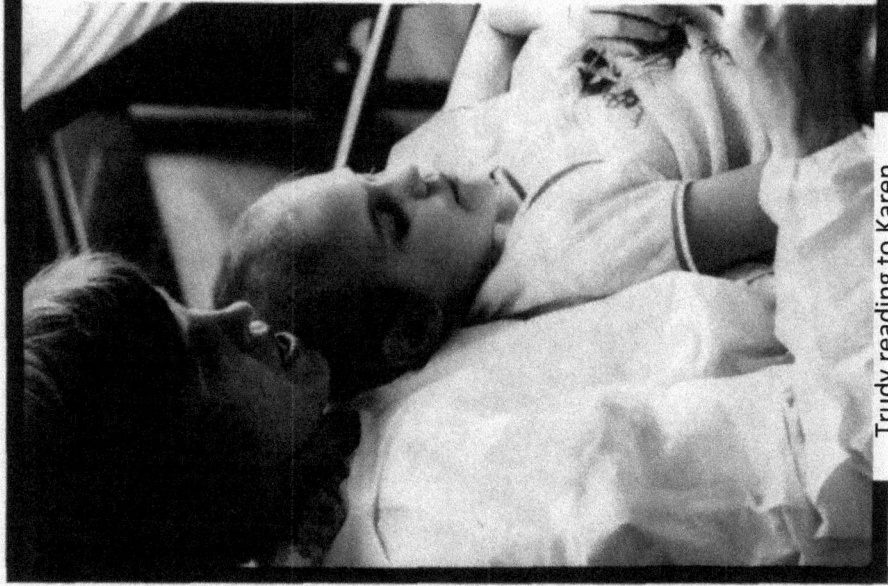
Trudy reading to Karen

Karen with Nurse Hilda on West

Mr. Rothra and Karen having school lesson at home

Waiting Karen's turn at outpatient
clinic, hoping she won't be readmitted

Familiar blood drawing procedure at clinic

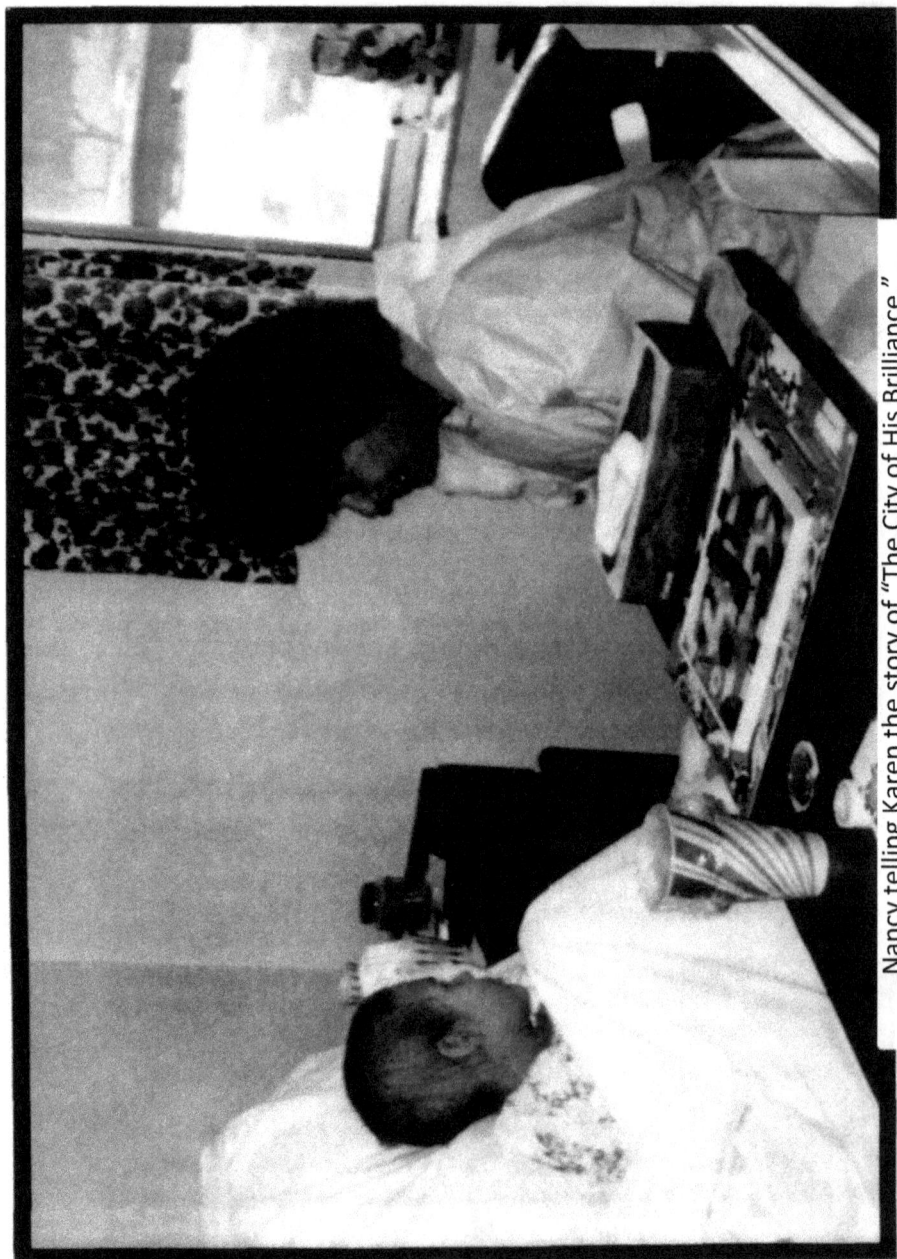
Nancy telling Karen the story of "The City of His Brilliance."

Karen

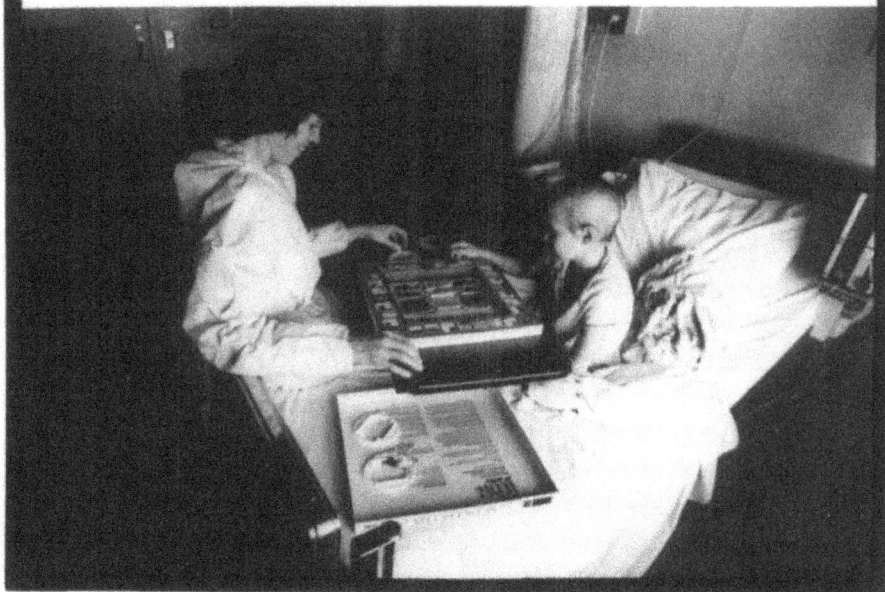

Playing a game in Karen's Room

Karen hanging favorite "Frosty" ornament
On Christmas tree her last night home

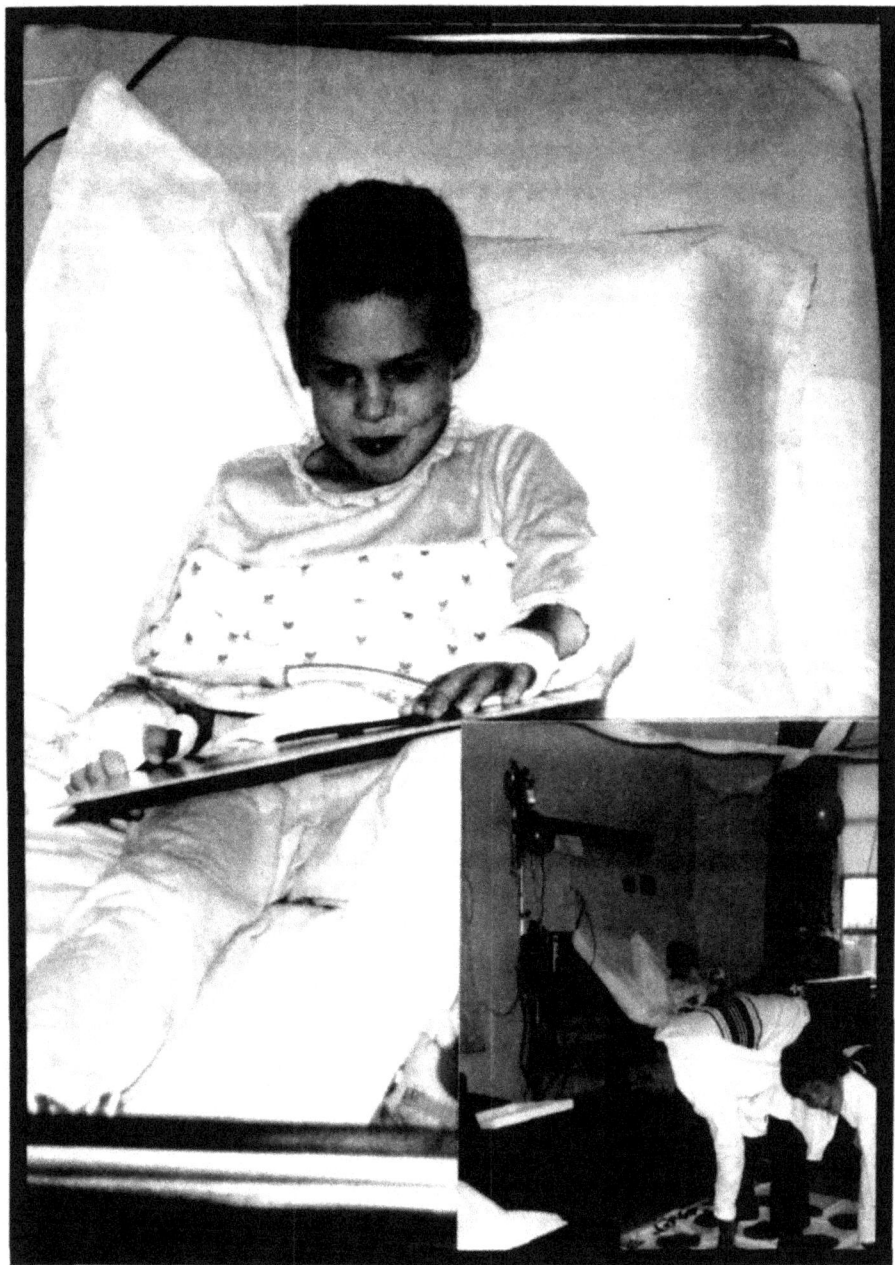

Family fun - playing "Twister"
at Karen's 7th birthday party

9
Lord of Glory

George would be starting his job in New Jersey on the second of January. In his final week, the scout staff gave us a going-away party. They made fond farewells to George, and gave a special gift to Karen.

The following day, George leaned his head into Karen's room with a big smile. "Hey, Karen," he said. "Remember that present you asked Santa about at the Christmas party?"

She nodded her head, "Yes."

"Well, God worked out a way for you to have it!" He walked in the room with the big box from the staff.

Karen's face lit up as he pulled out a color, portable television and set it up beside her bed. He turned it on. The reception was clearer than on the black-and-white wall television in Karen's room, and the color was excellent!

We rejoiced in the generosity of the scout staff who bought it for Karen, and for God's goodness in moving their hearts to do so.

On New Year's Eve, the entire family gathered in Karen's room and watched the Orange Bowl parade on the new television. The year before, we were all there in person to watch the bands and beautiful floats. Now pain stabbed my heart as I looked at Karen lying in bed and remembered what used to be.

While we watched the parade, I decorated the "open room" in honor of Karen's seventh birthday. Chris helped me to hang festive crepe paper from one corner of the room to the other, while George and Mike blew up balloons to hang around the room. Mother arranged a table for the food and set out the paper supplies.

On January first, I awoke eager to put the finishing touches on everything. After the usual morning routine, the family arrived. We made the coffee and punch and prepared the food. At the designated time, the nursing staff and other hospital workers came, bringing gifts for Karen. I lit the seven candles on the sheet cake decorated with butterflies and balloons, and we sang "Happy Birthday," as I carried the cake to her bed. Karen looked at the lighted candles, but did not have the strength to blow on them.

"You blow them out, Chris," Karen said. With one big breath Chris blew out the candles. We all clapped. At Karen's request, Chris opened her gifts.

While people ate, we brought out the game of Twister. Karen watched her Daddy, whom we all knew didn't like the game, play it just for her. George and Chris lined up on the Twister mat, Karen spun the needle and I called out the color for the hand or foot. As the game progressed, it was a funny sight to see the two of them twisted into odd-looking contortions on the mat. Ignoring her pain, Karen smiled.

Early the next morning, Mother and George came to the hospital to say goodbye. George was flying to his new job, and Mother back to teaching.

George drove Mother to the airport and came back so I could drive him to the airport next. After kissing Karen goodbye, we walked out to the car.

At first, George didn't turn on the key. Instead, he put his head on the steering wheel and cried from the depths of his heart. He choked out, "I can't go. I just can't go!"

I put my arms around George and tried to comfort him. "Oh, God," I prayed. "Give us your strength. Be with George and me. Grant us your comfort."

After a while, George turned on the key and backed the car out of the parking space. We drove out of the hospital lot in silence.

At the airport, we kissed goodbye. I'll call you tonight," he said.

He could get back right away, if necessary. It seemed foolish for him to stay. For the moment, Karen appeared stable. The doctors had encouraged George to take this job and had not talked of any immediate crisis.

"What good would it be to wait around for an emergency to happen?" I asked myself.

Even with these thoughts running through my mind, I drove away from the airport with a sinking heart. I felt totally depleted. "At least you haven't left, Lord," I prayed aloud.

When I got back to the hospital, I read Karen's blood report for the day. Her white count had risen to 31,000. Usually after chemotherapy the white count is below normal and, if the treatment has been effective, the white count will stay low. This number indicated that her count was already accelerated.

She was experiencing a great deal of pain and was given an injection of Demerol. Because of her low blood platelets, she bruised easily and her leg swelled painfully from the shot. Mercifully, she soon fell asleep.

Sitting in the rocking chair and looking out through the window as the light of the setting sun slowly disappeared,

I turned to observe Karen sleeping in bed. My heart was sick over her pain.

As the light slowly receded from the room, hope gradually receded from my heart. I sat there, silently rocking in the semi-darkness, with no prayer left to say. What more could I do? I was desolate.

Hilda walked into the room. She stood beside me, quietly sensing my grief, as I rocked on.

"Is there anything I can do?" she asked softly.

I shook my head, " No," still looking straight ahead.

Hilda continued to stand beside me faithfully, and I felt her love emanating from her being and permeating the room. She loved Karen, too. After a while she said, "I'll be at the nurses' station if you need anything," and she turned to leave.

"Thank you, Hilda."

As she opened the door, the light from the hall shone on Karen for a brief moment. Then it was dark again.

Later that night, George called and gave me the number where I could reach him. Before we said goodbye he prayed for Karen and for me. I reached over and placed my hand on Karen, feeling God's strength and love seep into us both as George prayed.

"Goodbye, sweetheart," he said. "I'll call you tomorrow."

Mr. Angulo arrived at his usual 6:00 A.M. time-right on schedule. He flipped the light switch on and said, "Good morning, Karen. How's my little friend?"

Karen was so familiar with the blood-drawing process that she automatically lifted her hand, hardly awake yet.

Mr. Angulo drew several drops of blood from Karen's finger, prepared it for evaluation at the laboratory and walked out of the room with a cheery, "Have a nice day," and flipped off the light.

I turned over in bed. Karen was already asleep again. Yesterday's blood report of 31,000 was still vivid in my memory. Was the white count holding? Maybe it started to drop.

I got up and dressed quietly, fixing a fresh pot of coffee in the little kitchen. When it was brewed, I poured myself a cup.

The change of shifts came. I sat at the nurses' station motionless, waiting. Everyone was going about his or her individual responsibilities.

Soon the computer started typing - exactly what I was waiting for! When Karen's report printed out, I looked quickly at the report of her white blood count. My heart sank: The count had gone up to 50,000!

Dr. Pefkarou passed by and I asked her what could be done.

"It's too soon for more chemotherapy," she replied. "We'll just have to wait."

I slowly walked back into Karen's room, my mind racing. Karen was beginning to wake up.

"How long can we wait?" I thought to myself. "If her white count continues to climb unchecked, she'll die. Yet if she's given more chemotherapy too soon, her system will be poisoned.

"Lord. Are you setting the final stage to perform your miracle?"

We were at a place in Karen's illness where everything that could humanly be done, both medically and spiritually, had been done.

"Lord, is there something more I should do? I could call Pastor Jerry, or the Muellers, or the elders from our church to anoint Karen with oil, or . . . ."

But God's hand of peace interrupted me, and my loving heavenly Father spoke to my heart. "This is my time now, Trudy. No man can do what I'm going to do."

I turned on the Christian radio station and heard a message straight from God to me. The very first words that came forth were: "There's victory in Jesus!"

"Praise His Holy Name!" I whispered.

God knew that I desperately needed His strength and encouragement, and He was preparing me for the events that were to come.

Nancy's arrival at the hospital was like a breath of fresh air. She came to share another chapter of God's story to Karen. "I know the Lord is giving me this story," Nancy said, "because on the days He doesn't give it to me, I just don't have it!"

In this part of the adventure, Karen came to a lake in which she saw herself reflecting great inner strength and beauty. She was wearing a radiant dress made of woven moonbeams, and she spun round and round in delight.

"What a beautiful story," I said, as Nancy finished.

"Yes," said Nancy. "The Lord gave me that picture of Karen. He especially pointed out her strength to me. He is working His strength within her as she endures pain and suffering, trusting in Him."

Mike and I both had dentist appointments the following day. I called my friend Evelyn and arranged for her to visit with Karen while I was gone.

She was delighted to help and brought phonograph records to play. It was a good idea, since listening was about all Karen could manage because of her pain. Her throat was so sore she couldn't even swallow her own saliva. It was easier for her to spit it into a tissue or basin. The only time Karen swallowed now was when she had to take pills. She tried hard to cooperate and to be brave.

Evelyn told me later how Karen enjoyed hearing the records and was especially thoughtful as she listened to one on which children sang Christian praise songs. "It was obvious that her mind was on things of the Lord. The world around her didn't seem that important," Evelyn shared.

When I arrived back at the hospital shortly after Evelyn left, I was unaware of the profound and precious moments that were to come.

I washed my hands and gowned. "Hi, Karen. Mommy's back!" I said, as I opened the door.

Karen was leaning back in her bed, which was raised to a sitting position. Karen turned to me with both arms outstretched. Pain and grief were in her eyes and tears rolled down her cheeks.

"Mommy, I'm going to die!" she cried.

My smile dissolved. A wave of shock surged through my body as I ran to the bed and hugged her. She cried intensely.

"Why do you say that you're going to die, Karen?" I asked, trying to control my emotions.

"Because I hurt so bad!" she cried.

I pulled the rocking chair to the side of the bed and gently lifted Karen onto my lap.

"Oh, Karen, I love you so much!"

"Mommy," she sobbed. *"I'm too precious to die!"*

Her words deeply moved me. The supernatural peace of Jesus settled over me, and I spoke, clearly and softly, "Oh, Karen. Yes, you are so very precious to Daddy , Chris, Mike and me. But you're even more precious to Jesus. I don't know what His plans are for you - whether to heal you here or have you grow up in heaven."

Karen stopped crying as I spoke.

"Are you willing to grow up in heaven, Karen?" I asked, softly.

She nodded yes.

"You know, heaven is such a wonderful place," I continued. "There's no more pain, or sickness or sadness there."

"But I'm too young to die. I need a family to grow up in."

"You have a family there too, Karen," I answered. "My daddy, your Grandpa Patterson, is there. And Daddy's mommy (your middle name Byrle was chosen because of her, you know) is there. And the disciple Andrew, who you've always wanted to meet. And ...." My voice weakened as I realized the weight of our conversation. I began to cry.

Karen raised her head. With great intensity and urgency she cried out, "Oh, God, heal me! I don't want to die!"

"Oh, heavenly Father," I prayed. "Heal our little daughter."

I didn't have the voice to continue. Karen and I cried together as we held each other tightly.

Then, with God-given wisdom and strength, Karen prayed a beautiful prayer of encouragement. "Oh, God, give us your peace and comfort. We know we can trust in you and that you are with us. Strengthen us and bless us. In Jesus' name we pray. Amen."

We continued to embrace each other and cry.

"Mommy," she cried out suddenly. "We've got to stop! We've got to stop this! Get the Bible and read."

I reached over to the bedside table for my Bible. Opening to Psalm 23 (RSV), I started reading, my voice quivering.

"Even though I walk through the valley of the shadow of death," the passage began. Somehow I was enabled to read to the end. "And I shall dwell in the house of the Lord forever."

I started to cry again and Karen said, reassuringly, "You can stop crying, Mommy . God said He's going to heal me."

Karen obviously had an inner peace and assurance. She looked calm, tranquil.

"When did He tell you?" I asked, wiping my tears with a tissue.

"When I was praying."

We rocked for a while in silence. "I want to talk to a doctor," Karen said. "I want to ask him about my medicine."

To my surprise, one of the team physicians was talking in the hall at that precise moment. Sitting Karen on the chair, I opened the door and put my head through the doorway. "May we see you for a minute?" I asked.

The doctor came in and sat down. Picking Karen up, I sat down with her on my lap. Karen looked directly at him and asked a question that I'm sure came as a shock to him.

"Am I going to die or do you have medicine to make me well?" His answer startled me, and I think even surprised him.

"You will be fine, Karen. You will be home in a few days."

"See, Mommy," Karen said with elation as he left. "The doctors have a plan!"

"Yes, and God has a plan," I answered.

Karen did not mention dying again. God had given her assurance that she would be healed, and the doctor had concurred. In Karen's mind, the issue was settled.

I walked into the hall, the discussion with Karen still heavy on my heart. Nurse Geri was there, and I shared with her our conversation, starting to cry.

157

"You and George have been super parents," she said, reassuringly. "If they were giving out grades, you would each get an A+!

"I'm not surprised that Karen realizes she is dying," Geri continued. "She's too smart not to know."

It was sad to watch Geri say a fond goodbye to her patient. She was leaving the next day to go back to school, and didn't think she would ever see Karen again.

"I need a shot," Karen moaned. This time she was given morphine.

"It should ease the pain longer," the doctor said.

With relief, Karen slept.

Again, I wept, "Oh God, I can't stand to see Karen in pain. Yet it hurts me to see her being given such strong pain killers as morphine. Do something, God! Do something!"

Karen's white blood count rose to 81,000! Each day, the count was becoming more deadly. Yet it was still too soon for more chemotherapy.

It was as though the final scene was being played in an intense drama. There were no actors other than Karen and God on the stage. No one else was to receive any glory, for it was out of man's hands.

Despite the seriousness of the situation, my spirit became surprisingly more elated, almost heady with the anticipation of a spectacular, cosmic conclusion.

My human emotions were numb: They could no longer hold my spirit in reserve. It didn't make sense to my reason, but the more hopeless Karen's situation became, the higher my spirit leaped with excitement. Surely, God was in control and nothing could thwart His plan.

Nancy and her teenage daughter, Stephanie, came to visit. Karen and I were happy to see them, and to listen to the next chapter in Nancy's continuing story of the City of His Brilliance:

Today in the adventure, Dogaphin, Karen and Ivac came to a roaring, raging river. The waters came from high on the Mountain of Difficulty and poured down to the River of Anxiety in the valley below.

Dogaphin found a log and used it to make a bridge for them to cross the river. Karen was afraid, but held tightly with her arms and legs as she began to inch across. Just as she got to the middle, a three-headed snake suddenly appeared and wrapped itself around the log.

"Oh!" Karen said. "A three-headed snake!"

"Tee-hee-hee," laughed the three-headed snake.

"My name is 'You'll Never,' " said the first head.

"Mine is 'Cause,' " said the middle head.

"And mine is 'You'd Better,' " said the last head.

"You'll never make it to the City of His Brilliance," the first head spoke again, teasingly.

"Cause you're too weak," taunted the middle head.

"You'd better go back," snickered the third head.

"Oh, Dogaphin, what will we say?" said Karen.

"Yes, we will make it," said Dogaphin. "Because we belong to Him. We will make it and we're going to go on."

And, as Dogaphin and Karen and Ivac repeated over and over again, "Yes, we will, because we belong to Him and we're not going back," the three-headed snake loosened its hold on the log, dropped into the river and floated away.

The three friends inched on across until they got to the other side.

As they sat there resting, they were filled with peace and joy. They knew that their faith had grown as they crossed the River of Anxiety.

I was amazed how this adventure so paralleled the anxiety which Karen had just faced over dying and the peace she was given when she trusted in the Lord.

Karen listened intently as Nancy talked. (Nancy told me later she could tell that Karen understood the truths shared in story form because Karen had experienced them. They had already been perfected in her by the trials and sufferings she had endured.) Nancy was amazed that Karen understood in a just a few, short years, spiritual truths that had taken her years to learn.

The story finished, Karen thought again of her pain. "I need a shot," she groaned.

"It's too soon for another shot, honey," I said.

Nancy suggested that we pray. She, Stephanie and I laid our hands lovingly on Karen.

"Dear Jesus," Nancy prayed, "we hold Karen before you and ask you to take away her pain. Hold her in your arms, Lord Jesus, and protect her. In your mighty name we pray. Amen."

Karen became calmer and more relaxed. "Keep thinking about Jesus holding you in His arms, Karen," Nancy said.

"He loves you so much," I added.

"Where is that Scripture verse about momentary affliction?" Nancy asked. "I thought about that while we prayed."

I checked the concordance in the back of my Bible. "Here it is: 2 Corinthians 4:17," I said. I turned to 2 Corinthians and read, "For this slight momentary affliction is preparing for us an eternal weight of glory beyond all comparison ..." (RSV).

"Oh, God, show forth your glory," I prayed.

Nancy and Stephanie said goodbye to Karen, and I walked them out to the hall. I wanted to share with them the conversation which Karen and I had had about her dying.

"I don't know why the doctor told Karen she would be home in a few days. Do you think he was just trying to encourage her?"

"I think he was speaking prophetically," Nancy said. "He's probably wondering why he said it that way too."

As we talked, Stephanie became very quiet and tears filled her eyes. Before she and Nancy left, we joined hands to pray. I appreciated the encouragement of Nancy's prayer and felt comforted.

As Nancy continued in prayer, she paused and asked her daughter, "Do you have a word from the Lord?"

Stephanie remained silent, so Nancy finished praying. I walked them to the elevator and hugged them goodbye. Later, Nancy called to tell me that, when they got to the car, Stephanie broke into tears.

"Oh, Mother," she cried. "I couldn't say anything when you asked. I was just too overwhelmed with God's glory and majesty. When Mrs. Colflesh started telling us how Karen said she was going to die, I felt angry at God. I said to Him, 'How could you do this, God? She's only a little girl and she loves you! How could you take her to heaven so soon?' "

"And you know, Mom," Stephanie continued, "He didn't answer my anger. He revealed himself to me, instead. I felt overwhelming love and peace. I was surrounded by His glory. He showed me that He was all majesty and power, that He was *God* and that whatever He did was best."

"It was a profound experience which Stephanie had with the Lord," Nancy concluded. "Karen has truly been a pathway of blessing to her."

10
Eternal Life

The phone rang in Karen's room. It was George. I put the phone to Karen's ear so he could talk to her. She listened but wasn't up to responding so I gave George our love and again, as he had done with each of his nightly calls, he closed with prayer. I was uplifted and strengthened: I knew God was using him to strengthen Karen and me spiritually, even though we were separated physically.

As I tucked Karen in for the night, she asked, "Mommy, when will I get to the City of His Brilliance in the story?

"I don't know, Karen," I answered.

"Well, when I get there," she said, "I'm going to be healed!"

"I know, honey."

The next morning, I read the report of Karen's white blood count. It had reached 120,000! In the face of hopelessness, I again experienced a strange sense of elation. "Lord, I know you're going to do something soon," I prayed. "You *have* to!"

The doctors came into the room on their morning rounds. Dr. DeLamerens was smiling. He picked up

163

Karen's hand and patted it. "Today, we can start chemotherapy," he said.

I was at once shocked and relieved. I hadn't realized more chemotherapy was a possibility. Apparently, enough time had elapsed since her last series so that she could have more.

"What a relief," I thought. "Maybe this is God's answer."

My friend Chris phoned. "Trudy," she said, "would you like for me to stay with Karen tomorrow so you can go home for a few hours?"

"That sounds great," I said. The last few days had been very tedious, because of meeting Karen's pains and needs, and my patience needed a rest.

I drove home the next day while Chris stayed with Karen. Both boys were with friends for the weekend. The place was quiet and I laid out in the warm Florida sunshine, grateful to relax.

As the sun set and the air became chilled, I went in to change my clothes and headed back to the hospital.

When I arrived, Karen was very fussy and demanded my attention. She was exhausted from the constant pain, and distressed about her weakened condition. Thankfully, I was refreshed and could tend to her patiently.

Nancy came to the hospital after dinner. Karen hardly noticed her and continued to cry in pain.

"I have a story for you that will help, Karen," Nancy said. As she began the story, Karen became quiet so she could listen.

On the way to the City of His Brilliance, Karen and Dogaphin were attacked by a swarm of tiny, flying horses with stingers in their tails. Each little horse had a different stinger!

When *pain* stung, Karen and Dogaphin felt pain; when *fear* stung, they felt afraid; when *hopelessness* stung, they thought, "What's the use!"

"Ouch! Ouch!" cried Karen. "They're stinging me all over. It hurts and I'm afraid. I don't like this. Ouch! Ouch! Dogaphin, *do* something. "

"Call on the name of Jesus!" said Dogaphin. "Call on the name of Jesus! The stingers are overcome by the blood of the lamb. We must call on Him. Save us, Jesus!"

"Jesus, Jesus, Jesus!" said Karen.

As they began to call on the name of Jesus, the horses flew a short distance away and buzzed around.

"Sing," said Dogaphin. Karen and Dogaphin began to sing, "'Jesus, Jesus, Sweetest Name I Know. Jesus, Jesus, Everywhere I Go ... .' "

As they sang, the little flying horses gave up and flew away.

"We *will* get to the City of His Brilliance," Dogaphin reassured Karen, when it was all over. "And *nothing* can stop us. There you *will* see Jesus and be healed."

After the story, Nancy prayed with Karen. Then she and I sang songs of praise to Jesus. Later, as we talked outside of Karen's room, Nancy said she could see Karen being attacked by "stingers" as she was in the hospital room that night.

"This has been a hard day for her," I said. "The praying and singing helped a lot."

"I could tell she felt peace when I said goodbye," Nancy said.

"When will the story be over?" I asked.

"I don't know," Nancy answered. "The Lord hasn't given me the ending yet."

I shared with her about Karen knowing that she would be healed when she reached the City. "When she gets to the City, Nancy," I asked, "do you know if she'll come back?"

"I don't know that, either," she answered.

We said goodbye and I went back into the room.

"I need a shot," Karen cried.

I checked with the nurse, who said it was too soon for more pain killer.

"I can't wait," groaned Karen.

"Jesus, Jesus," I called. "Help Karen!"

George telephoned. He had flown into New Orleans for a Boy Scout convention that afternoon and wanted me to know where he could be reached. I shared Karen's condition with him and related the distress I felt over her pain. Again, George prayed for us. Before he hung up, I wished him "Happy Birthday" for the next day. We always made a big celebration of family birthdays, but this year his birthday came in the midst of his new job and Karen's critical condition. It was too much to handle. Saying "Happy Birthday" was all I could manage.

"I'll call again tomorrow, honey."

After George hung up the phone, he told me later, he prayed that God would either heal Karen or take her to heaven. He couldn't bear to hear about her pain and asked that Karen be released from it.

You can have more pain medicine now," the nurse said. "I've called the doctor to come and give it to you."

"Oh, good," Karen said, relieved. "Tell him to hurry."

While the doctor was slowly administering the morphine through the i.v., Karen's nurse brought her some medication in a little cup; a liquid to help her mouth sores.

With a silly grin, typical of Karen when she felt well, she took the cup. Lifting it as if saying "Cheers," she paused a moment, dramatically threw her head back, draining the contents into her mouth. She switched it around a minute, and spit it back into the cup. Her action was so unexpected in the midst of the tension and pain that for a moment I was taken aback.

"You big silly!" I finally said, heartened at a glimpse again of the real Karen. "You're too much!"

I turned on the television after the doctor and nurse left the room. But there was nothing interesting on so I soon turned it off.

"Let's go to bed for the night, Karen," I said. "I'm really tired."

Karen felt like sleeping, too, now that her pain had abated. I lowered her bed and lifted the side rails.

"Help me straighten out, Mommy," she said. I moved Karen to lay her flat and noticed she gave no help.

"She seems so weak," I thought to my self. I pulled out my bed and was asleep in minutes.

"Mommy," Karen called, rousing me from sleep. "I need to use the bedpan."

I got up and helped Karen and then laid back down to sleep.

"Mommy," Karen's voice sounded again. "I need to use the bedpan."

I helped her again, supporting her weight in my arms.

"Oh, that's right, I just used it," Karen remembered aloud.

167

"That's all right, honey," I said, as I laid her back down. "Sweet dreams."

I got in bed and fell back asleep.

"Mommy," Karen's voice cried out again. "I need the bedpan."

"I'm going to call the nurse to help you, Karen," I answered, as I pressed the call button.

Belle, the night nurse who was with Karen the first night we were in the hospital, came to the door. I told her Karen's needs and she helped her.

"May I please have a glass of ice water?" I heard Karen ask Belle.

"Her voice sounds so clear and strong," I thought to myself.

Karen had never recovered the full use of her voice since the previous summer when she had the cobalt treatment for her throat problem. The best she could do was to speak in a hoarse whisper.

When I heard Karen speak to Belle, her voice was perfect. I was excited.

"Karen," I said. "Your voice sounds so good."

When Belle returned with the ice water. she helped Karen with it and then laid her down.

"Thank you very much," Karen said, sweetly, her voice still crystal clear.

When Belle left I said, "Karen, I'm very pleased with how pleasant you were. Have a good rest, sweetheart."

Belle walked into the room. I opened my eyes and saw daylight. I realized I had had a restful night. Karen had not awakened with pain and she had slept through the night. How glad I was, for we both needed the rest.

Belle left and returned in a minute with the nursing supervisor. I looked up and saw that they were both standing by Karen's bed and Belle was holding up the sheet.

"I wanted you to see this," she spoke quietly to the supervisor.

Their faces showed concern and I knew something was wrong. Springing out of bed, I hurried beside Belle and looked. Karen's bed was covered with blood. She had just had a massive hemorrhage and was lying in a pool of blood! I became weak with fright.

Karen was lying there resting peacefully.

"Wake up, Karen," Belle said, gently.

Karen's eyes moved under her lids but she didn't open them. Belle and the supervisor left quickly to call the doctor.

"Good morning, honey," I said, looking at Karen. "It's time to wake up." Her eyes moved slightly under her lids and then were still.

She couldn't wake up, and I started to tremble. Leaning across Karen, I hugged her. "Oh, Karen. I love you!" I said, kissing her cheek. I wanted to say more, but my voice was choked.

Pacing the floor and wondering what to do, I thought, "I'll call Nancy." She lived only a block away. "I hope it's not too early," I reflected as I dialed her number.

Nancy answered on the first ring.

"Nancy, I need you," I said. "Karen has hemorrhaged and is in a coma." I couldn't believe the words that were coming out of my mouth as my voice cracked.

"I'll be right there," Nancy said.

In the bathroom, I started to dress. A nurse was changing Karen's bed and gown. Even before I finished dressing, Nancy arrived.

As she came in the room, God's peace returned to my heart and I felt His strength flow into me.

Now, at last, the long wait was over. This was the day God had chosen to act. Throughout the long months of preparation, we had been waiting for this moment - the climax of God's mighty plan in Karen's life.

"On the way over, God showed me how to pray," Nancy said. "He said, 'Pray that Karen's blood stays within the limits I have set.' I remembered the Psalm that said that God has sent the boundaries of the sea and they can go no further" (Ps. 104).

"That's a good way to pray for hemorrhaging," I said.

We stood at the foot of Karen's bed while Nancy prayed, commanding the blood to stay within the limits God had set.

We moved closer to Karen and visited with her. There was a peace and calmness on her face. She did not open her eyes but, as we talked, I saw a tear, and then another, come out of her eye.

"Look, Nancy," I said, excitedly. "I know Karen hears us. Look at her tears. She's responding!"

The door opened and Dr. Pefkarou rushed in. "Good morning, Karen," she said, moving quickly to her bed. She asked the familiar, "How are you this morning?" while getting out her examining equipment from her black bag.

She listened to Karen's heart, which seemed to be strong, and took her pulse. She lifted Karen's eyelids and observed. I saw that one eye was dilated and the other was not,(a familiar warning sign of bleeding in the brain.)

The knowledge didn't register with me. "Why won't she wake up?" I asked the doctor.

"I'm afraid she has hemorrhaged into her brain," she answered.

"Look, there's another tear," I said. I knew Karen was aware of our presence.

"I'll be back shortly," the doctor said.

As she left, Joan and Chris came into the room and we embraced. Nancy had made a quick phone call to rally the troops. Shortly after that, Bev and Myrna arrived. Others came, as word of Karen's condition spread.

As the room filled with my friends, I felt an increase of the Lord's strengthening and peace. We read Scripture verses and Psalms aloud to one another. We sang hymns of praise and sang together in the Spirit.

Bev sang a word from the Lord, "I am coming with healing in my wings."

"Oh," said Nancy. "As you sang that, I had a vision. I saw Jesus in a rugged, shepherd's shirt with the cords open and untied at the neck. He was running down the mountain in great leaps and bounds. His hair was flowing out behind Him as He came, and He was happy and excited. He stopped halfway down the mountain and waited."

"Praise you, Jesus!" we exclaimed. Surely He was coming to bring Karen life and healing.

Man could give Karen no healing now; her situation was too critical. This was the moment when only God could raise her up, and only He could receive the glory.

Dr. Pefkarou came back into the room. "I'm going to give Karen her chemotherapy. Her white blood count is dropping," she said with a slight smile.

"Now don't worry, Karen," she continued. "This won't hurt. I'll do it slowly, just as you like," and gradually Dr. Pefkarou injected the medicine through the i.v. connection. With her other hand, she held Karen's wrist and counted her pulse.

Suddenly, she stopped the injection and leaned over Karen's chest, listening with her stethoscope. "Her heart's stopped!" she exclaimed. "Get the emergency tray," she called to the nurse. "Clear the room."

171

The nurse ran for the tray while the doctor started pumping Karen's chest with her hands, attempting cardiopulmonary resuscitation (CPR). My friends quickly evacuated the room.

I stood at the foot of Karen's bed, holding on to her feet and pleading for her life. "Oh, Jesus, Jesus, Jesus," I cried fervently, praying in the Spirit, unashamed at the doctor's wondering glance.

The nurse was back immediately with the emergency tray and the doctor made an injection into Karen's heart. It started to beat. With great relief, I relaxed my grip.

As my friends were praying in the hallway, Nancy told me later that the Lord spoke to her heart and said, "Today Karen is to enter the City of My Brilliance." Nancy experienced the most wonderful feeling of release in her spirit, but she began to cry because she understood that God was saying, *Release her and let her come home to be with me.*

I called everyone back into the room and asked Nancy if she would tell Karen her story for today. Nancy pulled the chair beside Karen's bed as usual while I sat on the side of the bed and gently rubbed Karen's legs.

"Today is an exciting adventure in our story, Karen!" Nancy began. *"Today you go to the City of His Brilliance!"*

Dogaphin and Karen climbed to the top of a long hill and, as they reached the crest, they saw The City of His Brilliance just ahead!

They were so excited, they ran and skipped all the way to the City, singing as they went, " 'This Is the Day That the Lord Has Made.' "

Eternal Life

Nancy started to sing and we all joined in:

> This is the day,
> This is the day,
> This is the day that the Lord has made;
> We will rejoice,
> We will rejoice,
> We will rejoice and be glad in it.

As we sang, tears streamed out of my eyes. "Nancy," I cried, "Karen really is skipping toward the city and she's singing this song right along with us. I *know* it."

"I know it, too," Nancy answered, her eyes glistening. She continued with the story:

> When Dogaphin and Karen reached the gates of the City, it was far more beautiful than they had ever imagined. Even more stunning than the Book had described.
>
> Karen walked through the big, pearly gate: The City of His Brilliance at last. It was so beautiful! Out of the center of the City rose a holy, radiant, glorious Light and it lit the entire City.
>
> All of the towers sparkled and gleamed in that light. The walls that surrounded the City were made of precious jewels, which sparkled. The streets were made of gold so pure you could see right through them. The streets all led in one direction - to the center of the City. Karen and Dogaphin began to sing, dance and laugh all at the same time as they traveled along the golden street.
>
> As they approached the center of the City,

they came to a beautiful garden with green, rolling hills. As Karen looked, she saw - in the center of the garden - the most beautiful fountain she had ever seen in her life. There were great sprays of water shooting high into the air and cascading down. More intricate, little falls of water and patterns of sprays came from the sides. As the water sparkled and the droplets fell in every direction, the Light lit them, and thousands and thousands of beautiful, sparkling rainbows shone throughout the garden.

Karen sat down on a log and reflected on what a wonderful place this was, and she thought and thought about whether she should stay or go back. As she was sitting there, Jesus came and stood beside her.

"Karen," Nancy said, leaving the story to speak directly to Karen, "I don't know the rest of the story. You see, I've never been there. But if you come back you can tell us about it."

We were all quiet. I reflected on the beautiful story, realizing that only Karen and Jesus knew the ending.

Our friends continued to come. The nurses put out extra gowns for everyone and provided the empty room next to Karen's as a place to contain the overflow of visitors. They gathered there to pray, and took turns coming into Karen's room.

Carol, the nursing supervisor, offered me her assistance. "Do you know where we can reach George?" she asked.

George had flown to New Orleans. I found the phone number of the convention hall and gave it to Carol. Together we went to the nurse's office to phone. I realized it was George's birthday. "Some birthday!" I lamented.

My heart raced as Carol made the connection for the call. "What will I say? How can I tell him the news?" I thought.

"Would you please have George Colflesh contact this number immediately?" I heard Carol say. "It's a matter of life and death."

Was I actually hearing those words? They couldn't really be describing Karen! My dulled senses couldn't fully comprehend them.

"They won't hold the phone," Carol said. "They will have George call as soon as he is contacted."

Returning to the room, I walked over to Karen. "She seems awfully hot," I said, feeling her head. Nurse Jannette got a thermometer and put it under Karen's arm. It quickly read 104 degrees.

Karen had already been given a suppository; but her temperature had not lowered.

Sam, the nurse's aide, and Jannette took off Karen's gown and pulled off the sheet. They got basins of cool water and put a water-repellent cloth under her. Then they started cooling her body with washcloths dipped in the water. Those they laid on Karen's circulation points, cooling them in the water as they absorbed the heat.

How peacefully Karen lay there as the nurses worked on her. Usually, Karen would be frantically asking if the process were done yet. Amazingly, Sam and I could even joke about how cooperative Karen was today.

Between the suppository and the cooling, Karen's temperature came down quickly and we covered her again with a sheet. We left her undressed to keep her cool.

Nurse Emmy came to stay with Karen. I hadn't seen her since she had worked with Karen the previous summer; now she had a nursing position with a nearby university. I found out later that she had kept in touch with things on West and had asked to be called if Karen became critical. When called, she excused herself from her job at the university to come to minister to Karen,

"There's a call for you out here, Trudy," Carol said, opening the door. "George is on the line."

I rushed to the phone. When I heard George's voice, I broke into tears. "Karen's in a coma," I cried. "But she's still alive. Her heart stopped once, but they got it started again."

"I'll get a plane right away," he said. "I love you, honey."

Our friends had gathered back in the room. I discovered that Victor had been called and was there. I hugged him with relief.

"I felt we should sing the song, 'Sing Hallelujah' when I got here," Victor said, "but I don't know all the words."

"Oh, that's the song 'We'll all go up to Zion,' " I said, and looked at Karen while I started to sing; the others joined in:

> We'll all go up to Zion,
> We'll all go up to Zion,
> We'll all go up to Zion,
> The City of our God.
>
> Sing Hallelujah,
> Sing Hallelujah,
> Sing Hallelujah,
> There's joy in the Lord.

176

I felt a release of joy as we sang about Zion. As the song ended, Emmy, who had been monitoring Karen's pulse, suddenly jumped up and started CPR heart massage on Karen. "Please clear the room!" she said.

I asked Victor to stay, while the others left. We prayed silently. In a few moments, Karen's heart was beating again on its own.

Relieved, I went to the room next door and told my friends that Karen was still alive. A few of them came back to the room with me. We stood around Karen's bed, talking quietly about things of the Lord. The rest of our friends stayed in the other room to pray.

Emmy continued to monitor Karen. Again, Karen's heart stopped and Emmy began heart massage. After a few moments, she called out to the nurses' station. "Page Dr. Pefkarou, Dr. Heart!"

Emmy sat by the bed and waited. I heard the intercom announce, "Dr. Pefkarou, Dr. Pefkarou. 'Dr. Heart.' "

We stood there, quietly praying.

Dr. Pefkarou was in the downstairs hall. She heard the page and knew that it concerned Karen. The elevator door opened and she ran in, pushing the second-floor button. When the door opened on the third floor, Dr. Pefkarou again pushed the button for the second floor but, because of the express system, the elevator went back to the first floor. In exasperation, she ran out of the elevator and up the nearby steps to the second floor.

While we waited, I watched Emmy and wondered why nothing was being done. I heard the page for Dr. Pefkarou again. Where was she?

"Oh, Jesus," I prayed. "Please come and give Karen life." Karen's color was slowly leaving her body and a bluish tinge colored her face.

Dr. Pefkarou rushed in and checked Karen for vital signs. After a moment, she reached across Karen's body and took my hand. Tears were in her eyes as she softly said, "I'm sorry."

My mind didn't register her statement. My emotions didn't react.

"May I stay here with my friends?" I asked.

"Yes. Stay as long as you like."

In a daze, I walked to the other room. I looked at my friends.

"Her heart stopped. She's dead!" I announced.

They put their arms around me and we cried together. We walked back to Karen's room. "Oh, she's beautiful," Bev exclaimed.

I looked at Karen. Her face glowed with a special radiance and was filled with peace. We stood around her bed, feeling the presence of God in a powerful, tangible way.

"Trudy," Marian said tenderly. "Even before you came in the room to tell us about Karen, the Lord spoke to several of us at the same time and said, 'It is finished.'

"He also gave me a wonderful vision of Karen going to heaven," she continued. "I saw a long, ivory stairway leading up to the throne of God. Karen was walking up the stairs, wearing a beautiful, white gown. Her hair was fully restored, beautiful, long and flowing. On her head was a wreath of white daisies, and here and there a touch of red from another flower.

"Flowers were being thrown on the steps as she walked, and lining both sides of the stairway were hosts of angels, blowing trumpets and singing praises to God.

"Jesus was sitting on the throne, and as Karen walked up the stairs, He stretched out His arms toward her and said, 'Let the little children come to me and forbid them not, for of such is the Kingdom of heaven.' "

Jesus emphasized the words *forbid them not* to me. I knew He was saying that this was His plan.

The vision filled me with joy beyond my grief. "Angels blowing trumpets! Jesus welcoming Karen home! Let's sing 'We'll all go up to Zion,' " I said, strangely rejoicing.

We joined our voices together as we stood around Karen's bed and sang:

> We'll all go up to Zion,
> We'll all go up to Zion,
> We'll all go up to Zion,
> The City of our God.
>
> Sing Hallelujah,
> Sing Hallelujah,
> Sing Hallelujah,
> There's joy in the Lord.

I knew that, as we were singing here, angels and believers were singing there, welcoming Karen into heaven. We were joining the heavenly throng who were celebrating her arrival. I was caught up in joy and filled with God's supernatural peace.

We joined hands and prayed. As our eyes were closed, two of my friends experienced a brilliant light passing between them. They opened their eyes to see if the sun had come out from behind a cloud. The light in the room was the same. Then they knew that the Light was Jesus.

At the same moment, the Lord gave another friend, Esa (who was praying for Karen at her home), a vision of what was happening. Esa shared with me later that she saw the hospital room and all of us standing around Karen's bed wearing our long, white hospital gowns. The room began to turn golden and to shimmer. She watched the room become filled with more and more light.

Then she saw Jesus at the center of this light. He moved to Karen's side, leaned over her and said, "I am the Resurrection and the Life. Those who are in me *never* die."

Esa saw Karen's spirit rise and join Jesus. Then He and Karen left together.

As we stood around Karen's bed praying, I lifted my hands toward heaven and praised God. I thanked Him for giving us Karen and I lovingly returned her to Him. The words came from deep within my spirit; not my mind. It was as though I were in two parts. I remember thinking how clear my voice was as I listened to my own words. I was full of joy and peace. I thought of Emmy sitting there on the corner of Karen's bed and was glad the Lord had brought her here this day. Surely, she was being blessed.

When I finished praying, I felt calm. God totally surrounded me with His strength and peace.

The nursing supervisor entered the room. "Do you have something you'd like us to put on Karen?" she asked.

I went to Karen's closet and got out her new tee-shirt - it had the word 'Jesus' on it - and picked out the new pair of pants which I had bought for Karen to wear home at some point. These clothes, along with Karen's favorite Mickey Mouse hat with the green sun visor, I gave to the nurse.

We left to go to the other room while Karen was disconnected from the i.v. and dressed. My friends gave me words of love and reassurance.

"God has called you to a new life now, Trudy," Arlene said. "He has called you to New Jersey to set you apart for a time unto himself, a special time of love and healing."

"It will be a time of rest and restoration," Bev added. I knew that I needed all of those things, for I was very weary.

"You may go back in the room now," the nurse announced.

As we walked into Karen's room, I again sensed God's sweet presence and peace. Karen had on her Jesus tee-shirt and her Mickey Mouse hat. I sat on the bed beside her and laid my hand on hers, receiving God's peace.

As my friends began to leave, several encouraged me to come with them for a quick lunch. Stepping out of the hospital, the air was chilled. Flo gave me her white blazer to wear. When I put it on, we realized it was a perfect match with my white slacks.

"How appropriate," I reflected. "The Lord clothed me in white today in honor of Karen's 'Homegoing' (for this time she was going home to heaven) celebration."

Soon after I left, George called the hospital. He was at the airport in New Orleans. The secretary asked Dr. Pefkarou to take the phone.

"I'm calling to see if there's any change in Karen's condition," he asked the doctor.

"George," she said, tenderly, "Karen's gone."

"I expected you would say that," he answered, solemnly. He hung up the phone in that lonely place and cried.

When I returned to the hospital, Dr. Pefkarou told me George had called and said she told him about Karen's death. She looked at me with tears in her eyes and said, "I wish it could have worked out differently."

I told her about Jesus and the angels welcoming Karen into heaven. The reality of what I was saying took my breath away, and I began to cry. I walked into Karen's room and again was filled with peace.

Velma and June had come to the hospital. They were sitting in the room, quietly waiting for me to return. They hugged me and held my hand. "God's peace has filled this room," they commented.

181

Hilda handed me a note. "Your pastor was here while you were gone and left this for you," she said.

I read Rev. Reed's note: "We are both weeping and rejoicing with you and for you. His presence is so real around here ... think how much more so for Karen right now. Call me; I'll be waiting and will come right away."

I talked with my friends for a few minutes and then remembered the boys! Chris and Mike were not aware of the rapid turn of events and I needed to tell them the news. My heart sank; If only I didn't have to tell them that Karen had died!

Velma said she would ride home with me. Before leaving, I asked Carol, the supervisor, if Karen's body could be kept in the room until George came.

"Yes," she replied.

I was grateful and began to gather some of Karen's things to take with me, but left the cards on the wall and asked that the Christmas tree be left. I wanted the room to still be decorated when George arrived.

By now, Mike would be at his job as bagboy at the local supermarket. Chris would be arriving home from school. As Velma and I drove along the freeway, I wondered what to say to the boys. Going into the busy store to find Mike was not something I looked forward to.

Driving into the supermarket parking lot, I found a vacant space right in front of the store and turned off the engine. Mike was loading groceries into a nearby car. It was God's arrangement for providing the parking space and sending Mike outside at that precise moment.

"Hi," Mike said, surprised as he saw me coming toward him.

Looking into his eyes, I said, quietly, "Mike, Karen is with Jesus in heaven."

His face turned white, and his lips trembled.

"Tell someone you have to leave," I said.

182

"I'll be right back," he said, seriously.

In a few moments he was with us in the car as we headed home to tell Chris.

"Hi, Mom," Chris said without looking up from his book as I walked in. "How's Karen?"

Chris was lying on the floor. "Get up, honey," I said. I wanted to be able to hug him.

He looked at me, his eyes questioning, as he got up.

"What's wrong?" he asked.

"Karen's in heaven with Jesus," I choked out, motioning for Mike to come over.

The three of us hugged tightly and cried. After a while, we sat down and I related the events of the morning to them.

Velma got a ride home as the boys and I drove back to the hospital to wait for George. A friend was going to pick him up at the airport and drive him to the hospital.

As we walked through the hallway of West, toward Karen's room, the glory of God's presence was flowing out of the room into the hall. The boys realized it, too, and sensed God's peace as they walked into the room to look at Karen.

When George arrived, I met him in the hall. Holding each other's hands, we walked into Karen's room. The shades were pulled and the room was lit by the soft - colored Christmas tree lights. Silently, we walked over to Karen and stood for a long time beside her.

"She looks so peaceful," George said.

Dr. DeLamerens walked into the room and came over to Karen. He picked up her hand and lovingly patted it, just as he had done for so many months on his daily visits.

We sat and talked awhile. Then, Dr. DeLamerens said that when we were ready, they would take Karen's body downstairs.

The boys waited at the nurses' station while George and I went to the hospital chapel to be alone. When we got by ourselves inside the chapel, we held each other and wept profusely.

After a while we walked back upstairs. Karen's body was no longer in the room. With the help of the boys and the nurses, we removed the many cards, the picture of Jesus with the children and the Scripture verses from the wall. We packed Karen's things and cleared the room.

"We'll call you about the funeral arrangements," we told the staff as we left. We knew that their hearts, too, were heavy.

As soon as we arrived home, we called Rev. Reed and he immediately came to be with us. As we discussed the funeral plans, I said, "It has to be a service of praise." My thoughts flooded with plans for the service.

We needed to share the glorious visions the Lord gave us of Karen going to heaven, and I wanted to sing some of the songs of praise we had sung in Karen's room.

"You and George work it out," our pastor said, "and we'll do whatever you like."

Next, we had the sad job of calling George's dad and my mother with the news about Karen. Other relatives and close friends also had to be informed. That night, we went to bed both emotionally and physically exhausted.

11
Home in Zion

My eyes shocked open the next morning, realizing that Karen was gone. An aching, searing emptiness rose in my chest; I could hardly breathe with the intensity of it. It felt as though my heart had been ripped apart. Tears flooded through my eyes as I sobbed in pain and anguish, encountering Grief face to face!

"Jesus! Help!" I cried inwardly.

George turned and held me tightly. I felt the strength of his arms and was comforted. God, too, was wrapping me in a thick, protective covering and the ugly, stark reality of Karen being gone was slowly closed out.

Many friends came to our house. They cleaned, made the beds, washed dishes, prepared food, answered the phone and helped wherever needed. It was good to be surrounded by their love and ministry.

Throughout the morning, the question kept returning to me, "Is there something still left undone? Are we to have one final prayer - a prayer for Karen's resurrection from the dead?"

As we gathered for lunch, I told my friends what I was thinking. I needed their counsel. "I know it seems like a wild idea," I said, "but from the beginning of Karen's illness, the thought of praying for Karen's resurrection has been with me. Perhaps God has brought us to this point for this very thing!"

"I thought about praying for resurrection when I saw Karen at the hospital," George added.

"What should we do?" I asked.

I looked around the table at our dear friends who had been so faithful with their prayer and support for many months. All were quiet, pondering the seriousness of the question.

"Well, 'We have not because we ask not,' " one person spoke out, quoting James 4:2.

"I feel excitement in my spirit," someone else said.

"I have a peace about it," responded yet another friend.

"I believe God wants us to pray for resurrection," agreed another.

"I don't know if I would ever feel peace if I didn't," I said. "This may be God's climactic plan for Karen and I wouldn't want to miss it."

An awesome excitement mounted as we worked out the plans for the resurrection prayer. We immediately thought of people to call, those who had partaken of Karen's experience and would come together in unity of purpose as the body of Christ to release God's power. Those who felt led to do so would meet with us an hour before visiting hours began at the funeral home on the following night.

I called Victor to tell him our plans and asked if he would lead the prayer time.

"I'll pray about it," Victor replied, "and let you know."

I felt a mixture of emotions within me. I didn't know whether to be sad or happy. The eager anticipation of our resurrection prayer covered any feeling of sorrow or pain.

Mother arrived from the airport. We had said goodbye just over a week ago. Now we hugged again, holding each other tightly.

George and I left for the funeral home to buy the casket and to make the arrangements.

"Bring in the clothes you want us to put on Karen," the director told us. I knew already what they would be. Back at home, I laid out the beautiful, new green velvet gown and peach blouse we had bought for Karen.

"Oh, Karen," I cried. "I wanted you to wear this for Christmas, but you were too sick. Then I hoped you would wear it for your birthday, but that didn't work out. But ... ," and the tears rolled down my cheeks, "I didn't plan for you to wear it for your funeral."

I chose Karen's necklace with the small heart and cross for her to wear, and a woolly, white puppet of a lamb to put under her arm. With its crossed eyes and whimsical face, it would add just the right touch of lightness. Karen was never one to be serious for long.

"I would like for Karen to have a garland of daisies on her head, too," I thought, "just as she was envisioned wearing on her way to heaven."

Telephoning Nancy, I asked if she could make a garland for Karen. It would be special if it came from her.

"Trudy, Karen has been purified through all the trials and sufferings she went through," Nancy said as we talked. "There was no further work God needed to do in her."

As Nancy said the word purified, a thought came to me. "Nancy did you know that the name 'Karen' means 'purity'?"

"I hadn't realized that!" she exclaimed.

We continued to share how precious Karen was to us. "I just remembered there's a Psalm about 'precious,' "

I said, and I quoted: "Precious in the sight of the Lord is the death of His saints" (Ps. 116:15) .

" 'Precious Purity!' " we both exclaimed together.

"That's Karen's new name in heaven!" I realized. 'Precious Purity' - what a beautiful name!"

That evening, my friend Susie called. "Trudy," she said, "when I heard the news about Karen I was filled with grief and began to cry. 'Why did you let this happen, Lord?' I asked Him. 'Was there something I could have done to make it different?'

"The Lord gave me the most wonderful picture as an answer. I saw Jesus sitting in a beautiful, daisy-filled meadow with green, rolling hills behind Him.

"Karen was skipping and playing close beside Him, picking and tossing daisies into the air and happily running back and forth. Then she ran over to Jesus and He picked her up and placed her on His lap. She threw her arms around his neck and they joyfully hugged each other.

"Karen was the picture of health with pink, rosy cheeks and beautiful peachy skin. Her brown hair was long and flowing and she was wearing a white dress. Her feet were bare."

"That's Karen all right," I said, thinking of the bare feet.

Susie went on, "I could see that Karen was ecstatically happy and totally healed. Even the memory of her pain and suffering was gone. She had total peace and total joy.

"Then Jesus turned to me and said, 'See how happy she is. See how happy!" And my distress over her dying left.

"Then a simple, lilting melody began to flow through my mind. It skipped up and down gracefully as I had seen Karen skip. The Lord gave me these words to go with the tune:

Home in Zion

"Jesus loves Karen.
Karen loves Him.
Together they are happy.
Together they are one.
La la la la la."

I hung up the phone. My heart soared to hear such heavenly, happy news of Karen. Our loving Father had surrounded us with glorious images of Karen, happy and whole for eternity.

"Lord, I think you've already shown me your plans concerning Karen and our resurrection prayer. Would it even be right to ask her to leave the glory of heaven and return here?" I wondered.

Yet I still felt an inner urging to have the prayer. "Perhaps there is more involved here than I can see, Lord," I thought.

The next day was filled with activity. George's sister, Eugenia, arrived. Friends brought food, plans were completed for the memorial service and other details were carried out.

Victor called to say that he and Sara would participate in the prayer for Karen's resurrection that night. "I'm really excited about it," he said. "God spoke to me through Scripture that this is the direction in which we should go."

"Thank you, Lord," I whispered, grateful for the confirmation.

I got out the Bible and looked up some verses. John 14:12 said, "Truly, truly I say to you, he who believes in me will also do the works that I do; and greater works than these will he do because I go to the Father."

We believed in Jesus, and one of the works that Jesus did was to raise the dead.

189

I read Matthew 10:8, which said, "Heal the sick, *raise the dead,* cleanse lepers, cast out demons" (italics mine).

"Lord," I prayed, "I don't know what I should do. You know what the best outcome of our prayer will be. Would you allow Karen to come back if we prayed, even though it may not be your plan?"

I read further. John 11 described how Martha came to meet Jesus. She told Him that if He had been there, her brother Lazarus wouldn't have died. The next verse virtually jumped out at me! Martha said to Jesus, "And even now I know that whatever you ask from God, God will give you" (verse 22, RSV). God had spoken to me!

Here was my answer and protection! We would ask that Karen be raised in the name of Jesus. Jesus knew whether or not this was the Father's will. If it wasn't, then he would not ask God to accomplish it. What a relief to know that I could rest in my trust in Jesus!

In the afternoon, George and I went to the funeral home to see that everything was arranged as we wanted. I walked into the room and saw the open white casket at the far end. "It's so little," I thought.

We walked over to see Karen. She was beautiful! The pink ruffles from her blouse added color and softness to her face. The daisy garland that Nancy had made was fresh and lovely on her head, covering where her hair had fallen out.

Adjusting the heart necklace, and turning it to show the cross, I picked up Karen's hand and saw the bruise where her last i.v. needle had been. It was skillfully covered by makeup. A look at her fingernails reminded me that I had planned to cut them. No need to do that, now.

How important all the little details of Karen's body had been to me. As precious as Karen was to us, so was her body. "Precious Purity," I thought, observing her face. It was radiating with beauty and peace.

After rearranging a few things, George and I left for home. On the way out, I turned to look once again at the little coffin.

"It's so hard not to have Karen with us, Lord," I prayed aloud. George put his arm around me as we walked to the car.

I had a great sense of expectation as we returned to the funeral home that evening. My mother and George's sister, Mike, Chris, George and I drove together.

The Muellers met us, and our other friends soon gathered. We stood in a semicircle in front of the coffin. Victor shared Scripture which the Lord had given him and led us in prayer.

We sang songs of worship and praise. We knelt as one before the Lord. We joined hands in unity and sang in the Spirit. Then we waited silently before the Lord.

God's presence was powerful. The Holy Spirit was revealing things to each of us. While kneeling and waiting, I sensed Jesus standing in front of me with Karen beside Him. He reached out His hands and placed them on my head. I felt His anointing touch as an electrical charge, then as a pressure around my head like a ring of fire. Had Jesus placed a crown of victory upon me? I wasn't quite sure.

"A great harvest shall come forth of many spiritual children," the Holy Spirit inwardly spoke to another friend.

Still there was silence. I looked at my watch. Visiting hours were about to start. I knew that God would accomplish His purpose whenever we asked Him. "We· need to pray specifically for Karen's resurrection," I said to Victor.

191

We gathered around Karen. One of the men prayed a prayer of resurrection and Victor spoke the words of faith, "Get up, little girl, in the name of Jesus."

I watched Karen intently. Would she move? It was as if my soul was on tiptoes of expectancy, watching for signs of life.

"Rise up in the name of Jesus!" Victor commanded.

Karen's form remained lifeless, yet I felt no disappointment. I walked over to Victor. "It is finished," I said. People were already arriving. I knew we didn't have to beg God. We had run out of time to ask further. He could have raised Karen at any time, but He didn't. People gathered in small groups and started to talk. George and I began greeting guests.

Victor and Sara soon felt it was time to leave. They came over to where we were visiting and gave us a hug goodbye. We thanked them for all they had done, and they said they would continue praying, then left for home.

To my surprise, the Muellers returned a few minutes later. "The Lord won't let us go home," Victor stated. "He said, 'Turn around and go back.' He isn't finished, yet. We'll go in the back room and pray further."

Just then, Jean, another friend who had left shortly after the prayer for Karen's resurrection, returned. "The Lord told me to come back and keep praying," she said. I led her to the back room where Victor and Sara were praying.

My mind was reeling. Was God still going to perform His miracle? Perhaps He wanted to raise Karen when the room was full of people! What a spectacular conclusion to a viewing that would be! Again, a sense of excitement rose within me.

George and I mingled among the many people who were coming and going, talking quietly and encouraging them. We shared God's vision of Karen's glorious entrance into heaven.

Hundreds of people came. Friends from church, women from Aglow, acquaintances from business, people from the neighborhood, school and the hospital were there. Karen had touched many, many hearts.

I walked toward the casket. Many baskets of beautiful flowers from friends surrounded Karen. The thoughtfulness of their expression touched my heart. My eyes fell on a small arrangement placed on the piano. A white, satin cross about a foot high was used as a background: Pinned onto it was a small corsage of baby-pink rosebuds.

I looked at the corsage and remembered! After Karen was born, my mother sent two corsages for us to wear home from the hospital to celebrate the occasion. They were made of baby-pink rosebuds.

"Jesus, did you send Karen a rosebud corsage to welcome her to her heavenly home?" I asked, my heart warmed with love and wonder.

Chris came over to me. "I just saw an unusual picture in my mind. I saw five chains lying lengthwise on the ground. They were being chopped in half, one by one."

I was excited! Something was happening. I told George, and we went to the back room to tell Victor and Sara.

"Praise God," they exclaimed. "The Lord. showed us we were praying against more ancestral bondages on your family. Now we know they're being cut. We'll keep praying."

Jean continued to pray as well.

Chris came over to me later. "The last chain's been

broken," he said. We went to tell our friends in the back room.

"The bondages have been broken," I shared. "Now it truly *is* finished."

"Lord," I thought. "You had more in your purpose for our meeting than we had planned. You said 'No' to Karen's returning, but used this whole experience to minister to us and our entire generational line, even children to come."

We had prayed for Karen's earthly life to be restored. Instead, God restored a new dimension of spiritual life and freedom to Karen's family here on earth.

As the hour grew late, people began to thin out. I sank wearily onto the couch. My emotions were numb, my body tired.

Velma stayed behind as the funeral home emptied. She and the family gathered around Karen's coffin. We joined hands as she offered a prayer for God's peace and strength to be upon us.

George and I lingered at the coffin as the others walked toward the door. We held hands and looked at Karen. Tomorrow, her body would be flown to Chautauqua, New York and buried in our family plot the next day. I knew it was the last time I would see her until I was in heaven, too, or until the Lord returned.

"It hurts so badly to say goodbye," I cried. George held me for a few minutes, then we turned and slowly walked toward the door.

We arrived early for the memorial service at the church. George and I stood at the back, and greeted people as they came.

"Shouldn't we go and sit down?" I asked. The rest of the family had already taken seats.

194

"Let's stay and welcome the visitors," George said. "It's important for them to see us."

I knew what he meant. Truly, God was holding us in His strength, comfort and joy. It was His gift to us to experience and His gift to others to see.

As we stood there, my heart was moved to see Hilda and Lisa (from the hospital) arrive. They had spent many loving hours ministering to Karen. What could I say to minister to them now? We greeted each other with a special hug.

"Don't be sad that Karen is gone," I said, reassuringly. "She didn't die from leukemia. Her sickness was allowed by God only as a vehicle for His purpose in her life. She's in heaven today because Jesus came for her."

As I spoke these words, I heard them myself for the first time. God was speaking to me as well as *through* me to them. I was astounded at the concept. It didn't make sense to my natural mind, but God put a "realization" in my heart that went deeper than reason. It was truly His revelation.

George and I took our seats as Rev. Reed opened the service with a word of welcome. "In the name of our Lord Jesus Christ and on behalf of the family of Karen Colflesh, we welcome you to this service of worship and praise to our Savior God; and in honor and loving memory of Karen, who is with the Lord.

"I would like to say just a word about the service. It is a mark of the faith and trust that George and his family have in that, not only have they borne a good witness before the world during a time of severe testing, but they have actually been able to plan this service by themselves and to ask a number of their friends to take part in it. God gave them the peace and the comfort that has enabled them to design a worship service rather than a time of mourning.

"Of course, we experience sorrow even as believers. We weep with those who weep and rejoice with those who rejoice. But we focus our attention today on the Lord Jesus Christ - who is the Resurrection and the Life. And, therefore, it is a service of worship and praise to Him and because of Him."

We asked Victor to read the Scriptures and he shared the following briefly: "Karen was like the martyrs and saints of old. She knew that her permanent home was not here, but looked forward to her home in heaven.

"As Abraham offered up Isaac in obedience to God, he knew that God could bring him back to life again. Jesus could have brought Karen back, but it served God's glory to allow her to die. Karen is now in the Promised Land."

Nancy came forward to share the last chapter of "The City of His Brilliance." Marian shared her vision of Karen walking the stairway to heaven with the angels rejoicing. And Susie related to the congregation her vision of Karen and Jesus in heaven.

As we had sung around Karen's bed while she ascended the heavenly stairs, so we sang again at the service: "Let's go up to Zion, the City of our God; sing Hallelujah, there's joy in the Lord."

During the singing one of our friends, who sat a few rows behind us, accompanied on her tambourine. "How appropriate," I thought, and realized anew that God's joy didn't depend on circumstances.

Then we bowed our hearts to our Sovereign Lord, singing as with one voice:

He is Lord! He is Lord! He is risen from the
dead and He is Lord! Every knee shall bow,
every tongue confess, that Jesus Christ is
Lord!

Reverend Reed came to the pulpit. He read from
Romans 8 and 2 Corinthians 4 and 5. These Scriptures
speak of the glory that comes out of suffering, how God
turns all things to good and how we are more than
conquerors through Christ.

"These passages," the pastor shared, "speak over-
whelmingly of the kind of God we serve: A Sovereign God
- One who holds all things in His hands, One who is
Sovereign in creation, One who is Sovereign in salvation.
He gives eternal life as a precious gift to those whom He
has known from before the foundation of the world. What
a beautiful, wonderful thing to know that our time and our
lives are not in the hands of hapless chance or even that we
are victims of ourselves - of our own mistakes and our
own ideas. But rather, our God is able to work all things
together for good, even sickness, death and sorrow, to
those who love Him and are called according to His
purpose."

Reverend Reed spoke further of God's desire that we,
like Karen, would all come to know and trust Jesus Christ
as our personal Savior and that we would live as she did,
to His honor and glory.

At the conclusion of the message, we rose as a
congregation to sing "Crown Him with Many Crowns,"
and magnified the name of Jesus as we sang. After the
benediction, our family stood at the front of the church to
receive the rest of the congregation.

During the triumphant, postlude music of Purcell's
"Trumpet Voluntary," friends and acquaintances

streamed forward to greet us. The atmosphere was one of praise and victory. People's hearts were touched and strengthened.

As we were about to leave, I saw nurse Holiday coming toward me. Tears were streaming down her face.

"Karen was so special," she cried.

"I know!" I said, softly. "I'm so glad you were part of her life. Can you come over to our home, Holiday? We have friends stopping in."

Our home was filled with loving friends when we arrived from the service. I took some food and sat to rest, my energy low. Holiday walked over to me and I smiled.

"You know, Trudy," she began, "Karen started me thinking about the Lord, again. I had drifted away from Him over the years, but last night I recommitted my life to Him."

"Oh, Holiday, how wonderful!" I exclaimed. I felt my energy level rising again. God had touched another life through our precious daughter.

The following morning was the day of Karen's burial in New York. We had decided not to fly north, and I felt a peace at not being there. The boys were in school, and George and I took Mother and Eugenia for a sail on Godsend.

While we were on the water, my thoughts turned to the graveside service which we had arranged for friends to conduct. My prayers joined with theirs.

"Look!" said George, interrupting my thoughts.

I looked over the side of the boat. To my surprise, a large dolphin was leaping in and out of the water, keeping perfect speed with our boat.

"Just like Dogaphin!" I exclaimed with delight. We watched as the dolphin accompanied us for several minutes before disappearing.

"Oh, God," I exuded. "You're so good to give us this special touch. You know how our hearts need encouragement. Thank you, Father, for reassuring us of your love."

I gazed across the water in the direction of the dolphin, now lost from sight. Our Precious Purity was home in Zion. We had done all that the Lord had shown us to do. Now we were sailing on. Even with George's new job, the coming move and the difficulty of adjusting to life without Karen, I was confident that more "Dogaphins" would unexpectedly leap to the surface, reassuring us of God's continual love and care.

12
Provider

George and I discovered that God was continuing His constant care for us, providing what we needed at just the right time. With gratitude, we realized we had received total payment for Karen's funeral expenses through the insurance policy, a generous financial gift from our church and independent donations from loving individuals. We knew, however, that paying the funeral expenses was nothing compared to the astronomical expenses from Karen's extended hospital stay. We did not begrudge a single penny that was spent in ministering to Karen's needs, but when added all together, we were astounded to find that the bill came to almost $56,000.

Thankfully, George's health insurance paid eighty percent and, for the last three months, Dr. DeLamerens new foundation covered the other twenty percent of the expenses.

All of this greatly reduced our debt, but still we owed thousands of dollars in accumulated hospital and doctor bills. When George phoned from New Jersey, he asked me to go to the hospital and find out the exact amount of our bills.

I wasn't sure how I would feel, returning to the hospital.

It had been only two weeks since Karen's death. It was a pleasant surprise, however, to experience peace as I again entered the "Hospital with a Heart."

I brought with me some of Karen's books and toys to donate and visited the staff on West. They were like family to us and it was very good to see them.

Next, I went to the business office and talked with the patient service coordinator. We had become friends during the past months.

"Esther," I said. "I need to know what our total bill is so we can start making plans for repayment." I knew the hospital would be patient with us if we continued paying a small amount each month, even if it was for the rest of our lives. I thought of the bitterness that could easily come upon parents who, after the death of their child, were left with only bills. If all the expense had resulted in returned health, it would have had a purpose to it, but to be left with no child and only debt was an extremely hard thing.

George and I had to turn our eyes to Jesus concerning our debts. We knew that God would be the source to meet our need. Just as we had trusted Him to be with us throughout Karen's illness, we trusted Him now to provide us with the means to pay the hospital expenses. We had learned the scriptural principle of sowing and reaping, and had been "sowing" money in the name of the Lord throughout the years. We knew seeds sown grow to a harvest, and we had planted to help meet our financial need.

"Trudy," Esther said with a smile. "I have good news for you concerning your bill. The trustees of the hospital met just yesterday, and they agreed to apply money given from an anonymous donor to cancel out your debt."

I was stunned. "You - you mean we don't owe *anything?" I* stammered, trying to take in the full weight of what she had said.

"That's right," she answered. "Not a thing!"

"Tell me more about this donor."

"The donor consists of a family whose own child died here. They have given money to the hospital, to be used towards the bills of other parents whose children die."

"What a blessing," I said. "Thank you so much!"

My heart was singing as I walked to the other end of the hospital to Dr. DeLamerens office. I needed to find out the balance of our bill with him. We had been paying him our insurance money, but we felt it didn't begin to cover the expert, professional service he and his staff had given us.

I sat down with the doctor's secretary. "What is the balance of our bill with Dr. DeLamerens?" I asked.

She looked lovingly at me. Karen had touched a place in her heart as well. "The doctor wanted me to tell you," she answered, "that you don't owe a thing."

"Not a thing!" I exclaimed.

"Not a thing," she smiled.

"Oh, thank you! Thank you so much!"

I left the hospital, hardly believing what had happened. God completely took care of everything we owed! He had seen to it that we could leave Miami debt free. He was giving us a fresh, new start. I called George as soon as I got home and told him the exciting news.

I attempted to bring our family life back to normal as much as possible without Karen or George being present. I encouraged the boys to continue their activities.

Mike asked if his school service club could come to our house for a party. "They couldn't find any place to meet," he said.

"Not here!" I reacted at first.

But the Lord reminded me that Mike needed my love and support, and this was one way I could give it. I knew that if Karen hadn't been ill I would have done more for him during the past months. This was his senior year in high school, and I realized it might be the only time he could have his friends over, since we hoped to be moving soon. Agreeing with the Lord, I offered our home despite my feelings, and found the evening spent with the lively, enthusiastic teen-agers to be a blessing.

Soon after this, Chris wanted me to come to the Sunday evening service to hear his choir sing. I was reluctant to attend because Karen's choir (that is, the choir Karen used to sing in) was also singing and I didn't know if I could handle it, emotionally. However, I went so I could encourage Chris.

As I waited for the service to begin, the children in Karen's choir filed into the row right in front of me. The faces of Karen's friends, who had faithfully prayed for her Sunday after Sunday in their classroom and had sent many cards and drawings to cheer her, were sweet to see.

Little Becky Sue saw me and turned around. With the innocence of childhood, she asked, "Karen died and went to heaven, didn't she?"

Other children turned when they heard Karen's name.

"You're her Mother, aren't you?" one asked.

"Oh, I know Karen," another said. "She's my friend."

They wanted to talk about Karen and heaven. God gave me the peace to tell them how happy Karen was in heaven-that Jesus was there, and that Karen was with Him.

"It's a wonderful place," I said. "And Karen is all well and will never be sick again. She's running around, playing games and having a great time. And if she falls down, she won't get hurt and she won't skin her knee."

"You mean like this?" Becky Sue asked, holding up a skinned knee, patched with a band-aid.

When I saw her knee, I realized God had led me to say just the right words to Karen's curious friends who wanted to know all about life in heaven. "Thank you, Lord, that I could minister to these precious, little children," I prayed.

I enjoyed hearing Chris sing in his choir. He gave me a special smile when he saw me. It was worth coming. At the end of the service, several teen-age girls came over to me. "Mrs. Colflesh," one of them said. "I want you to know that Karen did something very special for me."

"What's that?"

"Well, I used to be very frightened of death and the fact that someday I would die. But I'm not afraid any more, now that Karen has gone through it."

I thanked her for sharing that, and we talked about Jesus taking the fear out of death. I was glad to be able to talk with the children and teen-agers. It comforted me to minister to others out of my grief.

The next morning was a quiet one. The boys were both at school and I was alone. I made my bed and loaded the dishwasher.

Wandering aimlessly around the house, I stopped in front of Karen's room. I looked in at her pink-flowered canopy bed, all neatly made and unslept in. Cute stuffed animals and pretty dolls sat on her shelf, unplayed with and uncuddled.

Karen's favorite Mickey Mouse hat lay on her dresser.

TOO PRECIOUS TO DIE

"You don't need that now, do you, honey?" I said.

My heart ached. Picking up a piece of paper and a pencil, I sat on the floor in the middle of Karen's room. I wanted to put into words the grief I was feeling. Maybe it would help me to feel better.

Tears rolled down my cheeks as I wrote:

> I didn't get to hear you sing last night in
>   primary choir.
> I can't pick you up at school.
> We won't do any of the special things mommies
>   do with little girls
>   and that I so loved doing with you.
> Oh, God, it's so hard, so very hard; my heart is
>   breaking,
> and I am so lonely for her.
> Oh, God, reach into the depth of my sorrow
> and heal me with your sweet balm.

Another wave of grief hit me. I started to cry and write at the same time:

> It just can't be real, are you really gone
>   forever, my little one?
> Oh, loving Father, why didn't you heal her?
>   We trusted you to do that.
> Oh, loving Father, why didn't you raise her?
>   I knew you could have.
> Now Karen's with you - not with us.

"Oh, Father, I'm so miserable," I cried.

I wandered into the living room and sensed that it was important to turn on the radio. The dial was set to the Christian station and as soon as I turned it on, the words "Trust in Me" were sung.

Provider

I dropped to my knees, overwhelmed, awestruck. The voice was that of Andrew Culverwell, Karen's favorite singer; the recording was from one that Karen knew by heart. I listened to the words anew as I realized it was a message straight from the Lord, with love from Karen:

Trust in Me
When you know you're sinking.
Trust in Me
When things are falling apart.
Trust in Me
I will never leave you.
Trust in Me
You'll have such peace in your heart!

Several nights later, I turned down the covers and looked at the empty double bed. It was lonely without George, and it was lonely without Karen and I missed them both intensely. As I thought of my loneliness, I became aware of a deep, throbbing ache that seemed to center around my heart. For a while, it felt like I would break apart.

"This must be what a broken heart feels like," I cried aloud.

"Oh, God!" I cried out. "I can't bear this pain. Help me!" Gratefully, the pain eased and I crawled into bed and fell asleep.

The next morning, I awoke feeling rested, looking forward to the events of the day. My dear friends from Aglow were holding a "farewell luncheon" for me and I was eager to see them all again.

Before the end of the luncheon, everyone gathered around me to pray. As we all lifted our praises to Jesus,

His spirit filled us. I dropped to my knees. As my friends continued to pray, I felt the Lord's blessing fall upon me and His strength and healing flow through me.

"The Lord showed me a picture of a tree as we prayed," one of the ladies said. "It was lifted, roots and all, from Florida and planted in New Jersey. I could see that it was a fruit tree because, as it was lifted, one of the fruits fell to the ground. The words 'the planting of the Lord that He may be glorified' came to my mind."

"The fruit that fell must have been Karen," I said.

"Yes," she answered.

"And fruit doesn't fall until it's ripe," I reflected. "Another thing about fruit is that when it falls into the ground and 'dies,' the seeds bring forth a harvest. I'm believing that Karen's death will bring many, many people into the Kingdom of God."

"And God's promise," my friend said, "is to heal you from your grief. The Scripture I received is from Isaiah. Look how appropriate it is," my friend said excitedly, handing me her Bible.

I read the verse aloud:

to grant to those who mourn in Zion
to give them a garland instead of ashes,
the oil of gladness instead of mourning,
the mantle of praise instead of a faint spirit;
that they may be called oaks of righteousness,
the planting of the Lord, that he may be
glorified. (Isa. 61:3, RSV)

"Thank you, Lord," I prayed, "for providing all we need."

13
Comforter

"Hi, Trudy," Nancy's cheery voice sounded from the other end of the phone. "You had talked about spending some time together. Why don't we drive down to the Florida Keys for the day. I know a quiet place, along a beach by one of the bridges, where we can sit and talk."

"What a good idea," I answered. "The Keys aren't that far from us. It would be a good place for a restful retreat."

I felt like a little child again, going on an adventure, as Nancy picked me up for our "retreat." On the way, we stopped at an Amish farm and bought fresh-picked strawberries and homemade "sticky buns" for our picnic.

In almost no time, we parked at the beach and got out of the car to hike. We came to a cluster of mangrove trees, jutting their mass of tangled roots out over the water.

Nancy and I climbed over the roots and out to the edge of the trees, where we sat leaning against the trunks. We sat quietly for a while, looking out over the deep turquoise water and listening to the gentle lap of the waves around the roots. It was soothing and good.

"Nancy," I said, after a long silence. "Why didn't God heal Karen?"

She turned and looked at me, lovingly. "I don't know, Trudy," she said truthfully.

I talked about the Scripture verses and promises which the Lord had given us and how I had perceived and understood them. I wondered if Karen might have had a choice whether to be healed here or to enter eternal life. I questioned whether I had understood God's leading correctly, or maybe missed what He was saying to me right at the end of Karen's illness.

I talked, cried and shared my innermost thoughts and questions; Nancy listened, loved and comforted me.

We walked down the hill to the catwalk under the bridge. We watched the fishermen who were lined up at the rail pull in the fish. Pelicans, circling in the air, settled to float on the water beneath us.

"You know, Trudy," Nancy said, after a while. "There is something I saw the day Karen died that I haven't told you, yet."

I turned to look at her, questioning.

"Just before Karen died, I had a vision of Jesus standing at the foot of her bed. He was holding her little body across His arms. She lay there limp and naked. Her body was broken . . . oh, so broken.

"I looked at Jesus," she continued. "On His face was displayed fierce anger and judgment. From His eyes flashed the fire of righteous indignation. He spoke the words, 'Who dared do this to one of my little ones?'

"I had never seen Jesus like that before and I realized, for the first time, some of the awesomeness of God's anger against Satan at the final judgment."

"Thank you for sharing that, Nancy," I said, quietly.

As we stood there beneath the bridge, I felt a peace settle over me. So Jesus was angry over the leukemia that had debilitated Karen's body. Satan had touched one of Jesus' little lambs and would receive full judgment and punishment. I was comforted with the knowledge that there would be a day of reckoning, a day of justice - Satan would know God's wrath.

Again, I was reminded that, even though Satan had come to rob and to destroy, Jesus had come to give life, and to give it abundantly. He had rescued Karen from the power of evil and He had turned the leukemia (and death) into His servant - as a vehicle to fulfill His plans for her life.

"There's something else I've wondered about, Nancy," I said. "Do you remember the prayer which the Lord gave you on the morning Karen died-to pray for her blood to stay within the bounds the Lord set? Why do you suppose she continued to hemorrhage?"

"I've thought about that too, Trudy," Nancy replied, "and I think I have the answer."

"What is it?"

"We had a different understanding of that prayer than the Lord had. He *did* set the boundaries, only they weren't within the usual course. He chose Karen's hemorrhaging as a loving, painless way to call her home.

"When you think about it," Nancy continued, "Jesus' desire for us is, really, to complete our life here so we can be with Him in heaven."

She opened her Bible to John 17:24 (RSV) and read Jesus' words:

> Father, I desire that they also, whom thou
> has given me, may be with me where I am, to
> behold my glory which thou hast given me in
> thy love for me before the foundation of the
> world.

"To me, it's as if Jesus is sending me a postcard from heaven saying, 'Wish you were here!' His great longing is to have His loved ones there with Him. Truly, it is such a glorious, wonderful place that our life here is *nothing* by comparison. What we call life now is just a shadow compared to the abundant life of eternity. If Karen chose heaven, she chose correctly, for she was in God's will. Heaven is the best place to be. It's our final destiny and the fulfillment of our lives.

"God gave me the story of 'The City of His Brilliance' to tell Karen about heaven because Jesus yearned that she be there with Him. Someday we will be there, too, Trudy, and then there will be no more sickness or sorrow."

I felt lifted as Nancy explained. We walked back to the car and got in.

"I don't think I missed God's direction," I said. "I believe He caused me to hope in her healing right through to the end. It wasn't a stubborn, self-willed hope that denied reality but a God-given encouragement even in the midst of my fully knowing the seriousness of her condition. "

"We are a people of hope," Nancy said.

"And now my hope is not in Karen's healing, but in our victory through her death. I was never to stop having hope. Now I'm just to redirect it."

After our day at the Keys, I never again felt the need to question God about Karen's death. He had allowed me to speak it all out and listened patiently as I asked. I did not receive an answer for every question. However, I had received His love and reassurance that I could trust Him absolutely and that, even in Karen's death, He would cause it to work for our good.

Though I had stopped asking, "Why?", God sent answers for questions I had earlier wondered about.

I thought of my brother Jim's prophecy early in Karen's illness: "Because you have given her to me (that is, to God) I am giving her back to you."

I realized now that I had jumped to the conclusion that God's giving Karen back was a permanent arrangement. But now I knew that the prophecy was for a specific event which had been fulfilled after the August crisis - at which time the Lord gave us Karen for several wonderful months of health and happiness.

Now I understood that, even as Jesus reassured Karen of her healing during the August remission, and again at the end of her illness, He was speaking of spiritual healing - a healing far greater than the physical. Truly, from August on, Karen *did* receive great spiritual strength. And she ministered to all of us, especially to me on the day we talked about her death.

My friend Arlene called me on the phone.

"Trudy," she said. "I didn't remember this incident until after Karen's death, but I thought you would like to know about it. Remember when you and Karen brought us the 'promise cookies'?"

"Yes," I replied.

"Well, I picked up the last cookie to eat but, before I broke it open to see what Scripture verse was in it, I prayed, 'Lord, let this be a special word to me concerning Karen.'

"Then I unrolled the verse. What I read shocked me. It spoke of healing, but healing in such a total way that I knew it referred to more than earth could offer. God showed me then that Karen's complete healing would come through her death. I was so unprepared for that insight that it completely left me until just now, and I wanted to share it with you."

"Thank you, Arlene," I said, as I hung up the phone.

I realized, as God had shown Arlene, that His greatest healing does come through death. If Karen had been healed on earth, she would have struggled against sin as long as she lived and, in the end, died as we all must. But God, in His love and wisdom, had already taken her through death to her total healing in heaven where sin, disease and death could touch her no longer.

I was happy that one day nurses Lisa and Ella could come to the house to have lunch with me. I showed them Karen's room and we talked together about our special little girl. I shared the events of Karen's last night with them. "The last words I heard her say were 'Thank you very much . . . .' "

Suddenly, it was like the bridge I was walking on collapsed. My throat tightened with emotion and there were no more words, only tears. We all cried together.

The next morning, I thought again of my last hours with Karen. "I never got to say goodbye," I realized, with painful clarity.

Death was so final. No time was left. I felt so helpless. "Oh, God," I cried. "I never got to say goodbye to Karen!"

My heart was broken as I poured out these words on paper:

The days were full of caring and tending and
    talking and loving,
But you had much pain and that occupied
    your thoughts.
    I didn't realized you were leaving.
I kept waiting and hoping it would all
    be different soon.
Everybody was doing all they could, medically.

Comforter

We waited before the Lord in quiet trust,
So I wasn't expecting you to go.
I couldn't absorb the medical clues
  that you were slipping,
My mind was dulled to the seriousness
  of your condition,
And when you left,
I never got to say goodbye.

With that, I threw back my head and let out a long, mournful wail from the very depth of my being. The pain was too deep for tears.

After I quieted, God spoke to my heart. "What did you want to say to Karen?" I wrote down my thoughts:

I miss you.
I love you so much.

I'll think of you every day.
I'll be coming soon.

I looked at what I had written: It wasn't much, but it was very important.

"You know I'm not bound by time," Jesus said to me. "Nothing is beyond my reach. I want to take you back to Karen's bedside so that you can say goodbye."

I closed my eyes and saw the hospital room again. I was at Karen's left side by the head of her bed. My friends were standing around the bed, praying.

Jesus came to the bed and raised Karen to life. Then He turned Karen to me. She hugged and kissed me and said goodbye.

I talked to her and told her all the things I wanted to say.

Lovingly, I hugged her and told her to go with Jesus. I saw myself take Karen's hand and place it in the hand of Jesus. Together, they left for heaven.

Tears were in my eyes but, this time, they weren't tears of agony, they were tears of joy. Death was not as final as it had seemed. My Lord is Ruler over time and He had let me mentally relive a portion of it to accomplish something very important.

Even though I was experiencing grief, I found I was basically ignorant of the whole subject. A book, displayed in our church library, caught my attention: It was Joyce Landorf's *Mourning Song*. I found it to be a fascinating, helpful book on how to realistically deal with death and grief. As it explained, dealing with sorrow after the loss of a loved one is called "grief work."

"A very appropriate term," I thought, seeing it as something that could be faced and worked on.

There are typical stages that people go through in their grief. The first is one of shock, which is the body's physical and emotional protection. The reality of the loss is too great to absorb, and it is common to deny that it even happened. I realized that I had felt God's cushioned protection from reality for many weeks after Karen's death.

The book went on to say that many people prefer not to leave this first stage of grief. They pretend that life is still the same, even without their loved one. As a result, they never work through their grief and never experience healing from it.

As beautiful as God's protective peace was to me, He knew I needed to face a world without Karen and learn to live in it. He also knew my desire to face my grief and walk through it to the other side with Him. So, as

I was able, the Lord gradually unwrapped me from His protection.

The next stage, I read, is one of intense suffering and loneliness. In it are anger, questioning and depression.

I related to that. I was glad to read that it was a normal, healthy path to recovery. I was glad, too, that Jesus was with me and that I could trust Him to see me through safety.

The third part of grief work is the slow, gradual healing of the mind, soul and inner emotions. I was surprised to read that this process normally takes one to two years. (I was hoping it would not last that long.) For those who do not face their grief, it takes even longer.

A vital step in being healed from grief is forgiving. We must forgive God for allowing the death of our loved one. We must forgive the person for dying and we must forgive ourselves for any regret we may have.

Joyce Landorf's book explained that as we forgive we are set free to accept the reality of the death and to receive healing. A Christian's faith contains a wealth of restoration and the knowledge of his guaranteed life forever in Christ.

"Amen to that," I agreed. It was comforting to know there was a pattern to grief. Even Christians, with all the strength and hope of our faith, go through grief. But, with Jesus, we come out restored.

George flew home for a few days. I had been busy with friends and activities but was excited with the anticipation of being together with him again. I expected we would comfort and support each other and work out our grief together.

I was sure that we were experiencing the same feelings because, as Karen's parents, we went through her illness and her death together. But I was wrong. George didn't want to hear what I had been learning about grief and what I was feeling. He continued to avoid any discussion of Karen or our feelings.

Finally, I approached him with my questions and he lashed out defensively, "Don't talk to me about prophecies, visions, God's plan or heaven. Who knows what is going to happen! What difference does it make, anyway? God's going to do just what He pleases!"

I felt wounded. I hadn't expected George's angry reaction. Trying to think of something hopeful to say, I said, "We-we-will be-together again in heaven."

"Maybe *you'll* be, but I don't know if I'll *ever* see Karen again!" George answered vehemently. "Who knows if . . ." and his voice trailed off.

"I just don't want to say anything. I don't want to say things I don't mean," George said, his voice softening.

But his words filled me with fear. The alarming thought went through my head, "I've not only lost a daughter, I've lost my husband as well."

George was such a strength and support to me during Karen's illness. To see the contrast now was painful.

After that experience, George and I did not talk about Karen. Knowing that it would only hurt each other, we concentrated on other things.

It was a relief to wave goodbye to George at the airport as he headed back to New Jersey. Our time together was draining, emotionally. George's attitude threatened my emotional stability.

I didn't like the idea, but I realized that George and I each needed to work through our grief separately and that we could not support each other.

I was thankful to still be in our old home, surrounded by friends and activities. My heart went out to George in his strange, new place-without home, family or friends. But I knew I couldn't help. I prayed that Jesus would strengthen and comfort him.

As I prayed, the Lord reminded me that part of grief work is anger and that George was honestly expressing his built up hostilities. The words that comforted me most, however, were what Paul wrote in Philippians, "I am sure that he (the Lord) who began a good work in you will bring it to completion" (Phil. 1:6, RSV).

God showed me several weeks later that He had brought George through his anger. George sent me a copy of the letter he wrote to thank the many people who had donated blood for Karen.

My heart filled with joy as I read his words:

> Many lives have been touched through Karen's faith in the Lord throughout her illness and during the time she knew she was failing. We know that she has been healed and is home with the Lord. This makes heaven that much more precious for us to think about, as we know that we will be able to spend eternity with her.

Jesus was faithful to His word: He was leading George, as well as me, on the pathway to recovery.

Without difficulty, George and I found a home to purchase in New Jersey. Within three months, our Miami home was sold. Busy getting everything ready for the move, I appreciated the loving help of friends.

At the end of April, George flew in from New Jersey.

The moving company loaded the van. We said tearful goodbyes to our wonderful Christian friends and started the long drive to our new home.

We left behind that part of the Body of Christ who had walked and prayed with us through Karen's illness and death; we left behind our son, Michael, who was staying with friends so he could finish his senior year in high school; and we left without Karen.

"I don't know if I can take it, Lord," I prayed, through my tears.

"I have called you to New Jersey," He answered. "I am planting you there. That is the place in which you will receive my blessing now, not Miami."

"It is your presence, Lord, that I desire. Where you are is where I want to be."

As I reaffirmed my faith in His leadership, I felt peace in my heart and anticipation of what lay ahead. We were committed to God, and He was committed to us. Again, I would learn of His faithfulness to see us through the unexpected difficulty of grieving that lay ahead.

14
Healer of Broken Hearts

As good as it was to be with George again, I experienced the hardest part of my grief - the loneliness and separation from Karen - compounded by our move.

On our first Sunday in New Jersey, George drove us to a church he had been attending. On the way, he played a music tape of children singing praise songs. While it lifted George's heart to hear it, I reacted in just the opposite way.

I heard little voices sing:

His name is Jesus, Jesus,
Sad hearts weep no more.
He has healed the brokenhearted,
Opened wide the prison door,
He is able to deliver evermore.

As I fought back the tears, they sang the next song:

With healing in His wings,
With healing in His wings,
The Son of righteousness shall rise,
With healing in His wings.

It hit me even harder. I remembered the vision of Jesus running down the mountain to meet Karen on the day she died. He brought her eternal healing that day.

I began to sob. George turned the music off, and we drove the rest of the way in silence. I walked into church with my eyes red, attempting to smile when greeted.

Every hymn we sang seemed to talk about the joy of heaven - about meeting our loved ones or about Jesus coming again. I tried to sing, but my throat became choked and the tears flowed.

On Monday, I registered Chris at his new school. Returning to our quiet house and walking around aimlessly, I finally went out to the deck off the kitchen.

"Karen would have started school there today, too," I thought.

Sitting on the steps, I leaned against the railing. My heart was heavy. Sobbing, I told the Lord how I hurt and how much I missed Karen. His presence was with me and He listened and comforted me.

After my crying diminished, He spoke to my heart.

"Let's review the situation," He said.

As I listened, He reminded me of my commitment to Him as Lord. He explained that sorrow had an important work in my life, that Karen's life was fulfilled here, and He had a perfect plan and that there was fruit and joy to come. He reminded me of the Scripture verse: "Looking to Jesus the pioneer and perfector of our faith, who for the joy that was set before him endured the cross, despising the shame, and is seated at the right hand of the throne of God" (Heb. 12:2, RSV).

I remembered that Jesus had endured the cross for the *joy that was set before Him.* I, too, had a cross and pain to bear, but on the other side of the pain, He promised joy.

I sat quietly and waited. After I finished crying the Lord finished speaking but still I sensed there was more; I wasn't to go into the house yet.

A minute passed, and then another. Hearing a noise above, I looked up. A flock of honking geese flew over our house in a perfect V-formation. Joy welled up in my heart.

"There is *victory* in *Jesus!"* I exclaimed, excitedly. " 'Thanks be unto God, which always causeth us to triumph in Christ' (2 Cor. 2:14, KJV). Thank you, Lord, for the victory. Thank you for your special sign to me'" I went into the house rejoicing, my spirit lifted.

Each day was long and quiet. There was no busy phone with friendly voices, no activities in which to become involved, no get-togethers planned.

As I worked, unpacking and settling the house, tears would often flow. I thought about those hot and salty tears, coming from the depth of my being: they were doing an important work. The salt was tenderizing and the heat was melting all the hard and cold places of my heart so that compassion could flow. God was using sorrow to make my heart like His (Ezek. 36:26).

In the evenings, George and I would often go for a walk around the lake near our home. My heart was too heavy for me to smile as we passed our new neighbors. George would greet them for the both of us. I really didn't care. I felt wretched. Through my tears, I wondered if I would ever be happy again. George was a strength and comfort to me. He seemed to be already on the other side of the valley of grief and was extending his arm to help guide me through it.

I had asked the Lord to allow me to experience the depth of grief that was necessary for me to go through: I didn't want to ignore it or leave it too quickly. If my healing was to be complete, I needed to face grief fully and to work through it all the way. Joyce Landorf's book had made that clear. And Jesus promised, "I will not leave you ... desolate ... [nor] bereaved" (John 14:18, AMP). Jesus promised me and I knew that, in His timing, I would come through.

One morning, I read the words of Jesus: "Shall I not drink the cup which the Father has given me?" (John 18:11).

I reflected on those words for a long time. Jesus, the very Son of God-obedient and perfect in all ways to His Father's will - was given a cup of suffering by His Father, who loved Him. Jesus' cup was not given because of disobedience or for lack of love from His heavenly Father.

God's words began to speak to my heart and I took paper to write them down: "Trudy," my heavenly Father said, "I have a cup of sorrow for you to drink; not as a result of disobedience, not as a form of punishment, but because it is my will for you to drink it. Your obedience and love for me brings me pleasure and delight."

"Yes, Lord. I love you. I trust you. I serve you," I answered. "I will drink your cup of sorrow. I will drink it with acceptance and thankfulness."

I imagined myself reaching for the cup which He offered me, holding it to my lips bravely, though my knees were weak, and I could hardly breathe. Swallowing the sorrow, it was unbelievably hot and searing. It utterly took my breath away and I felt such pain I thought I would die.

But I did not throw down the cup. I continued to drink. An unusual strengthening and support flowed into me; a realization filled me that I was surviving in the very depths of anguish - and that in surviving this I could survive *anything.* I was standing, fortified. Wonderfully, such strength was being supplied that allowed not only survival, but victory - victory in the depth of grief, conquering in the midst of defeat, overcoming when all seemed lost.

As I continued to drink, I became aware of a sweetness within the sorrow. Its presence was unmistakable and I realized that it was Jesus himself, the Man of Sorrow who is acquainted with grief. I tasted of Him in a way I had never known before. I clung to Him as though my very life depended upon Him, and I focused on His sweetness, His strength and His comfort in my sorrow.

It was a glad day when Mike arrived at our new home after graduation. His happy, outgoing personality lifted the routine quiet of the house, and it was good to hear Mike and Chris interrelating again.

Summer came. The warmth of the sun and the beauty of our new surroundings were encouraging. Friends whom we had left behind continued to pray for us, telephoned and corresponded at precisely the times when their loving touch was needed most. God's tender hand of blessing was upon it all.

I began to write down the events of Karen's illness and death and all that the Lord did and showed to us throughout that time. So much had happened; I wanted to collect it in writing before time dimmed the memory.

As I wrote, I discovered a great satisfaction and peace came to my heart and I sensed my writing was a cathartic experience for me, bringing healing.

I wrote to Dr. Pefkarou at the hospital concerning some details I wanted to verify about Karen. I reread the words which poured out:

God has shown us many things already about Karen's sickness and death. Although it appeared that God was powerless to halt the progress of leukemia in Karen's body, I know that isn't so. Our mighty God is so powerful that all the atoms of all creation are held together by His will (Col. 1:17).

I believe that, in Karen's death, He has shown forth the power of weakness, the same apparent "weakness" He allowed when His Son died on a cross. He could have commanded 10,000 angels to free Jesus. He could have burned the earth to a crisp with His wrath. But He didn't, because His love had a greater plan-and that was to draw you and me and all of Adam's race into a personal relationship with Jesus, who is our Savior.

Out of the mystery of apparent weakness comes God's greatest glory and power. Christ rose from the dead; He broke the chains of sin and death and made a way for us to come back to the heavenly Father for all eternity.

I believe God has an even greater purpose in allowing Karen's death than in healing her. What may have seemed to be His weakness will one day show the greatness of His wisdom. At this point, I do not see His greater plan. But I do know that *"All* things work together for good to those who love God and are called according to His purposes" (Rom. 8:28), and that everything God does, He does in love.

"Thank you, Lord, for those thoughts and for the comfort they bring me," I prayed.

The warmth and cheer of summer cooled and faded into fall. We drove Mike to college in North Carolina, Chris started seventh grade and I was left in quietness and loneliness.

"How long, Oh, Lord, how long?" I cried.

Had grief completed its full work in my heart? Was I melted and broken enough before the Lord? Was I ready to be healed? I didn't know.

I opened my Bible to look up Scriptures on healing and mourning and discovered the following:

> He heals the brokenhearted and binds up their wounds. (Ps. 147:2, RSV)
> Blessed are those who mourn, for they shall be comforted. (Matt. 5:4, RSV)
> I will turn their mourning into joy, I will comfort them, and give them gladness for sorrow. (Jer. 31:13, RSV)
> And God will wipe away every tear from their eyes. (Rev. 7:17, RSV)

It was obvious that God was the One who brought about the healing, but I knew I could have a part by being open to receiving it. I wrote out the verses to read each day.

As the days went on, I wanted more and more to have a good friend with whom to share. I thought of Nancy and wrote to her about my feelings.

"All my friends are in Miami . . . . How I long to have a day with you again and talk and share. Remember the blessing and satisfaction of our day at the Keys?" I wrote.

Even as I penned those words, God was preparing the answer to my needs and, as yet, I was unaware of the joy that was being set before me.

Unknown to me, Nancy and her husband Ron were planning a fall vacation to New England. When she got my letter, she realized our home in New Jersey would be a perfect place to stop on the way. Just two weeks later, Nancy and I strolled together through a wooded path that was brilliant with fall foliage.

"It's hard to believe you're here," I said to Nancy with a happy smile on my face. "Isn't God good!"

"He's a *wonderful* God!" she said, rejoicing.

As we walked, I shared my thoughts and pains with Nancy. I told her that, as painful as grief was, I didn't want to rush through it - I wanted to be healed from the center outward.

"I've often wondered," I said, "how it will feel when I stop grieving for Karen. This may sound strange, but I don't know if I *want* to be healed if it means I would no longer have the tears of remembering her."

"I don't think being healed of grief means you won't still have tears," Nancy said. "It basically means not living and walking in constant emotional pain."

"You mean, grief would just be an occasional visitor rather than a constant companion?" I asked.

"That's a good way to put it."

"How do I know when I'm ready to come out of grief, Nancy?"

"God has set His world and His works in seasons. The book of Ecclesiastes has a whole chapter on that subject: It talks of a time to weep and a time to mourn, a time to laugh and a time to dance (Eccles. 3:4). I believe God has set a time clock within us and we'll *know* when our season is over. God is ready to heal your sorrow any time you're ready to let Him."

As Nancy talked, I felt an excitement stirring in my spirit. Maybe my season was over; maybe my sorrow would end soon? I felt hope bubble up within me as my heart cried out, "God, I'm ready to be healed!"

We walked through the woods to the edge of the lake and stood there watching the sun sparkle and dance on the water.

"Nancy, I'm ready to come out of mourning," I said.

She opened her arms to me and we hugged.

"Would you pray with me as I make this a commitment of my will before God?" I asked.

We joined hands and began to pray. Nancy thanked God because He had set all things in seasons and He had led me to this decision in His perfect timing.

I prayed, relinquishing to the Lord my sorrow, grief and mourning: I asked Him to heal me and bring my mourning to an end. As I did so, I fought against fear. Could life ever be normal again? Could I really be healed from grief when the greatest pain I felt was the separation between Karen and myself? How could that separation ever be changed?

Even as these questions were struggling in my mind, the Lord gave me instant understanding of a truth I only vaguely knew; *that we are not separated from those we love who are in Christ Jesus!*

A brilliant, circular light shone in my mind's eye, and I knew it was the City of God. A pathway was streaming out as a beam from the City. The light of the path was the same light as the City. We who belong to Jesus are traveling on that path of light through the world to our real home, which is in heaven. On this path there is no separation (as the world sees and experiences it) between the loved ones in the City and the loved ones who are still on the path. We are united, as the City and the path are united. There is access between the two in the communion of the Spirit. Just as the Holy Spirit is constantly with us, through Him we can constantly be in fellowship with all of our beloved - those on earth and those in heaven. There is no closed door. There is no separation. Permanent access is there.

"Thank you, Father, for that beautiful revelation!" I cried.

Even as God imparted His knowledge to me in a moment's time, my pain of separation was instantly healed and I knew that Karen and I were joined in His Spirit eternally.

"Oh, Father," I exclaimed. "Let me have a picture of Karen in heaven to hold in my heart. Let me see her as you do, so that I may rejoice."

I waited for pictures or thoughts to come, knowing that my ability was limited. What input or experience did I have that could express Karen as she is now?

"Father, I can't think of anything to say," I prayed. "But I'm going to speak forth words in faith and trust you to direct them. Here is how I see Karen," I began to speak. "I see her with her usual, bubbling personality-full of fun, telling jokes and saying cute things. She is a pure delight to the adults and angels of heaven. She moves easily among them and knows their acceptance and love.

"She leads and organizes small groups of children to play games such as . . ." and I found myself tripping over the word "softball."

"They won't have softball in heaven," I began to reason. But I felt God encouraging me to say the word, so I continued in faith, and said, ". . . to play games such as softball. She also climbs trees (I had no doubt about that), swims in the lake and splashes in the fountain of living water.

"She has a time of instruction and study, and learns quickly, with great interest and curiosity, asking many questions and understanding the answers.

"'Karen's major responsibility is to be at the throne of God. There, she worships with the throngs of saints and angels and rejoices in the presence of the Father. As a young handmaiden of the Lord, she is ready to carry out any errands or requests that might be made of her.

"I know there's something else Karen does at God's throne," I said, breaking into my thought, "but I don't know what it is."

"Oh! I know!" Nancy said excitedly. "God just showed me a picture. In it, He was sitting on His throne, surrounded by the twenty-four elders. They were conducting solemn and important business. Karen ran up to the throne and tugged on God's robe. With a radiant smile, He reached down and lifted her up to His lap, where she cuddled against Him."

My heart melted and my mind reeled within me at the thought of it. What a magnificent picture of the God of the Universe; the Mighty, Powerful Creator and Ruler with a Father's heart of love who reaches down in gentleness and joy, picking up the little children to cuddle on His lap!

God gave Nancy and me a picture of His ultimate power and His ultimate tenderness. Leaning against His great heart of love was our daughter Karen - Precious Purity!

Nancy's praises ascended with mine to God and we joined with the worshipers at the throne, glorifying and rejoicing in Him. We praised with our mind and spirit, lost in the wonder and joy of His presence.

As we praised the Lord, Nancy was given a picture of a heavy, dark cloak of mourning slipping off, leaving me clothed in a beautiful, white gown. In the vision, I started to dance and whirl. Sparkles of light, like stardust, spun off the gown and glittered in the air as I laughed and danced and praised the Lord.

Nancy began to sing a song we both knew, and I joined in:

> Put on the garment of praise and the spirit of heaviness is gone, gone from me. Dance in the Spirit and in the Heavenlies. Almighty God is He!

I woke up the next morning feeling light and free. Truly, the spirit of heaviness was gone! I had forgotten how good it was to feel joy in my heart, light in my eyes and a lilt in my step.

The great weight of mourning was removed. God had healed me! I was given, just as He promised, "the garment of praise for the spirit of heaviness" (lsa. 61:3, KJV).

"Praise you, mighty God, loving Father, who turns my mourning into joy, who gives me access into the Heavenlies and who holds on your lap our Precious Purity!"

15
King of Kings and Lord of Lords

I marveled at God's expression of love in arranging for Nancy and her husband to drive thousands of miles as His instrument of healing. An equally great wonder arrived shortly after in the mail.

A letter addressed from "The 700 Club" (the Christian Broadcasting Network), was addressed to George and me. During Karen's illness we sent out prayer request letters and up-dates on Karen to our loved ones and several ministries. We were on their mailing list.

I opened it and looked through it casually. At first glance, I thought it was an invitation to visit their television show when we were in the area.

I read the letter again, this time more slowly: "Your name has been mentioned as a potential guest of 'The 700 Club.' "

"*Guest*!" I exclaimed! "Oh, Jesus," I whispered, and dropped to my knees. "Look what you have done!"

The wonder of His power was awesome. "It isn't Karen you've called to be on 'The 700 Club,' it's George and me!"

I thought back to Psalm 57, which the Lord had given to us at the beginning of Karen's illness. Indeed, He had walked us through this Psalm verse by verse in a personal way. As I read verse 9, "I will thank you publicly throughout the land. I will sing your praises among the nations," I remembered thinking that Karen would be miraculously healed and sent forth as an evangelist to our country and to the world. One way to reach the world for Jesus was via Christian television, and I had envisioned Karen giving her testimony on "The 700 Club."

In part, "The 700 Club" letter read:

> Currently the program is aired on more than
> 120 television stations and 3500 cable TV
> systems, as well as 130 radio stations. In
> addition we are in foreign markets such as
> Japan, Taiwan, Manila and Puerto Rico.

"I had no idea, Lord," I prayed in awe, "that you planned for George and me to 'thank you publicly throughout the land, and sing your praises among the nations' [Ps. 57:9, TLB]. This must be how you intended for Karen to be 'an evangelist' to hundreds of thousands! Even though she is in heaven, *we* can share her testimony on earth."

Quickly, I phoned George at the office and read him the letter. He, too, was awed at the wonder of God's plan. Our mutual response was to write to the Christian Broadcasting Network (CBN) and explain that we were deeply touched to be asked and would be available if they decided to invite us.

We expected to hear from "The 700 Club" by mail, but one day the phone rang with a special message. The cheerful voice at the other end said, "Hello, Trudy, this is Jackie Mitchum from 'The 700 Club.'"

She told me they would like very much for George and me to be on their program. I said we were very honored and would love to come.

"Let's see, now," Jackie said. "I know this is looking

ahead, but the date I have available for your program is January 9. Would you be able to come then?"

"January 9!" I exclaimed. "That's the day Karen went to heaven!" .

"Oh, my goodness! I had no idea. Will that be too difficult for you this year?"

"Oh, no. It's perfect! God had it planned all along! I can't think of any place I'd rather be than on 'The 700 Club' that day."

"I've got holy goose bumps," Jackie said.

"Me, too!" I agreed.

As I hung up the phone, I was again overwhelmed at God's goodness and love. He was reassuring us again that Karen's death was, indeed, part of His glorious master plan and that His hand of blessing would be upon us as we spoke on "The 700 Club."

Before fulfilling Psalm 57 on "The 700 Club," we would pass through the holiday season. As good as it was to be healed of grief, I found that I especially needed God's comfort as Thanksgiving and Christmas approached. These times held special family memories, and I was more acutely aware of Karen's absence.

In the midst of inviting relatives for Thanksgiving at our new home and planning the menu and fun family events, I began to cry. Running to the bedroom, I closed the door and poured out my tears and feelings to my heavenly Father. In the quietness that followed, He spoke to my heart: "I love you, my daughter. How precious you are to me. How precious is your little daughter, Precious Purity, who is with me now.

"All the saints rejoice in her presence. I know it is beyond your understanding, but all of heaven rejoices in her presence. Truly, she is loved and adored, even as you are also loved and adored.

"I have not placed a separation between heaven and earth. As she is loved here, you are loved there. I hold you each in my arms and I draw you together in me, for you, also, I have placed on my throne.

"Reign well on my behalf among those whom I give you. I have placed the earth before you to speak of my goodness, and I am able to save to the uttermost all those who would come unto me!"

I knelt in silent wonder before my heavenly Father. When I got up, I felt cherished and restored.

The prayers, phone calls and letters from our many friends encouraged and supported us as Christmas drew near. Christopher's enthusiasm in gift making projects lifted my spirit and I joined in his excitement to prepare for Christmas.

George, Chris and I tramped through the grounds of a Christmas tree farm searching for the right tree to saw down for our living room. It was fun getting the tree, but when we got out the box of ornaments my eyes filled with tears.

"Lord," I cried inwardly, "I can't face seeing Karen's favorite Frosty-the-Snowman ornament. What am I going to do?"

"I want you to hang it this year, Trudy," He answered.

I gulped. Perhaps it would be best, I realized, to face directly the thing from which I wanted to run.

"Chris, I'm going to hang Frosty this year," I said.

"Hey, I thought it was my turn!" he objected.

"I know, honey, but I *have* to do it this year."

"Sure, Mom. It's okay."

I unwrapped the tissue paper from around the smiling Frosty bulb and hung the ornament on the tree. Then, standing back from the tree to observe my placement, I prayed, "That wasn't so hard after all, Father. Thank you!"

God sustained us with His peace as Christmas came and went. Now our thoughts were turned to the coming television appearance. I was both excited and nervous. It was going to be such an important event, truly part of God's great plan coming out of Karen's sickness and death.

"Oh, God," I prayed, "I don't want to fail you."

God reassured George and me that He would not let us fail and that He would give us the words to say. One day, a Scripture from the Psalms stood out clearly to me.

"That's your direction for us, isn't it, Lord!" I said, as I read excitedly:

> All thy works shall praise thee, 0 Lord; and thy
> saints shall bless thee. They shall speak of the
> glory of thy kingdom, and talk of thy power; To
> make known to the sons of men his mighty
> acts, and the glorious majesty of his kingdom.
> (Ps. 145:10-12, KJV)

"We're to bless you for your power and works on our behalf so that the glory and majesty of your kingdom will be expressed."

Even knowing the direction in which the Lord would have us speak, I spent several restless nights thinking about what I would say, depending on what the host of the show, Pat Robertson, would ask.

Two days before we left for our "700 Club" appearance, I awoke with God's peace in my heart. I knew that many friends throughout the country were praying for us, and I felt the power of those prayers.

We had a smooth flight to Virginia. After an enjoyable dinner with Jackie Mitchum, the program coordinator, we went to our hotel.

"Lord, I'm trusting in you," I prayed as I lay in bed all night, waiting for morning. But I must have dozed just before dawn, because I awoke remembering having had a vision of a field. In it were many bales of wheat, harvested and lying ready. A large section of the field had been harvested already, but there were still more sections of wheat, ripe and ready to be gathered.

"Why, Lord!" I exclaimed. "You've given me a vision of what you're going to do today as we share Karen's story. You are going to gather many into the kingdom because Karen is a laborer in the harvest. And, even after this show, there will be more harvesting to come."

I lay there, thinking excitedly of what the Lord was going to accomplish. Then I remembered the date. The sun was beginning to shine through the window; as the bright streaks of the new day streamed into the room, thoughts of this date a year ago pierced my heart. Tears welled up within me as I remembered Karen's death.

"Oh, God!" I cried. "How am I ever going to talk to hundreds of thousands about you and Karen *today?*" "Trust me," He answered, and I forced myself to concentrate on Him.

I was grateful to be at the studio finally. At least, it would all be over soon. The make-up artist prepared me for the bright lights of television.

"You wore just the right clothes," he said. "The texture and color blend perfectly with the colors of the studio background and will show well under the television lights." He was looking at my soft, violet blouse and matching long tweed, plaid skirt.

"Thank you, " I said, remembering that my friend Eileen and I spent a whole day shopping and had asked the Lord to show us just the right outfit. I was feeling better moment by moment.

Pat Robertson came to greet us. We were impressed with his personal warmth and energetic vigor for the Lord.

Ben Kinchlow, the co-host of "The 700 Club," prayed with us before the show. George and I watched the television backstage as the show opened. I heard the announcer say, "CBN presents 'The 700 Club.' On today's program, George and Trudy Colflesh discuss their daughter's affliction with leukemia and her subsequent death."

As my eyes filled with tears, I wondered if I would be able to say a single word.

Pat and Ben opened the show. The director came backstage and motioned for George and me to come out.

"You're on, Lord," I prayed. We took our positions in the chairs and waited for the commercial to finish.

Pat introduced us and welcomed us to the show. He held up Karen's picture for the audience to see, and the camera zoomed in, filling the entire screen with Karen's smiling face.

Pat talked first to George and then asked me a question. Words that I hardly thought about came pouring out of me. It felt almost as though I were a spectator, but it was my own voice speaking, and it sounded confident and relaxed.

Pat continued to ask questions and make comments. George and I shared about Jesus bearing the burden and being present with us in power throughout Karen's illness; how He delivered her from evil and restored her life when her heart stopped.

We shared the belief we had held that Karen would be healed in order to be an evangelist. We also related our acceptance of God's greater plan to take her to heaven. We told about the glorious visions of Karen going to heaven and we explained that it was just a year ago this *very day* that God called her home to be with Him.

The conversation between Pat, George and me flowed as if it were a well-rehearsed script. We knew that the Holy Spirit was directing.

I even heard myself laughing with the joy of the Lord as I told about our singing Karen into heaven and all the angels rejoicing.

Pat leaned forward in his chair and looked directly at the camera. "Before we go on," he said, "I want to talk to some of the people in the audience, those who are watching right now. You know, the question of death isn't pleasant. You may be thinking, 'You Christians are nuts. You're laughing about something you should be crying about.' But, no; we don't cry because we know that we are surrounded by a spiritual world that is *the real reality.* What we see here in this life is human flesh, aging, sickness and death.

"These are *not* the reality. The reality is spiritual life. That's why Jesus said, 'If anybody believes in me, he can never die.' Jesus knew the power of the invisible world; He knew we are really surrounded by heaven. He yearns for the time when we can 'punch through the curtain,' if you will, and get into that other world.

"And little children so often see it. We adults don't always see it because we're too sophisticated, too worldly-wise, too tainted with sin. But these fresh, little children see the heavenly world around them and they want to be in it. They see that it's a better world than the one we're living in. They're not afraid of it; instead,

240

they see somebody who loves them and calls to them.

"But when you get like most of us are, tainted by sin, filled with our own self-will, at this point, we've got to be born again and become like a little child. That's what it means: You've got to be born from above to enter into that spiritual world. The Bible says, 'except a man be born again he shall not see heaven, and shall not enter it.'

"Now, how do you get born again? By giving your heart to Jesus Christ, by accepting Him as Savior, by becoming as a little child, by saying, 'I'm going to turn away from the things that have crowded me and filled me with the pollution of the world of death.'

"Now let me ask you; Have you been born again? 'Well,' you say, 'I'm a good church member.' But that doesn't mean you've been born again. There are good church members all over this world who have never truly shed this old life and taken on the new life.

"If you die," Pat said, looking directly at the television audience, "will people stand around and clap their hands and shout praises to God because you've gone home? Or will they be filled with sorrow and sadness, knowing you left them and that they'll never see you again?

"There are only two places to go to after death. One's heaven, to be with the Lord forever. The other is hell which is to be separated from the Lord forever. There is no other choice, no intermediate stage, no second chance.

"Would you like to have Jesus as your Savior right now? Would you like to *know* that, if you died today, you would go to be with Him forever? Would you like the assurance that the day of your death would be your coronation day? Won't you like to know the taste of Life, the taste of that everlasting world that is the true reality?

"I know you want this. Pray with me now. Simply

repeat these words after me: 'Lord Jesus, I'm a sinner. Jesus, my life hasn't been lived for you. I have the scent of death about me because I am so much a part of this world. Lord, I want to be a part of the *other* world, I want to be a part of the world of Life, of joy, sunshine and happiness.

" 'So, Lord, I turn away from the sin and selfishness that has taken control of my life. And I exchange it for the joy of *your* life. I take you now as my Savior, because I believe that you died for me and you rose again so that I might live.

" 'Lord, at this moment, I ask you to come into my heart. Fill me with your Spirit, Lord Jesus. Live your life in me and through me, and I will live for you. I will serve you all the days of my life.

" 'Thank you, Jesus, that you've heard my prayer. Thank you, Jesus, that you have come into my heart.' "

After Pat's beautiful prayer, he shared and prayed with those from the television audience who just made that commitment. He shook our hands and thanked us for coming. A commercial followed while we exchanged places with a guest minister who was to appear next on the show.

Backstage again, I was exhilarated! Our part was over and the Lord saw us through! We prayed that many, many hearts would be touched by the broadcast.

At the conclusion of the show we talked to people in the studio audience.

"As you spoke, I realized," said one lady, "that Karen *is* an evangelist. What you shared about her was so real, it was like she was there herself telling people about Jesus."

We flew home to New Jersey with happy hearts, marveling in the greatness of God's plan. Satisfaction and joy welled up within me. Karen's life and death had reaped a great harvest, and others were still to be touched. I knew it was well with my soul.

A local Women's Aglow Fellowship invited me to speak shortly after we were home from "The 700 Club." I just finished the final touches of dressing when Eileen burst through the front door with excitement. She had arrived to drive me to the meeting.

"I've come to help you dress," she said.

"But I just finished."

Eileen put her hands on my shoulders. "No, you haven't." She closed her eyes and started to pray. "Lord, I ask you to clothe Trudy in your full armor. I place upon her the helmet of salvation and the breastplate of righteousness. I wrap her in the girdle of truth and slip on her feet the shoes of peace. In her left hand I place a huge shield of faith to douse all the fiery darts of the enemy. And in her right hand I put the sword of truth, which is the Word of God. And over all, I place on her the sparkling garment of praise to reflect the light of Jesus. And now, Lord," she paused momentarily, "may Trudy and Karen go forth as partners to present your Word and your gospel message."

"Now I *do feel dressed*," I rejoiced as Eileen finished praying. "But what was that about Karen and me being partners?"

"The Lord gave the idea to me. He must want you to realize that you and Karen are part of a team."

"That's exciting!" I exclaimed.

Many ladies gathered for the Aglow meeting and as we sang and worshiped, I sensed God's presence. His peace fell upon me as I rose to speak. I knew He was ministering to people's hearts while I shared Karen's story. Many ladies were in tears as I told of

Karen walking the beautiful stairway into heaven.

"God showed me that Karen's death was not an accident or a mistake," I continued. "But rather, a vehicle to accomplish His purposes. He used the number seven, which shows perfection and fulfillment, to speak to us. The day Karen died she was exactly seven years and seven days old. Her life was not interrupted; Rather, it was completed. From the very beginning, she was a chosen child of heaven.

"Throughout the entire experience of Karen's illness and death, my faith was strengthened and I learned many things about our God. I found that He was faithful to lead us every step of the way. He did not let us miss His guidance or fail Him. Looking back, I know there was nothing left undone and, thankfully, I have no regrets.

"As God's people, we will have trials and suffering. Jesus himself suffered and we will too, not because of God's anger toward us or our disobedience to Him but because it is a necessary part of our discipline and growth. It is God's purpose to mold His likeness and glory within us. Through suffering, rightly received, Godly fruits will be produced.

"I did not choose or want this suffering but when it came I did not rebel against it. Instead, I turned to God knowing that He loved me, that He desired my best and that I could trust Him.

"If we resist hardship and suffering, raising our fists in anger toward God and closing ourselves off to Him, our hearts will turn hard and bitter and the loving purposes of the Father will be thwarted.

"Our Lord Jesus Christ has called us to trust Him completely, to offer Him our lives, our loved ones, our circumstances, our plans, our hopes and desires; and to be willing to take the suffering that will inevitably come,

244

trusting that His loving purposes will be greater than our understanding, knowing He will be with us totally - redeeming the situation and bringing forth good from the evil. For the joy that was set before Him, Christ endured the cross, scorning its shame, and is now honored in heaven at the right hand of the Father (Heb. 12:2). We are called to fix our eyes on Jesus, not on the suffering, knowing there is great joy ahead for those who endure. Jesus has called us to overcome, in His power, any hardship or suffering He allows in our life. He has called us to walk in victory, for we are more than conquerors in Jesus.

"There is victory over the hardships, victory over the trials, victory over the disappointments, and when our life on earth is ended, there is victory over death. Truly, there is victory in Jesus, for He is Lord!"

As I concluded, I asked those who wanted to receive Jesus as their Savior and Lord to raise their hands and told them that we would pray together. I was thrilled to see hands lifted throughout the audience.

Many people spoke to me afterwards. One of the Aglow officers shared a vision that at once humbled and excited me.

"While you were speaking," she said, "I saw an arc of light around you. It was a heavenly cloud of witnesses testifying to your message. Your face was shining with that light."

"Oh, Lord," I prayed. "You have allowed me to reflect your glory so that I might declare your praise. Heaven and earth were joined to glorify your holy name."

Isabel, the president of Aglow, handed me a thank-you note. God showed her His plan for Karen and me, and she wrote, "This is only the beginning of Karen's ministry through you. You are in Christ and Karen is in Christ as *one!"*

I thought again or what Eileen had prayed – that Karen and I would go forth as partners to present God's Word.

"Oh, Father," I prayed. "Indeed you *have* joined us together in Christ."

When I got home, I looked up Jesus' prayer for His disciples:

> That all of them may be one, Father, just as you are in me and I am in you. May they also be in us so that the world may believe that you have sent me. I have given them the glory that you gave me, that they may be one as we are one. (John 17:21-22, NIV)

"Thank you, Jesus, for the blessed oneness that I can experience with you and Karen, and all who love you, so that others can see and know your love," I rejoiced.

I continued reading the Scripture. Jesus said, "Father, I want those you have given me to be with me where I am, and to see my glory ...."

"Why," I realized, "that's the same verse that comforted me when I was thinking about Karen's death. It was Jesus' great desire that Karen be with Him in heaven. Even now, I know He is rejoicing in her presence as she rejoices in His."

"How good it is, Lord, that Karen can be with you and can behold your glory." Although I prayed with a thankful heart, tears suddenly came to my eyes. I thought about what I was missing in not having Karen grow up here on earth.

Jesus spoke lovingly to me. "Don't grieve for what has not been, but rejoice for what will be."

Music started going through my mind. It was one of the songs from the Children's Praise album, but it suddenly became very personal as I heard Karen herself sing it to my heart.

"I love being alive. I love being alive. Mommy, I love being *alive!*"

I wiped my tears. "Yes, Karen. You are alive. You *were* too precious to die. You didn't stay dead. You came alive again to a wonderful life eternal that can truly be called living.

"Some wonderful day, my Precious Purity, I too will share the joy of heaven with you and we will be alive together, forever more, for all eternity!"

I began to pray, "Lord Jesus, until that precious day, keep Karen and me joined in your Spirit and embraced in your love, where neither life nor death shall ever separate us from each other or from you.

"I exalt you, Lord Jesus Christ, King of kings and Lord of lords, at whose Name every knee shall bow in heaven, and on earth, and under the earth, proclaiming you Lord, to the glory of God the Father!

"Let that day be soon, Lord, when the whole earth is full of the knowledge of you as the waters cover the sea.

"Be exalted, O God, above the heavens! Let your glory shine throughout the earth!"

AMEN

It was Karen's desire to see all people experience the joy and salvation of the Lord Jesus Christ. She was concerned that no one be left out of heaven because they had not made the choice to invite Jesus Christ into their life to be their Savior and Lord.

247

If you have never taken this step, I urge you to do so now by sincerely repeating the prayer at the end of this book. Then you, also, can experience God's peace which passes all understanding, and know the tremendous love He longs to share. You will experience abundant life now, and after you die, eternal life in heaven.

It is my prayer that the brief life of Karen Colflesh, our Precious Purity, lead you to receive the Savior she loved, the Lord Jesus Christ.

Yes, be exalted, O God, above the heavens. May your glory shine throughout the earth (Ps 57:11, TLB).

Dear Lord,

I have never considered your rightful claim on my life, but have lived selfishly, without regard to you. I am a sinner, Lord. I am sorry for all the things I have thought, said, and done to hurt you, others, and myself.

I repent of my sins. Please forgive me for all of my sins through the provision of Christ's death on the cross.

I cry out to you, Lord Jesus, to be my Savior. Only you can save me from sin's punishment of Hell. Wash me clean, cleanse me and bring me into a relationship with you and with my heavenly Father.

I acknowledge that you died and took the punishment for my sins, that you rose again, and that you live forever to destroy the power of sin and death over me. Fill me with the Holy Spirit and make me what I ought to be.

Lord, I will live for you and serve you all the days of my life. Thank you, Jesus, for loving me and saving me. Thank you, Jesus, for coming into my heart. Amen

Also Available

Trudy Colflesh has also written books on emotional healing. The Soulcry Books are a poetic expression of the deep longings and cries of the soul and the response of a loving God who hears and cares.

Book 1
Emotional Numbness, Shame, Confusion, Escape, Anger, Loneliness, Lostness

Book 2
Abandonment, Emotional Wounding, Relationships, Fear, Sadness, Rejection

Book 3
Enmeshment, Identity, Pain, Inadequacy, Shame, Dependency, Dissociation

Book 4
Sexual Abuse, Denial, Ritual Abuse, Dissociation, Betrayal, Control, Identity, Trauma

Book 5
Dissociation, Suffering, Ritual Abuse, Sexual Abuse, Forgiveness, Comfort, Healing, Joy

Book 6
Shame, Failure, Perfection, Ritual Abuse, Anger, Dissociation, Sexual Intimacy, Truth, Acceptance

Book 7
Worth, Denial, Dissociation, Ritual Abuse, Rejection, Sexual Abuse, Surrender, Love, Healing

Book 8
Enmeshment, Self Worth, Suffering, Occult Bondage, Generational Iniquities, Mercy, Freedom

Available: www.Encouraginghope.com/books

About The Author

Trudy Colflesh has had a tender heart and sensitive spirit since childhood. She grew up in the home of a Presbyterian minister and saw her parents seek to meet others' needs in Christian love and service.

Trudy became active in service herself in high school and college. She graduated from the College of Wooster, Ohio, married her college sweetheart and worked several years in a Presbyterian church as a Director of Christian Education.

For many years, Trudy was a stay-at-home mom and active in volunteer church service. She and her husband, George, have two natural children, Christopher and Karen, a son Michael, adopted when he was ten years old, and have fostered two young boys.

When Karen was almost seven, she became ill with leukemia and despite doing all possible to save her, she died within seven months. Out of this painful time, Trudy wrote the book *Too Precious To Die* and traveled around the country speaking at Women's Aglow Fellowships and appearing on CBN and other TV and radio programs.

Having opportunity to minister to hurting people, as she herself was healing, Trudy felt the Lord calling her to go into the field of counseling. She went to graduate school and earned her Master's degree in Counseling at Montclair State University, New Jersey, in 1990 and became a Licensed Professional Counselor.

Since that time, Trudy has worked as a Christian Counselor, ministering hope and healing to countless clients. As she has listened to her own wounded soul and pursued recovery, as well as listening to the hearts of her clients, Trudy began writing poetic expressions of deep emotional wounds, as well as God's loving responses to our distress.

She knows with certainty that out of the painful issues of life, comes a sure belief that Jesus Christ knows our broken heart's pain, hears our soul's cry and brings us His Presence to comfort and heal.

"And we know that in all things God works for the good of those who love him, who have been called according to his purpose." (Romans 8:28)

Trudy is available for telephone counseling and coaching. If you would like to set up an appointment, please contact her at Trudy@Encouraginghope.com. Comments or questions may also be addressed to Trudy at this location.

www.ingramcontent.com/pod-product-compliance
Lightning Source LLC
Chambersburg PA
CBHW071409090426
42737CB00011B/1404